She Dared to Succeed

# She Dared to Succeed
## A Biography of the Honourable Marie-P. Charette-Poulin

*Fred Langan*

University of Ottawa Press  2023

 Les **Presses** de l'Université d'Ottawa
University of Ottawa **Press**

The University of Ottawa Press (UOP) is proud to be the oldest of the francophone university presses in Canada and the oldest bilingual university publisher in North America. Since 1936, UOP has been enriching intellectual and cultural discourse by producing peer-reviewed and award-winning books in the humanities and social sciences, in French and in English.

**Library and Archives Canada Cataloguing in Publication**
Title: She dared to succeed: a biography of the Honourable Marie-P. Charette-Poulin / Fred Langan.
Names: Langan, Fred, 1945- author.
Identifiers: Canadiana (print) 2022042876X | Canadiana (ebook) 20220428808 | ISBN 9780776637983 (hardcover) | ISBN 9780776637976 (softcover) | ISBN 9780776638003 (EPUB) | ISBN 9780776637990 (PDF)
Subjects: LCSH: Charette-Poulin, Marie-Paule. | LCSH: Legislators—Canada—Biography. | LCGFT: Biographies.
Classification: LCC FC636.C43 L36 2023 | DDC 971.064/8092—dc23

Legal Deposit: Third Quarter 2023
Library and Archives Canada

© University of Ottawa Press 2023
All right reserved.

Printed in Canada

**Production Team**
Copy-editing              Tanina Drvar
Proofreading              Céline Parent
Typesetting                Édiscript enr.

**Cover Image**
Bernard Poulin, *Portrait of Marie*, oil and coloured pencil on paper, 24" x 20", 2022.

The University of Ottawa Press gratefully acknowledges the support extended to its publishing list by the Government of Canada, the Canada Council for the Arts, the Ontario Arts Council, the Social Sciences and Humanities Research Council and the Canadian Federation for the Humanities and Social Sciences through the Awards to Scholarly Publications Program, and by the University of Ottawa.

# Table of Contents

| | | |
|---|---|---|
| List of Figures | | vii |
| Prologue | | xiii |
| Foreword | | xvii |
| Chapter 1 | Deep Roots | 1 |
| Chapter 2 | Growing Up in Sudbury | 7 |
| Chapter 3 | University Life: A Tale in Three Parts | 21 |
| Chapter 4 | A Single Mother Returns to Canada | 31 |
| Chapter 5 | Radio-Canada: Reclaiming Life | 41 |
| Chapter 6 | Bernard and Family Life | 53 |
| Chapter 7 | CBON (C'EST BON): The Birth of Public French Radio in Northern Ontario | 61 |
| Chapter 8 | Going Home | 73 |
| Chapter 9 | The NABET Strike | 79 |
| Chapter 10 | Head Office | 85 |
| Chapter 11 | Vice-President, Human Resources and Industrial Relations | 99 |
| Chapter 12 | Life after Radio-Canada | 107 |
| Chapter 13 | Called to the Senate | 115 |
| Chapter 14 | Work and Life in the Senate | 129 |
| Chapter 15 | A Franco-Ontarian Fights for Canada | 147 |
| Chapter 16 | The Law | 153 |
| Chapter 17 | President of the Party | 165 |
| Chapter 18 | The Senate Expenses Scandal | 177 |
| Chapter 19 | Enter the Auditor General | 193 |
| Chapter 20 | The Aftermath of the Inquiry | 213 |
| Chapter 21 | Elaine and Valérie | 237 |
| Chapter 22 | A Busy Post-Senate Life | 245 |
| List of Interviewees | | 259 |

# List of Figures

**Chapter 1**
Marie-Paule at five years of age, 1950 — 3

**Chapter 2**
137 Drinkwater, Sudbury, where City Hall is now located, 1946–1970 — 8
Marie, as Director of Radio-Canada in Northern Ontario,
 and David Schatzky, as Director of CBC in Northern Ontario, welcome
 Premier Bill Davis to the CBC/Radio-Canada station in Sudbury, 1981 — 10
Marie wins first prize at school in English Literature; an edition
 of the collected works of Shakespeare, with an inscription from
 her teacher, 1962 — 15
Marie-Paule's high school graduation picture (grade 13) from
 l'Académie Sainte-Marie boarding school located in Haileybury,
 Ontario, 1963 — 16
Marie-Paule, a Sudbury playground supervisor, with the members
 of her baseball team, which won the City Trophy in the summer of 1961 — 18

**Chapter 3**
Marie worked on weekends as a receptionist at CKSO Radio and Television
 in Sudbury, to help pay for her university tuition. The station asked her
 to help with commercial campaigns, 1964 — 22
Marie graduates *magna cum laude* from Laurentian University in Sudbury,
 1966 — 24
Graduation photo of Marie published in the yearbook, 1966 — 26

**Chapter 4**
Marie with her daughter Elaine, 1972 — 32
Elaine with the Franco-Ontarian singer and composer Robert Paquette, 1982 — 35
Elaine and Catherine de Hueck-Doherty, 1982 — 36

## Chapter 5
Marie as Producer of a weekend radio show at CBOF, the Radio-Canada station in Ottawa (the National Capital Region). She had suggested that the show, titled "Radioactif," be aired in a public space—it became one of the first live radio shows aired by CBC/Radio-Canada, 1974    43

Marie makes the cover of the December 1974 television guide of *Le Droit* newspaper (with a two-page story inside)    48

## Chapter 6
In August 1976, Bernard is interviewed by Marie who is seeking researcher-interviewers for her new four-hour daily magazine show, "Place 1250." Bernard sketched it from memory after the interview    55

Bernard resigns from his new position as researcher-interviewer when Marie states she did not date employees. The National Arts Centre tickets for the date on which they went after Bernard's resignation    56

Wedding Portrait, 1977    57

## Chapter 7
Family Portrait, 1980    65

Valerie wearing her CBON sweater, 1980    67

The CBON afternoon show "TNT" becomes a favourite of high-school students throughout Northern Ontario—here, in Kapuskasing in 1980    69

Marie and her team celebrate the fifth anniversary of the CBON radio station as well as the fact that its morning show is recognized as the best morning radio show in Canada (Prix Marcel Blouin), 1983    70

## Chapter 8
The family with Aunt Germaine, 1995    74

*Blueberries* by Bernard Poulin    76

## Chapter 9
Cartoon gift—depicting Marie as quite capable of running the radio station all on her own if need be—given to Marie by radio announcer Christiane St-Pierre during the NABET Strike of 1981    80

## Chapter 10
Marie on the cover of *Liaison* magazine following her appointment as Associate Vice-President responsible for French regional broadcasting in Canada, 1984    90

Marie, Bernard, and Maô, their chow-chow, 1996    92

As Associate Vice-President of French Regional Broadcasting and guest of honour of the Junior Hockey Tournament opening game in Matane and Rimouski, (Québec), Marie is asked to drop the puck. Alongside her is Maurice "The Rocket" Richard, 1985   93

Marie and Pierre Juneau, president of CBC/Radio-Canada, receiving a medal of recognition from the Conseil de la vie française en Amérique. Alongside them are Raymond Marcotte, Director of the Saskatchewan Radio Station and Jean Hubert, President of the Conseil de la vie française en Amérique, 1987   98

## Chapter 12

As Deputy Secretary to the Cabinet at the Privy Council Office, Marie assists in preparing the book Prime Minister Brian Mulroney was writing on his accomplishments, 1993   111

## Chapter 13

Marie receiving an honorary doctorate from Laurentian University, 1995   117

Prime Minister Jean Chrétien tried to reach Marie to invite her to represent Northern Ontario in the Senate; this was the fax received by Marie, in Italy, 1995   119

Marie with Monseigneur René Audet, celebrating their forty-five-year friendship as well as his spiritual guidance and mentoring, 2003   121

Marie, in the Senate Chamber, being escorted to her swearing-in ceremony by her sponsor, Senator Leo Kolber, and Senator Joyce Fairburn, Leader of the Government in the Senate   122

On the day of her swearing in, Marie was welcomed to the Senate by Speaker Gil Molgat. Present for this occasion: Paul Belisle, Clerk of the Senate, Raymond Bonin MP for Nickel Belt, Marie, Nathalie Grimard, Marie's executive assistant, Michel Lamoureux researcher, and Jean Pelletier, Chief of Staff to Prime Minister Jean Chrétien, 1995   123

Paul Desmarais, of Power Corporation and Jean Chrétien, then Minister of Justice, receive honorary doctorates from Laurentian University. Marie was then the managing director of the CBON radio station in Sudbury, 1980. Father Lucien Michaud, President of the University of Sudbury, Henry Best, President of Laurentian University, Paul Desmarais, Marie, and Jean Chrétien   125

Marie and Bernard accompany the Right Honourable Jean Chrétien and Madame Aline Chrétien during her first official function as Chancellor of Laurentian University   127

## Chapter 14
Marie and Bernard wishing Prime Minister Chrétien a Happy New Year,
    December 1997 — 130
Elaine on the water, 1986 — 131
Marie welcomes Governor General Michaëlle Jean to the Senate, 2005 — 134
Welcoming the Prince of Wales to Canada, 1996 — 135
*The Right Honourable Jean Chrétien* by Bernard Poulin, 2010 — 137
Marie visiting an underground mine in Sudbury, 1997 — 138
Celebrating the first National Aboriginal Day in Canada on June 21, 1996
    [now referred to as National Indigenous Peoples Day] — 143
Marie and some of her colleagues welcome a delegation of parliamentarians
    from Japan in the Chamber of the Speaker of the Senate, 1996 — 145

## Chapter 15
Marie and her parents, Alphonse and Lucille Charette, on the
    tenth anniversary of CBON, 1988 — 148
Marie is awarded the distinction of Officier de la Légion d'honneur
    by the president of France, via his ambassador in Canada,
Philippe Guelluy, 2003 — 151

## Chapter 16
Marie with Premier Jennifer Smith of Bermuda, 1999 — 158
Marie named as the Person of the Year by Richelieu International, 2008 — 160

## Chapter 17
Marie with the Mayor of Xi'an, visiting China's Terracotta Army, 2005 — 168
Marie welcomes Edna Bélisle, wife of the late senator, to her home — 171
Marie, as candidate for the presidency of the Liberal Party of Canada,
    speaking at the National Convention in Montréal, 2006 — 173

## Chapter 19
Family Christmas dinner at the Charette-Poulin home, 2012 — 197
Marie speaking at the Queen's Jubilee Dinner in Sudbury, 2012. — 207
Marie welcomes the President of the United States of America,
    Barack Obama, to the Senate, 2009 — 211

## Chapter 20
Marie with Senator Linda Frum in Saudi Arabia (on their Blackberrys)
    while their camel ride awaits, 2011 — 223

As a member of a Senate delegation to Morocco, Marie paid a courtesy call on the Crown Prince of Morocco who, a few weeks later, acceded to the throne as King Mohammed VI, 1999 — 229

Marie with former President (2007–2014) and Prime Minister (1984–1986 / 1995–1996) of Israel, Shimon Peres, 1999 — 230

## Chapter 21

Marie's favourite place is in or on the water, despite occasional bouts of sea sickness, 1997 — 238

Marie is introduced to the Prime Minister of the United Kingdom, Tony Blair, by Prime Minister Jean Chrétien. Also in attendance are Minister Denis Coderre and Senator Frank Mahovlich, 2001 — 240

Marie and Bernard alongside the Speaker of the Senate Noël Kinsella, and his wife Ann at the Negev Dinner in Ottawa, 2011 — 243

Valérie and animals are always one — 244

## Chapitre 22

Marie with her coffee and newspapers and Laurier, with his milk bowl, begin their day, 2013 — 246

Marie and Valérie, 1979 — 248

Marie receiving an honorary business degree from Collège Boréal President Denis Hubert-Dutrisac, 2013 — 249

Marie with former Governor General David Johnston, sharing Northern Ontario memories, 2018 — 255

The Poulin family, 1996 — 256

Bernard and Elaine, 1976 — 257

The Poulin family, 2019 — 258

# *Prologue*

THE RELATIONSHIP between achievement and service is complicated. This is particularly true for women.

Women are generally—not always—recognized for what they provide to others as mother, wife, nurse, and teacher, for example, but recognition for the many contributions they make in other roles, such as lawyer, doctor, scientist, musician, businessperson, artist, politician, academic, etc., is acknowledged far less frequently. The personal achievements of women are celebrated and rewarded far less commonly than are those of men. Indeed, women who accomplish great things are often stigmatized for their success.

Marie-Paule Charette is a woman of tremendous achievement. She has served as a social worker, a pioneering radio programmer, a media executive, the president of the Liberal Party of Canada, a lawyer, and a parliamentarian in the Senate of Canada. She has sat on the boards of several corporations, organizations, and not-for-profits. In all these roles, she has accomplished something truly extraordinary: inspirational personal achievement through public service.

It was not easy though. As a single mother in the early 1970s, she was shunned and as a working woman she encountered gender discrimination, sexual harassment, mockery, shaming, and intimidation. As a senator she faced the painful public trial of a politically motivated investigation.

Through all this, she persevered, and her legacy of actions and initiatives continues to benefit many.

Summer 2023

# *Foreword*

I AM HONOURED to provide a foreword to Marie's story. Although I have played a very small part in her life, she made an outsized impression on me. Her friendship brought with it generosity, enthusiasm, and loyalty. I was fortunate to be able to enjoy that friendship.

I first met Marie as one of my constituents in Ottawa South. At the time, she was an influential senior public servant and former broadcast media executive. My admiration for her would grow when I saw her in action, receiving an Honorary Doctorate; she demonstrated herself to be accomplished, smart, confident, and articulate in both official languages. It came as no surprise to me to learn, a few months later, that Prime Minister Chrétien had called her to the Senate to represent Northern Ontario. She was an ideal nominee to represent, not only the region where she grew up, but also Franco-Ontarians specifically, as well as professional women generally.

Being in the Liberal Caucus, in which I served as a Minister, and Marie as a Senator, allowed us to work together over the years. But it was not until 2003, when I chose to challenge the presumed coronation of Paul Martin – as the successor to Prime Minister Chrétien—that I discovered what a valuable and courageous friend I had in Marie. We knew we were running against the odds, but we believed we were helping to build and grow the Party. We realised we had been naive and were disappointed when many of my friends and supporters were treated harshly by the Martin team, even after the leadership was safely in Martin's hands. Marie was one of those whose professional and political opportunities were directly affected by supporters of the new leader.

Senator Poulin's balanced approach to issues, her personal and professional ethics and her hard work were unrelenting, despite the many challenges and the opposition she faced. Undeterred and persistent, she sought and won election as the President of the Liberal Party of Canada – the first Francophone woman to hold that post. Then, at the age of fifty-nine, she returned to university to obtain a law degree. Marie wanted to be more than just a rubber stamp as a legislator, she was intent upon understanding the legal context and procedures that impacted her work in the Senate.

After her retirement from the Senate in 2015, Marie remained undaunted by the challenges and difficulties she encountered over the years. She remains a positive example for—and a mentor to—young women and men who wish to pursue and succeed in their fields of endeavour. Marie's story is one of hard work, dedication, commitment to excellence and loyalty to her friends, her beliefs, and her principles.

And what an asset she is as a friend! In my experience, when things get tough, you definitely want Marie on your team!

Hon. John Manley P.C., O.C.

# Deep Roots

WE ARE SHAPED by our families and by the places where we grew up; Marie-Paule Charette's hometown, Sudbury, and Northern Ontario, shaped her. Her ancestors had been in Canada more than 300 years, arriving at Île d'Orléans in 1647 from Larochelle, in France, and settling initially in Quebec City. A century or so ago, they settled in the Sudbury area, which was a small work camp on the transcontinental railway built by the Canadian Pacific Railway (CPR).

The Canadian Pacific Railway, or CPR, the railway that connected British Columbia to Ontario, Quebec, and the Maritimes, was conceived by Sir John A. Macdonald as a massive nation-building project. Thousands of men worked on the rail lines that approached Sudbury from the east and west. Many of those men were French Canadians from Quebec. Once the railway was finished, some left, but a substantial number stayed and worked in the mines and farms as the area developed. Eventually, they brought their families and settled permanently in Northern Ontario.

The first passenger and freight train arrived in Sudbury in December of 1884. It must be admitted that, at the time, it was little more than a whistle stop, like so many other stations built every two hundred kilometres or so—a place to take on water and coal for the steam engines. Many of the other railway depots would end up becoming ghost towns, but Sudbury thrived. Government surveyors had come across the vast mineral deposits in the area in the 1850s, but it was not until the building of the CPR that mining was feasible. With the arrival of the railway, the area was soon transformed. Until recently, mining was the engine that drove the city's economy, allowing it to grow and prosper.

The CPR, though run by a group of mainly Scottish Presbyterians, asked the Jesuits to set up a mission in the area to serve the Catholic workers building the transcontinental railway. Father Joseph Specht SJ celebrated the first Mass in Sudbury in March of 1883. His replacement was Father Jean-Baptiste Nolin. He settled in Sainte-Anne-des-Pins and built a small chapel there, a log church where the Church of St. Anne stands today, where the Charette and Ménard families were baptized and married, and where they are buried.

By 1884, there were fifty families in the new parish, and the Jesuits provided schooling for the children of the workers. They continued to do so until they established the Collège Sacré-Cœur, a private boarding school for boys, which offered le *cours classique*, eight years of secondary and post-secondary teaching. The objective was to build a religious and Francophone elite in Northern Ontario. The college became the gathering place for Francophones in Sudbury, as the Jesuits would invite musical and theatre groups to perform in the college auditorium.

"Cultural events were organized, sometimes on a bi-monthly basis. The number of plays and concerts I attended as a little girl was outstanding because we never missed going to the Collège Sacré-Cœur for events," says Marie. "They also organized sports events—they had this huge field outside, which became an ice rink during the winter for hockey and curling. The Collège Sacré-Cœur became the founding college of the federation of Laurentian University in 1961."

The Church of St. Anne was another focal point for the development of the French-speaking community in Sudbury. It was the only Roman Catholic church in Sudbury until 1917, serving emigrants from Italy and other parts of Europe and the Francophone population. Language was not a problem; in those days, the Mass was in Latin, the language of the Catholic Church.

★ ★ ★

Marie-Paule Charette was born at the peak of the summer solstice, at noon, on Thursday, June 21, 1945, at Hôpital St. Joseph in Sudbury, Ontario. She was baptized seven weeks later, on August 13 in the Church of St. Anne. The priest who baptized her was a Jesuit, a religious order that had a long history in Northern Ontario. The Jesuits would come to play a significant role in Marie's life and the life of Sudbury.

The Charette family lived in the town of Garson, now a part of Greater Sudbury, then a village on the city's outskirts. Marie's parents, Lucille Ménard and Alphonse Charette, were Francophones. The Charette family always spoke French at home, though Francophones from Sudbury are fluently bilingual, part of the reason so many of them have gone on to success, not just in Sudbury but in the greater world.

There is a long history of Francophones in Northern Ontario, and Marie's family, on both her father's and her mother's side, have been a part of that history for generations.

★ ★ ★

The Sun King, Louis XIV, sent the first of Marie Poulin's maternal ancestors to New France in 1665. He was a soldier named Ménarde, (the second "e" was later dropped). There were skirmishes between the Iroquois and the colonists of New France, and the monarch sent 1,200 soldiers in support of his subjects. After surviving a brutal winter, the French eventually prevailed. A treaty was signed with the Mohawks in 1667, allowing the French to extend their commercial activities to the North, the Great Lakes, and the Mississippi.

France therefore ordered its soldiers home, but the king offered land and pay for a year if they stayed in the sparsely settled colony. Monsieur Ménard elected to stay, and he was given a piece of land along the Richelieu River, which runs from the St. Lawrence River in the north to Lake Champlain.

Marie's mother was a Ménard, descended from the soldier who landed in Quebec in 1665. The Ménard family hailed from a community north of Montebello called Saint-André-Avellin, located 131 kilometres east of Ottawa-Gatineau, along the Ottawa River.

During the First World War, Ludger Ménard went downriver to work in a foundry in Hull. It was a prosperous time, but there was a major recession after the war, and he found himself out of work. He even travelled to Montréal and crossed the St. Lawrence River on the winter ice road to see if there were any opportunities in south shore Longueuil. There were none. That is how Marie's maternal grandparents ended up in Northern Ontario in the town of Hanmer. The couple had six children, five girls and one boy. That boy died at about two years of age, during the influenza epidemic that swept the world a century ago; a tragic omen of the modern pandemic. The five girls all lived long, healthy lives.

Marie-Paule at five years of age, 1950.
Source: Family Collection.

Ludger Ménard became a carpenter in the Sudbury area, where there was a fair amount of construction. At that time, Sudbury was booming with the growth of International Nickel and other mines. Like all the family, he was entrepreneurial. He started small, for a time operating a pool hall in Hanmer, then expanding and starting his own contracting company.

★ ★ ★

The first Charette arrived in New France in 1647. His name was Pierre Choret; the spelling of the name changed many times over the years. When a priest entered the name in the parish records at baptism, he would spell it the way he heard it, since the early settlers may not have been fully literate and did not know the difference.

Marie's great-grandfather, Alphonse Charette Sr., called *Senior* to distinguish him from Marie's father, Alphonse, was born in Le Bic, Quebec, part of the city of Rimouski since 2009. It is a farming community on the shore of the St. Lawrence, where the river is wide, salty, and with a tide. It is a place of spectacular natural beauty and near du Bic National Park.

But you cannot eat beauty, and so he moved his family to Northern Ontario a short time after the building of the Canadian Pacific Railway. Charette Senior settled in a place called Gogama, north of Sudbury, where he went into the forestry business. One of the main wood products needed at the time was railway ties and later beams to support mining operations.

Marie's grandfather, Émile, was nine years old when he moved with his father to Northern Ontario. He had been to school in Quebec but never in Ontario. He had trouble reading and writing. Émile was naturally clever and learned the lumber business from his father and from working in a sawmill. Despite his lack of education, he prospered, and later managed to buy a farm in the village of Hanmer, about 32 kilometres from the centre of Sudbury. That is where he raised their fifteen children. Alphonse (junior), Marie's father, was the eldest.

The Charette and Ménard families would come together in marriage and become pillars of Sudbury and Northern Ontario's strong Francophone community.

★ ★ ★

Gilles Charette, one of Marie-Paule's brothers, shares some of his memories and research into his immediate family. "My mother was born in 1911, and my father was born in 1910. I also know that my Charette grandparents got married in January 1910 in Le Bic because that's where his wife was from. Her name was Marie Bérubé. The Bérubé and the Charette families were in Le Bic, and within ten years both families had moved to Northern Ontario.

"My grandfather Charette and my grandmother Marie Bérubé were intent on getting their children educated way beyond primary-level schooling."

Marie-Paule points out that the children from that branch of the family were super achievers. "All the men and women were highly educated; one became a doctor, and another had a PhD in agronomy and became dean of l'École d'agronomie de l'Université Laval. Don't forget that Laurent Charette was a youngster ('un p'tit gars') from Sudbury," says Marie-Paule.

"My father wanted to be a pharmacist. He wanted to go to Collège Bourget and take a Bachelor of science degree to then attend pharmacy school. But once at Rigaud, he was given tests. He had a lot of trouble with written French because he had never been schooled in French. The fathers concluded he wasn't bright enough, and put him in the business school. It was the biggest disappointment of his life.

"I found that out only when he was dying. I asked him if he hadn't been in business, what would you have liked to be. He looked at me, and his eyes brightened up and he said, 'A pharmacist, like Mr. Michaud, and to have run a pharmacy.' Then I asked him why he didn't do it, and that's when he told me the story of College in Rigaud.

"Our father returned to Sudbury and began working for his relatives and his father," says Gilles Charette. "My parents were married in 1936, and moved to Timmins, because his uncle thought that he was being ripped off by the manager of the grocery store. My father went up there and fired the manager.

"He came back to Sudbury and was given a job in another grocery store belonging to another one of my uncles. I'm not sure which one because he had uncles on his mother's and father's side," says Gilles, who laughs when he thinks of the number of relatives he and his family have in Sudbury and Northern Ontario.

"The Ménards and the Charettes hail from Hanmer and Sudbury, so you can just imagine the numbers of cousins, aunts, uncles, and a host of relatives from marriage we had in that area. It's unbelievable. I've never had a clear picture of the whole thing.

"Then," says Gilles, resuming the story, "an uncle of my father's, who owned a huge poultry farm on the outskirts of Sudbury, asked my father to manage it. The farm had approximately five thousand hens and produced thousands of eggs a day. These chicks had to hatch at a fairly constant temperature all the time, so electric power was crucial to us. Whenever there was a power failure, it was almost a disaster, and during the Second World War, things were difficult. I still remember the tanks rolling down Falconbridge Road. Marie-Paule was born while we lived on that farm.

"In 1946, my father decided to build a feed mill. He needed a siding for the boxcars to get to his place arriving with oats, wheat, and barley, which would be milled and bagged in his building and sold. It was a big business to start with.

> "I am always surprised by people who are not involved in their communities. It's as though they are missing out on one of the key opportunities of life: to meet new people and learn new things and get the feeling of contributing to a better way of life where you live."

> "You know, in the early years, what people were developing was like the Wild West, a mining town with huge entrepreneurial spirit. Nobody depended on anyone to make a living or give them a job, they made their own way."

However, increasing emissions from Inco's refining operations made farming increasingly difficult in the Sudbury area, so my father diversified into the flour and industrial equipment business, making full use of his prime location in town."

★ ★ ★

The people who came from around the world to work and prosper in Sudbury impressed Marie.

"One of the hallmarks of Sudburians of all denominations and cultures is that they are involved in the community. I am always surprised by people who are not involved in their communities. It's as though they are missing out on one of the key opportunities of life: to meet new people and learn new things and get the feeling of contributing to a better way of life where you live. I am particularly impressed with the Italian, Irish, Polish, Ukrainian, and the Finnish communities in Sudbury. I started with Italians because I think they were the ones who were the most united and they built things that are still there today, like the Caruso Club. The Irish community in Sudbury was also very strong. They are the ones who built Christ the King Church, the most important English Catholic church in Sudbury."

Mitch Spiegel, a local businessman and a friend of Bernard and Marie from their days in Sudbury, also knew Marie growing up in Sudbury. They even dated for a while, which at the time was a bit worrisome for their parents, since the Charettes were Catholic and the Spiegels, Jewish. Marie and Mitch could not have cared less.

Spiegel, has his own view of why there are so many Sudbury success stories: "I've always said that our best export is our entrepreneurs, unfortunately. We do have a long list. You know, in the early years, what people were developing was like the Wild West, a mining town with huge entrepreneurial spirit. Nobody depended on anyone to make a living or give them a job, they made their own way. That's why I think we produce such good people."

## Growing Up in Sudbury

MARIE-PAULE CHARETTE grew up as the fourth of five children and the family's only daughter. The family lived in downtown Sudbury; the father had moved the family from the poultry farm he ran during the war to be close to his business in the city centre.

The Charette family lived at 137 Drinkwater Street. The neighbourhood was as Canadian as you could get: English and French, immigrants from all over Europe, children playing together in the street. It was one of four houses torn down in the 1960s and 1970s as part of a redevelopment project; today there are municipal offices where the Charette house once stood.

"I loved it there. We lived next door to a Finnish family; the family to our right was Italian, and the Polish church was just down the street. Another family was Ukrainian, and an Asian family lived opposite us," says Marie.

At home, the Charette family spoke French, but in Sudbury's multilingual streets, English was the common language of play. "I spoke English all the time when I was outside. That's where I learned English, and I didn't learn it until I was six years old."

Their neighbours on Drinkwater Street included the Desmarais family. The Desmarais family went on to have a huge influence on Sudbury. Jean Noël Desmarais was one of the founders of Laurentian University; his son Paul would go on to become one of the most successful businessmen in Canada. His other two sons were equally successful: Jean would become a senator, and Robert, a judge.

"Marie had two older brothers, Gilles and Raymond—we used to chum around together, and we went to school together as well," says Judge Desmarais. "I would go to their place, and they would come to ours. Marie was

137 Drinkwater, Sudbury, where City Hall is now located, 1946–1970.
*Source*: Family Collection.

> "I wanted to do everything my brothers did, and my parents thought that was great. I would wash the car [once a] week when it was my turn, and I painted [the] outside [of] the house as my brothers did."

probably five or six years old at that time. She was a cute little thing. Her parents [...] were well-respected people—in the French-Canadian community, in particular, but [also] in Sudbury at large."

Wanting to be one of the boys, Marie-Paule grew up a tomboy. I was focused on baseball, cowboys, and Indians; I didn't care what I looked like. I wanted to do everything my brothers did, and my parents thought that was great. I would wash the car [once a] week when it was my turn, and I painted [the] outside [of] the house as my brothers did."

While this changed as she grew older, she picked up many things from her brothers. As you will learn later, she is hard to shock. And she still has an interest in some things that are perceived to be more masculine than feminine—cars, for instance.

"My memories of childhood are extremely happy. One of the things I liked was [sitting] at the dinner table [with my family]; my brothers were much older, so the discussions were about cars and hockey. To this day, I love cars. I don't even own a car anymore, but I would take a car show over a fashion show any day."

The man who had the most influence on her was her father. Dedicated to his Francophone roots, a successful small businessman and a leader in Francophone Sudbury. Alphonse Charette was very involved in the community. "My father had a dream: he wanted Francophones to be able to be born, educated, do business, be cared for, and die in French. He said that to me so often," says Marie.

"He became involved with the Caisse Populaire, bringing in the first *caisse* [credit union] to Sudbury. He felt strongly that Francophones should have access to credit to set up their businesses and send their children to private schools for Francophones. In those days, there weren't any French-language, publicly funded, secondary schools.

"He was also very involved in the coopérative funéraire, a popular funeral home in Sudbury, which was, once again, based on the co-operative movement. He wanted Francophones to have access to a funeral home that was governed by Francophones. So that was number two.

"He then got involved in the development of the nursing school in Sudbury, where nursing was taught in French to young women. Then, he got involved with a small group of men, a secret society called La Patente. They worked underground with different governments to bring in public funding for the school systems in French. That group worked very closely with then premier Bill Davis.

"Eventually, French-language secondary schools became publicly funded . My father was very proud of that, [though] he never looked for public recognition. He did all of this *pro bono*; he was running a small business and had he spent all that time on business, I'm sure we would have been wealthier," chuckles Marie.

"This was a courageous political decision on the part of Premier Davis: stand-alone publicly funded secondary schools. Today, there are 105 francophone high schools in Ontario," says Marie. "I had the opportunity to thank him personally in 1981 when he visited CBC/Radio-Canada in Sudbury during the election campaign."

> "My father had a dream: he wanted Francophones to be able to be born, educated, do business, be cared for, and die in French. He said that to me so often," says Marie.

Marie, as Director of Radio-Canada in Northern Ontario, and David Schatzky, as Director of CBC in Northern Ontario, welcome Premier Bill Davis to the CBC/Radio-Canada station in Sudbury, 1981.
Source: *Sudbury Star*.

One of the men Alphonse worked with on the Franco-Ontarian cause was Hector Bonin, father of Raymond Bonin, Liberal MP for Nickel Belt from 1993 to 2008.

"Around the time Marie and I were born, our fathers were working together on causes that promoted French in the community," says Ray Bonin. "Francophones were a minority in Sudbury, and it was therefore difficult to access services in French. Those were the days when Francophones and Anglophones didn't get along as well as they do now, and these businessmen used to meet to try and find ways to help young professionals get ahead."

Their work seemed to pay off. The Francophone community produced many successful individuals.

"Our fathers [...] believed in building institutions; they believed in our place in Ontario, but had to fight for it. This was more or less a clandestine organization or group. The francophone community in Sudbury was open to the English-speaking world around them but was determined to preserve its French-speaking heritage. It is one of the reasons that most Franco-Ontarians are strong federalists," explains Bonin.

"Thanks to their efforts promoting institutions and individuals, we grew up involved in the French cause. Still, I believe Sudbury is a success story both for Francophones and Anglophones. I always say, 'no one will respect you if you don't respect yourself,' and I believe our fathers respected the Francophone community; as a consequence, the Anglophone community saw that we were not just looking for a free ride.

"I keep saying *our fathers* because, in those days, [it was the men] who went out to those meetings three or four times a week; the mothers managed the families. I'm sure that my mother did as much for the francophone community as my father did, but in a different way. My father would also organize breakfasts, which he called *déjeuners causeries*, a breakfast where you have a discussion. He had a grocery store in those days, so he donated some of the food, and the women were always there to prepare it and take care of things."

Jim Gordon was mayor of Sudbury in the 1970s, and was elected in 1981 to the provincial legislature. He eventually retired from provincial politics and served as mayor again from 1991 to 2003. An Irish Catholic, he kept close to the French-speaking electorate in Sudbury. He provides additional context to Bonin's recollections: "Sudbury was originally built for the Irish and the Francophones. Those were the two strong groups. The one thing about the Francophone community in Sudbury is that they are very family oriented, and they have a real closeness that you don't see in other cultural groups. There are also a lot of successful people from that community. Paul Desmarais is a good example. Also, there was a home builder who came from just outside Sudbury, Robert Campeau."

★ ★ ★

Marie's mother stayed at home until her younger son was born, but soon afterwards, she returned to teaching. As in many families, mother and daughter had a special bond. "As a child, I was very close to my mother. Every Saturday morning, from the time I was very little, she would take me to Mass, and then to Kresge's to the little counter where she and I would have breakfast together. We did this until I was thirteen years old, when I left for boarding school," says Marie.

The elementary school was about four blocks away from the Charette family home, and Marie walked there every morning. To this day, she still goes for a morning walk. "In Sudbury, I went to a Catholic primary school called St. Thomas. There was an English section and a French section; I was in the French section. I'm still friends with a girl I went to primary school with, Sister Superior Rachelle Watier. She's the superior of the Sœurs de la Charité congregation; her office is in Ottawa, and she and I have always remained friends."

As head of her order in Ottawa, Sister Rachelle is as successful in her own vocation as Marie has been in hers. She remembers Marie-Paule Charette from

> "Mr. Charette was community-oriented, and I think she took that from him; he was involved in many [...] organizations, and that formed her, who she was, and who she is."

the first day of school. "I've known Marie since grade 1. Even at that time, she was a sociable and affable little girl and was seen as a leader. She was a relationship person even then."

She thinks Marie learned loyalty to the community from both her parents, but she noticed it more particularly in her father. "Marie's father was a businessman, and that had an impact on her. Mr. Charette was community-oriented, and I think she took that from him; he was involved in many [...] organizations, and that formed her, who she was, and who she is."

One of the Charette's neighbours was Jean-Paul Jolicœur, who became a priest and is now a monsignor living in Sudbury as an official of the Diocese of Sault Ste. Marie, which stretches from North Bay to White River. "I've known the Charette family for a long time. They were pillars of the community here, especially the Francophone community. Marie's dad, Alphonse, was quite involved with the community in Sudbury and in the church. That's how I met the Charette family. I also knew their relatives, the Ménard side of the family. After I was ordained, I ended up marrying them and baptizing them and burying them. Most of them were neighbours of mine when I was growing up," says Monsignor Jolicœur.

Religious orders played key roles in the Francophone community of Sudbury: the Jesuits through parishes and education; the Grey Nuns of the Cross, now called the Sisters of Charity of Ottawa (Sœurs de la Charité), through healthcare and education.

The Grey Nuns ran l'Hôpital St-Joseph; the General Hospital, now known as the St. Joseph's Health Centre, was run by the English nuns, the Sisters of St. Joseph.

Marie's mother, Lucille, was involved in many church-related groups, and she was determined that Marie, too, be closely involved in the Church. "When I was born because my parents were so happy to have a daughter, they dedicated me to the Virgin Mary for two years, and I only wore blue and white during that time," says Marie. "On my second birthday, we were living in the centre of the city. A creek flowed behind our house, but I was not allowed to go near it. One day, my mother found me sitting by the side of the creek with my feet in the water—I loved the feeling of the water on my feet. Anyway, she picked me up, and brought me to church, where she rededicated me to the Virgin Mary until the age of six."

One of the reasons her mother was so protective of her only daughter was that there was a sexual predator in the extended family. Marie would never have believed it if this same person had not attacked her when she was twenty-five. "My mother herself was fondled by this man as a child. She took good care of me. It was probably one of the reasons she sent me to boarding school as a young teenager," says Marie.

When Marie was thirteen years old, her parents decided that it would be a good idea to send her to a boarding school. The education of their children was vitally important to Marie's parents, and although the Charettes were not wealthy, there was no question that Marie and her brothers were to attend a good, French-language, private school. Alphonse Charette would go to the Sudbury Caisse Populaire at the start of the school year and borrow the money he needed for his children's education, since tuition had to be paid in advance.

L'Académie Sainte-Marie, located in Haileybury, Ontario, 220 kilometres northeast of Sudbury was their school of choice. Lucille Charette was impressed with the academic record of its graduates, and she wanted her daughter to have the same advantages. Lucille also liked the fact that at a boarding school Marie would have fewer of the usual distractions that teens might otherwise have and which might keep her from studying.

Marie-Paule's mother invited a woman who had graduated from the school to come over to the house to meet with Marie. She was sold on the idea. "L'Académie Sainte-Marie was run by les Sœurs de l'Assomption de la Sainte Vierge from Nicolet, Quebec," says Marie. "The woman who came to tea to tell me about the school talked about the fact that these nuns were forward thinking. They not only wanted the girls to be successful in a profession, they wanted the girls to become intellectually proficient and well-read. They wanted them to play sports, learn music, and be active in theatre. They offered a well-balanced educational program.

"I still remember arriving at school and looking at the grounds. [...] I couldn't believe it: there was a lake, tennis courts, basketball courts, and shuffleboard courts. It [seemed] huge. [In reality, it] was a small school of about 175 students."

The girls at the school were not all Francophones from Northern Ontario. About half of the students were from mining communities in Northern Quebec. At first, these young women were a little intimidating; they were more stylish than the Ontario girls, and spoke a different type of French, having come from all-Francophone communities. Their English was often poor to non-existent.

"They were completely different from the Northern Ontario girls. They [...] were more sophisticated [...] dressed extremely well whenever they went out, and were from well-to-do families from places like Val-d'Or, Rouyn-Noranda, and Ville-Marie," recalls Marie.

Marie-Paule took to the boarding school and was seldom homesick. "There were moments of loneliness on certain Sundays or on Mother's Day, and I always loved coming home for Christmas." She received a few visits from her parents too. "My parents would come maybe once or twice before Christmas. They would rent a motel room, and I would get permission from the nuns to sleep over with them. We had a lot of fun because they would take me out to the restaurant, and it was always a lovely visit."

Overall, Marie enjoyed her time at the school. "It was a discovery for me to live in an environment with girls; it was completely new for me. The discussions were different. I was always in awe and learning every day," says Marie. "There were huge dorms, and you only had a white curtain to separate one little bed from the other—very little space. In my second year, I was given the bed next to the window, which was a privilege because I was able to sleep with my window open and look out at the night when everybody was asleep.

"The typical day at school started at five thirty. We had to hurry up and get ready for Mass; we had very little time. No showers in the morning, and you did everything quickly: you'd put on your school uniform, which was a white blouse and a navy-blue tunic. To this day, my favourite colours are blue and white," says Marie.

In an all-girls' school, Mass was one of the day's highlights because it included that rarity: boys their age. In those days, girls were not allowed to serve Mass, only boys.

"The Haileybury altar boys were good-looking, which was definitely a distraction. Discussions after Mass always centred on the altar boys. After Mass, breakfast was held in two big rooms, where you would wait to line for your porridge and toast. Everyone brought their dishes from home, and you would always wash your own dishes after each meal.

"After breakfast, we would go outside to get some fresh air, and we'd go walking, or if you had time for a tennis game, you could do that. There was a study period from eight to nine. Classes started at nine and went until noon. [After] lunch, [we had free time] to chat, to walk or run or whatever you wanted to do. We'd then come back at one o'clock until four o'clock. It was very intense. [...] I had piano lessons until four thirty. Then there were days when I didn't have piano lessons, where I had a basketball game or worked on a Shakespearean play or a French play. We put those on twice a year, one in English and one in French, and I would play in both. And Saturday mornings were slower because there was time dedicated to doing a little bit of a cleaning job somewhere in the boarding school."

Coming from Sudbury gave Marie one big advantage: she spoke fluent English. She had the same English teacher every year, not a nun, but an educated woman who lived in the village. She passed on her love of Shakespeare to her students,

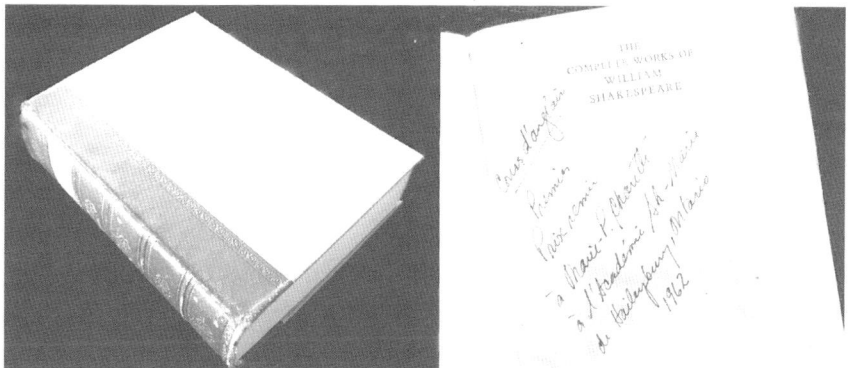

Marie wins first prize at school in English Literature; an edition of the collected works of Shakespeare, with an inscription from her teacher, 1962.
Source: Family Collection.

and to Marie-Paule in particular. One year, Marie-Paule was first in English—her prize was a book of the collected works of Shakespeare, with an inscription from her inspiring teacher.

Apart from the education she received, Marie-Paule Charette's five years at l'Académie Sainte-Marie gave her something she never knew she would need: a profound knowledge of Northern Ontario and the mining districts of neighbouring Quebec. She talked to the girls at school, visited them on holidays, and met their families.

Years later, when she was setting up Radio-Canada's new station in Sudbury, she knew the station had to serve the entirety of Northern Ontario. She knew where Francophone families lived and worked, and that meant she knew where to put the "repeater" antennas to broadcast over a wider area.

And when Prime Minister Jean Chrétien called her to the Senate in 1995, he wanted her to represent, among other things, the people of Northern Ontario and Franco-Ontarians from the whole province. She knew Sudbury, of course, and because of her years at l'Académie Sainte-Marie, she knew the rest of Northern Ontario, who the other Franco-Ontarians were and where they lived.

Marie-Paule Charette graduated from grade 13 at l'Académie Sainte-Marie with top marks. The results came in the mail. When Marie-Paule opened the envelope in front of her father and read him the results, he said: "Let's go celebrate, let's go have Chinese food." So she and her father went out to celebrate; Lucille was in Toronto, taking a summer course to become a specialized high-school teacher.

"At the restaurant, my father asked me what I was going to do. Would I go to teacher's college next year? No, I wanted to go to Laurentian University. His

Marie-Paule's high school graduation picture (grade 13) from l'Académie Sainte-Marie boarding school located in Haileybury, Ontario, 1963.
*Source*: Académie Sainte-Marie.

reaction was, 'You want to go to university. You're going to get married. Why would you want to go to university?' I said I wouldn't be a good teacher, and I would not have been a good nurse, so I said I'd like to go to university like my brothers, Raymond and Gilles. Gilles was the smart one in the family, and had been a model to me. I could see my father saying to himself, 'Oh my God!' so I told him, 'Dad, could we make a deal? I'll pay my tuition and expenses if you support my wish to attend university, and I'll live at home and not in residence.' He said, 'You know what? You're on; this is a great deal.'"

Marie-Paule was a hard worker, and not just at school. Her first job had been at the local candy store near her primary school, when she was twelve years old.

She got her second job two years later, during summer vacation from boarding school, working as a counsellor at the Sudbury Île-aux-chênes day camp. She then worked for Sudbury Recreation Department as a playground supervisor.

"The park I was assigned to was located in the Moulin à fleur, a predominantly French-speaking neighbourhood, which was considered pretty rough. Of the twenty or so members of the team, I was the only Francophone. Whenever I attended meetings with the other supervisors, I could tell that there was a little bit of snobbery regarding the neighbourhood I represented."

One of the girls who worked with Marie was Polish; she didn't speak French, but she was wonderful with the children.

The two of them came up with a way to teach the other playground supervisors a lesson. Marie-Paule had played baseball all her life, so she decided to build a team and coach the players. The trouble was, there were no players. She went door to door in the three streets of the Flour Mill District and left a piece of paper with whoever answered the door, asking if there were any boys in the household who played baseball.

It worked. A gang of them showed up at the playground and Marie-Paule spent bright Sudbury summer nights coaching them. Some were big hulking seventeen-year-olds who could really hit it out of the park.

You can guess the rest. Marie-Paule's well-trained players swept the end-of-season tournament and won the inter-park trophy.

The head of the Recreation Department, a friendly man named Bob Bateman, asked Marie-Paule how she did it. When she explained her system to him, his response was: "What are you doing next summer?" He wanted her to be the supervisor of all the playgrounds. It was a great offer, but she had found another job, one that would take her all the way through university and prepare her for a future career.

"I wanted to do more than work in the parks. I went to CKSO, a radio and television station, where I was hired as a receptionist," says Marie.

She worked on weekends and holidays, and with the money she made from her job and a provincial scholarship, she was able to finance her university studies without any help from her family. She started university when she was eighteen years old.

"Working, for me, has always been an enjoyable experience, and to this day I enjoy it," says Marie. This assertion is unsurprising for a woman who works seven days a week. "I remember when an insurance company launched its 'Freedom '55' campaign, promising people a chance to retire at fifty-five. I couldn't believe it. I would say to people: 'What's wrong with working?' What is it about working just to be able to retire? Then that whole TGIF [Thank God It's Friday] thing came out, and again, I was astounded. You don't work for weekends; you live seven days a week."

Marie-Paule, a Sudbury playground supervisor, with the members of her baseball team, which won the City Trophy in the summer of 1961.
*Source*: Family Collection.

Marie's desire for a career is something she learned from her mother. "When [my mother] decided to go back to teaching, she realized that she wanted to teach high school, but she only had a certificate to teach in primary school. In the mid-1950s, my brother André, who was the youngest in the family, developed severe allergies. He was told that he had to get treatments in Toronto. My mother and father decided that André would spend his summers in Toronto to receive the treatments he needed at SickKids Hospital; meanwhile, she would register at the Ontario Teachers College. She took summer courses while André was being cared for at the hospital. They would spend weeks in Toronto.

"I was twelve or thirteen years old at the time, a young teenager, working summer jobs. In the evenings, my father and I used to go to the drive-in. We saw every movie in the book. It was so much fun. That's when I became close to my dad. It was during those summers that he became my mentor. We started going out to lunch or dinner and we did that the entire time my mother and brother were away.

"My mother studied for about three summers to obtain her secondary school teaching diploma. She then began teaching at a high school near Sudbury. She was ahead of her times. So was my father, encouraging her."

Years later, Alphonse Charette was reading the *Sudbury Star* and spotted an ad for a job in Toronto with the federal government, working in Revenue Canada's Excise Duties and Taxes. He had a business degree from the college in Rigaud, and decades of experience. He was confident he could do the job. He also knew that he would have to move soon. His business—and his house—were being expropriated as part of the urban renewal plans in downtown Sudbury.

"I was a student at the time at Laurentian University," says Marie. "I drove my mother and father to Toronto and brought my father to his interview. While we were in the city, we drove around, and he said he might like living in Toronto."

Lucille was still teaching high school in Sudbury, but there was a new Francophone school opening in Toronto. They felt that there was opportunity for both of them in the city. When Alphonse was offered the position, he accepted. His wife and the rest of the family remained in Sudbury, and he commuted between Sudbury and Toronto for two years, leaving very early Monday mornings and coming back every Friday night.

"My parents moved to Toronto in the early 1970s and my mother began teaching at the first-ever francophone high school in Toronto: École secondaire Étienne-Brûlé. They found a beautiful small house in Don Mills, which was also close to the francophone church. They loved living in Toronto."

André, the youngest brother, was still a student when Alphonse and Lucille moved, so he applied to the University of Toronto in engineering. He lived partly in residence and partly at home. He then moved to Montréal for an engineering job.

In 1983, Alphonse and Lucille returned to Sudbury to live on one of Sudbury's many lakes. André moved in with

> "My mother studied for about three summers to obtain her secondary school teaching diploma. She then began teaching at a high school near Sudbury. She was ahead of her times. So was my father, encouraging her."

> "I discovered the importance of caregivers in a family. André, in my mind, was an angel. He could make my mother laugh, and yet he had to change her diapers. That takes a special person, a very giving person."

them when he went back to Sudbury a few years later. He then found a teaching position at Sudbury's Cambrian College.

"While André was living with them, my father became sick, and he was the one who took care of him until he passed away. He then took care of my mother until she passed away. Both of them were able to die at home thanks to André," Marie observes. "I discovered the importance of caregivers in a family. André, in my mind, was an angel. He could make my mother laugh, and yet he had to change her diapers. That takes a special person, a very giving person."

# University Life: A Tale in Three Parts

THERE ARE MANY PIVOTAL MOMENTS IN LIFE—Marie figures there have been seven major ones for her.

One of the most dramatic occurred in 1963, in a classroom at the fledging Laurentian University in Sudbury. It was a small class; there were maybe twenty students in it because philosophy was not that popular. Marie remembers the incident as if it were yesterday.

"At Laurentian University, I was interested in the basic courses: French, English, philosophy, psychology, sociology, research, and so on. During the philosophy course, we had our first test. I was always nervous during tests, and was fully focussed. The professor, who was also a priest, felt that I was concentrating too hard. [He] tapped me on the shoulder and said, 'Marie-Paule, you don't have to work that hard. I know you're just here to find a husband. So, relax, you'll do okay.'" But Marie-Paule did not relax: the remark shook her to the core.

She was eighteen years old when she was confronted with the fact that women were not always treated equally. She had grown up in a household of four brothers, and her parents had treated her as an equal to her siblings. They did not push her to become a nurse, a teacher, or a nun, though there was little chance of the popular Marie-Paule entering a religious order, even though she was and remains a practising Catholic to this day. Alphonse Charette had come to terms with his daughter's—then unconventional—decision to go to university.

When Marie-Paule graduated *magna cum laude* three years later, the priest who had quipped that she studying merely to find a university-educated husband—a common stereotype back then—apologized. "I'm so proud of you," the Jesuit said to her. Marie-Paule replied, without sarcasm or anger, "Father, I will never be able to thank you enough for saying what you said to me."

She explains her reasoning: "That priest gave me the best possible gift; he gave me the hunger to succeed. I hadn't had that passion before that; I wanted to enjoy university, have fun. There were very few women, so I was going out every Saturday night on a different date; I was having a hell of a good time. But him saying that put a hunger in my belly to learn, do well, and succeed."

This, according to Marie, was the first pivotal moment of her life. "I realized that my professor didn't see me the same way he perceived the young male students. He

> "I realized that my professor didn't see me the same way he perceived the young male students. He was a fantastic philosophy teacher, but he was stuck in the past. Maybe it was a pivotal moment for him too."

was a fantastic philosophy teacher, but he was stuck in the past. Maybe it was a pivotal moment for him too."

Marie-Paule Charette spent three years studying seriously while working part-time to pay for her studies. After working as a camp counsellor, she found a job as a receptionist at CKSO.

"It's where I fell in love with broadcasting," says Marie.

She worked every weekend for a dollar an hour. It does not sound like much, but a fully qualified carpenter made just a little more than two dollars an hour in 1964.

"It was the perfect job for me. It was much quieter in the broadcast centre on the weekend than during the week, so I was able to bring work on my university assignments," says Marie.

Marie learned much more than broadcasting. "Working there, I learned that information is power. As a

Marie worked on weekends as a receptionist at CKSO Radio and Television in Sudbury, to help pay for her university tuition. The station asked her to help with commercial campaigns, 1964.
*Source*: Peter Orfrankos.

receptionist, I became aware of everything that was going on in the station and in every office of every manager."

She learned the value of discretion as well. She remembers one incident in particular. "The wife of the station manager called and asked to speak to her husband. I said he was in a meeting and told her I would leave him a message, knowing all the while his mistress had come in fifteen minutes prior. There was no way I was putting the wife through to the office. True story."

The girlfriend walked past the reception desk on her way out, then, half an hour later, the manager left. Marie handed him the telephone message form, without making eye contact. The manager knew Marie knew. Because of her discretion he always treated her with respect.

"The life lessons I gained: One: information is power. Two: discretion is key in every workplace. Three: broadcasting is such an important part of people's lives."

Marie wanted to go into journalism, but there was a problem. There was only one Francophone school of journalism: Université Laval, in Quebec City. "I didn't want to go to Quebec City because I thought it too far. So, I decided to go into social work. I found that social work gives you the techniques for interviewing, which I wanted to master. I didn't know that I would be going into broadcasting. It was, to me, an unattainable goal; how do you get into it and how do you start?"

She would soon find out.

★ ★ ★

Marie-Paule graduated from Laurentian University *magna cum laude* in 1966. She wanted to do a master's in social work, and so applied to the School of Social Work of St. Patrick's College, in Ottawa, an English-language institution, and the Université de Montréal.

"I learned that if you worked for an employer who wanted you to pursue your studies, they would hire you for the summer and would give you a small bursary for your studies, but you had to sign a contract whereby you would return to them afterwards," recalled Marie.

> "I learned that information is power. As a receptionist, I became aware of everything that was going on in the station and in every office of every manager."

> "The life lessons I gained: One: information is power. Two: discretion is key in every workplace. Three: broadcasting is such an important part of people's lives."

Marie graduates *magna cum laude* from Laurentian University in Sudbury, 1966. Marie attends a special lunch hosted by Senator Rhéal Belisle (far right) and his wife Edna Belisle (third from right). In 1995, some twenty-nine years later, Marie-Paule is called to sit in the seat Senator Belisle occupied from 1963 until 1992.
Source: Laurentian University Archives.

"I called my mentor, Monseigneur René Audet, who was then Assistant Bishop of Ottawa, and explained the system. He said to leave it with him. He was a close friend of the Executive Director of the Children's Aid Society of Ottawa, Joseph Messner. He recommended me to Mr. Messner. The next thing I knew I was hired for a summer job in Ottawa, and at the end of the summer, they offered me a bursary for $1,800 in support of my master's. I signed an agreement with them which stipulated that, at the end of my master's program, I would return to the CAS for two years or reimburse the money."

Circumstances changed, however, and eventually Marie had to return the bursary. The Ottawa school accepted her, but she decided to try to get into the Université de Montréal. She knew it would be difficult; though her marks were spectacular, she worried there was a bias against Francophones from outside Quebec.

"I really wanted to live in a francophone environment. I had not yet received an answer about my application, so I called the Dean of the School of Social Work and made an appointment. She agreed to see me. I took the night bus from Sudbury, a twelve-hour ride to Montréal. Once I arrived, I freshened up and took a city bus to the Université de Montréal," remembers Marie.

"I was outside waiting for the appointment, and she called me in and asked what I wanted to talk about. I told her I wanted to explain why I had applied to the Université de Montréal.

"She had my transcript in front of her, so she saw that my marks were very good. I told her about living as a minority in Sudbury, and that I was interested in experiencing living in a French environment. But I said that rumour had it in Northern Ontario that the university didn't accept students who are not from Quebec very easily.

"She asked me where I had stayed the night before. I told her I had not stayed in Montréal because I couldn't afford a room and that I had taken the bus from Sudbury and arrived that morning and that I would be catching the next bus back to Sudbury at four o'clock that afternoon."

This story, told in a straight, quick way, just the way Marie remembers it now, shocked the Dean of Admissions.

"The dean looked at me and said, 'You mean to say you took the bus from Sudbury to Montréal, you slept on the bus, and you're going to take the bus back home tonight? You want to study here that badly?' I said yes, and she said, 'You don't have to wait to be informed that you are formally accepted; you're in.'

"I didn't walk out of there, I flew! I was so proud to have been accepted.

"When I moved to Montréal from Sudbury, my biggest surprise wasn't the French environment at all; it was the fact that it was such a big city compared to Sudbury. I'd walk down the street and I had nobody to say hello to. In Sudbury, you always knew someone, either in a store or on a corner. In Montréal, it was a totally different environment and feeling."

It was 1966. Marie was twenty-one years old and she immediately joined the Montréal student life. She shared an apartment with Thérèse Daoust, a young woman she had met while working one summer at the Children's Aid Society in Ottawa.

Marie then took a ski trip that would change her life forever.

"We went to Saint-Sauveur. It was my first experience skiing north of Montréal; there was a special price for

> "The dean looked at me and said, 'You mean to say you took the bus from Sudbury to Montréal, you slept on the bus, and you're going to take the bus back home tonight? You want to study here that badly?' I said yes, and she said, 'You don't have to wait to be informed that you are formally accepted; you're in.'"

> "In Sudbury, you always knew someone, either in a store or on a corner. In Montréal, it was a totally different environment and feeling."

students. On the bus, I was sitting with one of the students with whom I shared all my classes, Hugues Quirion," remembers Marie.

The next pivotal moment in Marie's life can be summarized as follows: young love and a hurried marriage.

"Hugues was quite a bit older than I was, but it was fun on the bus, and he taught me a lot of skiing tricks. We came back on the bus together and by the time we got back to Montréal, I was madly in love with him. We married three months later, as students."

Marie's parents were upset that their only daughter was marrying so quickly, marrying someone she did not know that well, as well as someone they had never met.

Her older brother Gilles felt the same way. "Hugues was a nice guy, good-looking and everything. Marie came to me and asked my advice, and I said that knowing someone for three months is a very short time when you plan to spend the rest of your life with them. But she stuck to her guns and married him, which was a huge mistake. He

**MARIE-PAULE CHARETTE**

"Ce qui vaut la peine d'être fait vaut la peine d'être bien fait.

Bachelière "magna cum laude" et "maxima charmae", Marie - Paule nous arriva de l'Académie Sainte-Marie pour se lancer en psychologie. Choisie 'Frosh Queen" dès son arrivée a la Laurentienne, elle accéda l'année suivante au poste de secrétaire de l'AGEUL. Comme finissante, elle fut elue vice-présidente francaise de la classe de graduation de l'Université de Sudbury, et secrétaire de l'Exécutif de graduation de l'U.L. Avec son départ, il se fait un certain vide . . . peut-être est-ce son rire caractéristique ?? May we wish the best of luck to Marie-Paule at the University of Montreal where she will be studying to obtain her Master's of Social Work.

Graduation photo of Marie published in the yearbook, 1966.
*Source*: Laurentian University Archives.

turned out to be not who she thought he was," says Gilles. "Before the wedding, he was an angel, he was a talker. Afterwards, he became the devil."

That crisis was still a few years away.

Marie and Hugues had to finish their university courses and earn their master's degrees. In Marie's case, there were two years of formal classes and then an internship, called a *stage* in French, a word often used by Anglo-Quebecers as well as Francos.

Marie's *stage* was at the Montreal General Hospital. It was an English hospital, but had many Francophone patients. While working there, it started to dawn on Marie that social work might not be for her. She could not get the problems of the patients out of her head.

"I learned a lot, but I have to admit that it was during my internship that I really started wondering whether social services was the appropriate profession for me," says Marie. "One of the things I discovered at the Department of Social Work within the hospital was that I would take my patients' problems home with me. The strength of a social worker is his/her empathy. But you need to protect yourself so that you don't take those problems home with you. You need to separate others' problems from your own personal life. I found out quickly that I was unable to do that."

Marie might have been having problems at work, but on the home front, things were going well.

"Hugues and I had lots of friends, and we had a very busy social life. We were both writing our theses. Hugues was originally from the Beauce region. He had been with the Dominican fathers for nine years, but had not been ordained as a priest. We were into sports; in the winter we did a lot of skiing. In the summer, we were able to rent a small cottage at lac des Deux Montagnes, which I just loved because, coming from Sudbury, where you have more than 330 lakes within the city itself, to be able to spend a summer on the lake is really a treat. We sublet our apartment, which was near the university, to students who took summer courses. This allowed us to rent that little cottage," says Marie.

When Marie and Hugues finished their master's degrees, they were both hired to teach at the Université de

> "Hugues was quite a bit older than I was, but it was fun on the bus, and he taught me a lot of skiing tricks. We came back on the bus together and by the time we got back to Montréal, I was madly in love with him. We married three months later, as students."

Montréal for a year. During that time, they escorted a group of twelve students on an Quebec-France exchange. That government-sponsored trip was part of their teaching duties at the university.

★ ★ ★

Then two major events occurred: Marie became pregnant; and Hugues decided he wanted to pursue a PhD in social work. He was accepted at a few universities, and chose Berkeley in California.

Marie gave birth to Elaine at Hôpital Sainte-Justine in Montréal in July 1970. Three weeks later, in August, they left for Berkeley.

It helps to be twenty-five and have the energy and optimism of youth.

Was she excited to go? "Oh my God, yes. This was 1970. There had just been the 1968 student demonstrations in France. This was the era of demonstrations, and Berkeley was a hot spot. I was looking forward to learning, and I had never lived outside of Canada, so it was a new and exciting experience for me," recalls Marie.

"We did not have an apartment waiting for us in California. We knew only one couple, the McPhersons, who were from Ottawa, and were able to stay with them for three days. He was a Berkeley student doing his doctorate in social work, like Hugues. We found a small house, which was owned by a dentist. Hugues didn't speak English very well, so I went to the dentist's office to negotiate the rental; it was a really cute little house, which we got for almost nothing. There was even a fireplace in the living room, which you appreciate on some winter nights in California.

"It was like school for me, like learning a whole new culture. I felt comfortable because I spoke English quite well, while Hugues improved rapidly his spelling because he was taking classes and had to study in English.

"During the first few months, he wrote his papers in French and I would translate them into English. I was really doing a lot of his schoolwork. Someone later asked me why I just hadn't also applied to the PhD program. I said, 'You're absolutely right, that was a major error on my part.' I was already doing so much of the work, and I was learning, and it was very interesting.

"For the first few months, everything went extremely well. We made new friends. Elaine was a very good baby, and we had a good family doctor and pediatrician. California was very alive. There was a place called People's Park, where the public concerts were given and where many demonstrations were held by groups like the Black Panthers. I remember going to People's Park often to see what was going on.

"We didn't go to San Francisco very often, even though it was just a bridge away, because we were on a tight budget. Some mornings I would take Elaine to a public pool. I really enjoyed the weather and the swim.

"In August 1971, my grandparents celebrated their wedding's fiftieth anniversary, and my parents invited me to go back to Canada with Elaine, whom they hadn't seen in a year, for a visit. I discussed it with Hugues. He was in school, so I went by myself with Elaine. I had a lovely visit. I was glad to be back home. I was away for maybe two weeks.

"When I arrived in Berkeley, it was very late, and I put Elaine to bed. When Hugues and I went to bed, he took his wedding ring off and put it on the bedside table. I asked him what he was doing that for. He explained that it was just uncomfortable on his finger."

Then came the biggest shock of Marie's young life.

"The next morning, I got up earlier than Hugues. I was sitting in the living room in a comfortable chair giving a bottle to Elaine. Hugues got up and came over to stand right in front of me and said, 'I don't believe in fatherhood anymore. I don't believe in marriage anymore, and I don't believe in God anymore.'

"I burst out laughing—I think that's my defence mechanism in difficult situations—and said, 'Hugues, I wish you had said this to me two years ago.'

"At that moment, I felt as though someone had pulled the rug out from under my feet," says Marie.

Not only had Hugues rejected his wife, his child, and his religion, he had totally embraced the counterculture of the era. The boy from Beauce, who had once prepared himself for priesthood, had gone full-blown hippie: drugs, sex, communal living—the works.

"In the following days, he tried to convince me that for our marriage to survive we would have to move into a commune—they were very popular then in Southern California. Hugues was looking more and more like a hippie, letting his hair and beard grow. But so was I—my blonde hair worn long, wearing headbands and jeans and tie-dye shirts. But while I was going to parties, I was extremely troubled. I was adrift.

"I had an appointment with my family doctor, a woman, and confided in her. The first thing she said was, 'I trust that you are using protection because sexual disease is widespread, and you have to protect yourself. Your husband is sleeping around, and he might catch something.' I followed her advice. Then I decided to speak to a friend I had made in Berkeley, named Sumi Kastelic. Her husband Frank Kastelic was studying with Hugues, and she was working full time.

"We went for lunch. I told her that Hugues had admitted to me that while I was in Canada, he had run around every night picking up women and having fun and, as he had said to me, 'discovering a new way of life and really enjoying it.'

"Sumi went silent at the table. Her jaw just dropped, and she said to me, 'Did you know that Hugues came to dinner every night while you were away? He would leave around eight thirty and say he had to go home to study.' She was shocked. 'That's what he was doing while I was cooking dinner for him every night?'

"Sumi was furious with him. She felt she had been deceived and asked if she could tell her husband. I agreed. I told her I wasn't ready yet to share this with anyone else. "She said to me very clearly, 'You have to leave to protect yourself and protect Elaine.' They had no children and never had any, but were very attached to Elaine, who was such a cute one-year-old," remembers Marie. The Kastelics were very supportive, and Sumi even came to visit Marie in Gatineau, when she was destitute and living on her own with Elaine.

"We had planned to go back to Canada for Christmas in 1971, and we did; I stayed in Toronto with my parents while Hugues went to Montréal to do interviews. Elaine became very sick while we were in Toronto. She had whooping cough and had to be hospitalized and put in an oxygen tent. I would spend all day and part of the evening with Elaine.

"My mother started asking, 'Where's Hugues?' I said he was in Montréal and that he had meetings. She felt ill at ease because I was always alone at the hospital with Elaine.

"Hugues did come back before she was released from hospital. When she was released, a good friend of ours—a Dominican priest who Hugues had known for many years and who had blessed our marriage—wanted to see us. One evening we were sitting on the sofa, the three of us—me, Hugues, and the priest Pierre Letellier. He asked how we were doing in Berkeley, and I said we weren't doing too well because Hugues had decided that he didn't want to continue the marriage the way it is.

"He said, 'Come on, Marie, this is your imagination.' I said that Hugues was running around quite a lot and he has discovered a new way of life. "Pierre looked at Hugues and asks, 'Is this true?'

"'Yes,' he admits, 'it's true, and I don't want to continue the marriage the way it is.'

"Pierre was taken aback. He started crying and was very upset. He asked what he could do to help us get back together, and that's when Hugues said, 'Well maybe Marie should stay in Canada and I will go back to Berkeley alone.'

"I said, 'Maybe you're right, Hugues. I hadn't thought of that.'

Marie thinks that there it might indeed be wise to remain in Canada, though that is incredibly hurtful to hear. Indeed, she could stay in Canada, and it would probably be preferable to do so. And yet, struggles with the idea, as she can't bear the thought of her friends and family finding out about the end of her marriage. In 1972, it was humiliating for a woman to be on her own.

The shock of rejection was a pivotal moment for Marie Quirion. The kindness of friends and the wisdom of a professional helped with healing.

# A Single Mother Returns to Canada

IT WAS JANUARY OF 1972. Marie Quirion was on a train from Toronto to Ottawa, with her baby daughter, Elaine, on her lap. She was not going back to Berkeley; Hugues had returned to California on his own.

Marie was travelling with Father Letellier. "He was very upset because he couldn't believe that Hugues had suddenly decided that he no longer wanted to be a father or a husband and that he no longer believed in God. It was a very sad trip from Toronto to Ottawa for me, and for Pierre," recalls Marie.

"I had found friends that I could live with, Paul and Mireille Leguerrier. When I arrived in Ottawa, Paul was waiting for me at the train station. He didn't know what had happened. I had called him in distress the night before, so he met me at the station and took me and my luggage, one suitcase, to their home in Hull.

"I told them my story. They were saddened because they were both very good friends of Hugues and me. I didn't have a penny to my name, but they said it was okay. They offered to let me to stay with them for free and assured me that things would work out. I had been there for a week or ten days when they advised me to get help because they saw that I was not in good shape.

"They knew of a psychiatrist, Dr. Josefine van Husen, who had treated one of their friends—tragically, her baby had died while she was giving it a bath. They didn't know the doctor, but seeing the positive impact the psychiatrist had had, they felt maybe I might benefit from Dr. van Husen. The next day, I made an appointment. I think the work she did with me was a pivotal moment in my life."

Despite her Dutch surname, Dr. van Husen was German; her maiden name was Zimmerman and she spoke with a strong accent. She was an atheist, and while she did not believe in God, she did believe in healthy eating. She thought it was necessary for a healthy mind and a healthy body.

"One of the first things she said to me was: 'You are not depressed; I do not believe in depression. I think you are having to adapt to too many changes at once, and that can be overpowering. I will give you tools to manage those changes,'" says Marie.

"Dr. van Husen had a huge impact on me. She taught me how to have a much more regular schedule: going to bed earlier, getting up earlier, and making sure that Elaine had a regular schedule and so on. She taught me how to eat healthier

Marie with her daughter Elaine, 1972.
*Source*: Photograph by Bruno de Vinck.

foods. She refused to put me on any type of medication. She got me walking much more, every day. She got me to socialize, go to places to meet new people, and apply for a job. She made me realize that I had to branch out on my own, even if I couldn't afford to live on my own."

Dr. van Husen told Marie she was going to do more than pull her out of the slump she was in. "I will teach you to fly, Marie."

"When I was called to the Senate in 1995, I received a card in the mail. In it was written: 'Dear Marie, My sincere congratulations, I knew you could do it. You can fly.'"

"A few weeks later, I tried to call her to thank her, but her husband told me she couldn't talk to me because she was unwell. I never forgot that she had taken the time to write that card." Dr. Josefine van Husen, a woman with a brilliant mind, was ravaged by Alzheimer's Disease. She died in August of 2013.

★ ★ ★

Following Dr. van Husen's advice, Marie began looking for a job. Her friends helped her find a part-time job at the Centre des services sociaux de Hull.

"I worked with families of children with disabilities. They struggled with so many difficulties. That's when I discovered how difficult it is to have a child with a disability. In those years there were so few services for families with children in need," says Marie. She was over-qualified for the work she was doing since she had a master's degree.

That degree qualified her to teach at the CEGEP level, and she soon landed a second part-time job teaching at night at an *école* polytechnique in Hull. There, Marie taught interviewing techniques, how case workers should speak to people who come to social services offices. She taught that one night a week.

However, not only were both jobs only part-time, but they were also temporary. The child who grew up in a happy, middle-class home in Sudbury was struggling for the first time in her life.

Marie also began looking for a place to live. What the Leguerriers did was set her up with a cousin called

> Dr. van Husen told Marie she was going to do more than pull her out of the slump she was in. "I will teach you to fly, Marie."

Dorothy O'Shaughnessy. Despite her Irish name, Dorothy did not speak a word of English. This is quite common in Quebec. In the middle of the nineteenth century, many French Canadians adopted Irish Catholic orphans whose parents had died on the plague ships while trying to escape the Irish Potato Famine. Those who were old enough to remember kept their Irish surnames.

"Dorothy was originally from Shawinigan, and she generously offered to share an apartment with me even though I had Elaine. There were two bedrooms on the third floor of a four-storey apartment building. It wasn't a five-star, but it was convenient and not too far from work," says Marie.

"We decided to give one of the bedrooms to Elaine; that way, when she woke up in the middle of the night, she would not wake Dorothy. I would be able to get up and take care of Elaine. She and I shared the second bedroom with beds that I had found at the Grey Nuns' Mont Saint-Joseph orphanage in Ottawa, which was closing. They were two small single beds, thirty-six inches wide, which we placed at either end of the bedroom. I have never forgotten Dorothy's generosity.

"Hugues had kept everything that had belonged to me and Elaine in Berkeley, so I had no furniture. While carrying in the few boxes we had, I was laughing about it in the corridor. I remember saying to Dorothy that this was the lightest move I had ever made in my life. The door of the apartment next door suddenly opened, and a very loud man's voice said, 'That can only be the laugh of Marie-Paule Charette from Sudbury.' I turned around and there was Ted Beauparlant, one of my classmates from Laurentian University. I hadn't seen him in five years. I hardly knew anyone in Hull, and there was someone that I had known for years living right next door to our new home. It was very heartwarming."

### Two Women Who Helped Each Other

Though Marie was poor at this stage of her life, a friend convinced her she needed a cleaning lady. That woman was Adrienne Morissette. She agreed to work for fifteen dollars one day a week. It gave Marie the time she needed to work and look after baby Elaine.

"This woman knew poverty and she recognized poverty. Adrienne became a key mentor for me in life and taught me so many things," says Marie. "She taught me how to make a tourtière and pickled food in the old French-Canadian way. She taught me how to wash and dry clothes so you wouldn't have to iron very many of them. She taught me how to survive, how to cook, and how to organize myself."

Adrienne even gave Marie valuable career advice.

"I was doing a job at Radio-Canada and another job was opening up so I asked her whether I should go for it. Her advice was, 'Yes. If you don't get it, you've lost nothing. You've got to be bold in life.'"

Elaine with the Franco-Ontarian singer and composer Robert Paquette, 1982.
*Source*: Family collection.

It turned out this wise woman could not read or write. One day, before going to work, Marie left Adrienne a note. At the end of the day, she came home to an embarrassed Adrienne, who confessed she could not read the note.

Later, Bernard offered to teach Adrienne to read and write, but she always said she was too busy. "When we moved to Sudbury in 1978, she was still cleaning our house once a week, and by then she had been with me a good five years. I went down to the basement one time, and I heard her sobbing, 'You are my family, and I am losing you.'"

Marie shared the apartment with Dorothy for a full year, then, as Marie was making more money, though still working two part-time jobs, Dorothy moved to a smaller apartment downstairs to give Marie her own bedroom. It was still stressful, but things were far from the disaster it had initially been.

Marie reduced the tension in her life by visiting Madonna House, a Catholic lay religious community at Combermere in the Madawaska Valley, a two-and-half-hour drive west of Ottawa. Madonna House was founded by Catherine Doherty. Born in 1896 into a family of minor nobility in Russia, she was a nurse in the First World War, escaped the Russian Revolution, immigrated to Canada, ran a soup kitchen in Toronto, and ended up in New York City where she did similar work. It was in New York that she married a journalist named Eddie Doherty.

Elaine and Catherine de Hueck-Doherty, 1982.
*Source*: Family collection.

Eventually they moved to the small town of Combermere, Ontario, where she opened Madonna House.

Marie was introduced to Madonna House by Hugues, in 1967, the year they married.

"When I found myself alone, I reconnected with Madonna House. In fact, Catherine Doherty was Elaine's godmother. Every summer Elaine and I would spend a week or two at Madonna House; it played a huge role in my life's learning."

Marie met a Belgian couple at Madonna House: Baron and Baroness de Vinck. Marie became close to the two of them, in particular Catherine, a poet and author of sixteen books of poetry. Born in 1922, she worked and lived in the United States until she passed away at the age of ninety-nine, in December 2021. She was sitting at her computer writing a poem the day before she died. She would have turned one hundred in just a few weeks.

Baron José de Vinck had built a cottage in the village near Madonna House. "They would go there every summer with their family, and I would join them there with Elaine. It was the only vacation I had, and it was with them," says Marie. The dinners and time she spent with the de Vincks and their children helped both Marie and Elaine. "They took me into their family. What a gift! They played a huge role in my life at the time."

Catherine Doherty was made a member of the Order of Canada in January 1976 and is being considered for canonization. She died in 1985.

Around the same time the de Vincks entered her life, helping Marie to overcome a difficult period in her life, Marie, herself, began aiding some of her troubled friends. Quite by chance, Marie discovered that one of the women she knew well had been sexually abused since childhood.

Her friend was on her way to visit her parents, and Marie suggested they have lunch upon her return. The day of their luncheon, Marie went to her house as agreed, but her friend did not answer. Worried, Marie tried the door. It was unlocked. Marie let herself in and, before she could call out, she heard sobbing coming from the bedroom.

"I sat next to my friend and asked what was wrong. I asked if I could help, but she said no. Later that night, she said that she thought she needed help. So, I suggested Dr. van Husen and she agreed to see her.

"A week later, I got a call from Dr. van Husen asking for my help. She told me she was breaking client confidentiality, with the permission of her client. She told me that my friend had been abused by her father since she was a little girl and was still being abused as an adult. That's why she had come home from her weekend visit so upset. The doctor told me my friend's problem was that she felt responsible and guilty."

There was a clear link between of social work, psychiatry, and faith.

> "If you compare yourself with others, you may become vain or bitter, for always there will be greater and lesser persons than yourself," is Marie's favourite line. "I never wanted to feel like a victim, and that line was my inspiration when I was poor and alone with Elaine."

"'I can't deal with guilt, only a Catholic priest can,' said Dr. van Husen. She asked me for the name of a Catholic priest that I knew and trusted, one who, in my opinion, was very open-minded. 'She needs to be blessed by a priest,' Dr. van Husen told me. And van Husen was an atheist. Being a Catholic, I knew quite a few priests, so I gave her the name of one and his phone number. A month later, my friend was a changed person. She eventually met someone, and they now have a child. It just changed her life."

Dr. van Husen may have been an atheist, but she believed in the ability of people to use their faith to help with some of their psychological problems. She knew the basis of faith and the importance of prayer. She thought the Roman Catholic Church made a big mistake when it reformed so many things at the Second Vatican Council, known as Vatican II.

Marie recalled the conversation with Dr. van Husen from 1972. "Marie, do you realize that the Catholic Church has made three major mistakes." Marie asked, "What are they?" She answered, "Number one: they are not encouraging confession anymore, and that is probably the worst thing that could be done because everyone has something to confess, and everyone feels guilty about something. Guilt is like a beast; it eats a person from the inside. The Catholics have been lucky because they have been able to get rid of the beasts on a regular basis."

Marie says, "There she was, telling me about the psychological benefits of confession. She talked about guilt and the harm it does to one's physical and mental health. To me, there's a huge difference between being treated by a psychiatrist and a psychologist. One of Dr. van Husen's greatest strengths was that in her work with patients she really relied a lot on her medical training, not her psychiatric training. Hearing her talk about confession as a healthy way of maintaining physical and mental health was astounding to me.

"She said the second bad decision the Church had made was to stop encouraging the Rosary. I asked why. 'The Rosary is the biggest natural calmer there is in the world,' said Dr. van Husen. Now what we do is take pills to calm ourselves. She said, 'Catholics who said their Rosary never needed that type of medication because they had a natural way to calm themselves.'

"The third bad decision the Church made, in her opinion, was getting rid of Latin. She said, 'The Catholic Church had a universal spiritual language; it was the only institution in the world that had a language to communicate internationally. They got rid of their communications tool.'"

Marie's Catholicism evolved along with many others after the revolution of Vatican II. She is now "a woman of faith." She has not kept up with the practices of her youth, when Mass was in Latin, and does not go to church on a regular basis but, she takes the time to read a prayer book twice a day. The prayer book is called Prier chaque jour; it is similar to the breviary that priests read every day.

The breviary was given to her by her spiritual director, Monseigneur René Audet, whom she met in 1959 at l'Académie Sainte-Marie when he was a priest. Eventually he became a bishop. He and Marie remained close until his death in 2011.

"I was so fortunate; I had two fathers, and both were my mentors for more than fifty years," says Marie.

The breviary follows the calendar of the Catholic Church and contains, for every morning and evening in the calendar, a prayer, a hymn, a psalm, letters to the Corinthians, a prayer of thanks, the Lord's Prayer, and a closure. Reading all that takes about fifteen minutes in the morning and at night.

"Prayer has a deep calming effect," says Marie.

Hanging on the wall in Marie's home office in Ottawa is the secular prayer "Desiderata," written by the poet Max Ehrmann. Its opening line is: "Go placidly amid the noise and the haste and remember what peace there may be in silence."

Marie saw the poem in a store in Berkeley in 1971. It may have been written in the early 1920s, but its message is pure sixties, and pure Berkeley to boot.

"If you compare yourself with others, you may become vain or bitter, for always there will be greater and lesser persons than yourself," is Marie's favourite line. "I never wanted to feel like a victim, and that line was my inspiration when I was poor and alone with Elaine."

# Radio-Canada: Reclaiming Life

MARIE-PAULE CHARETTE was not cut out for social work. Working with the families of children with disabilities, she took their problems home with her. At this point in life, she needed some luck if she was going to make a change. She had a wide group of friends in Ottawa and Hull, and one of them, a technician at CBC/Radio-Canada, told her there was an opening for a researcher/interviewer at the French-language TV station in Ottawa. He told Marie he thought she would make a good interviewer, and she agreed that he could put her name forward.

She had an interview with the producer and landed the job right away. It was a contract position, which meant she was not on staff, but it held the promise of exciting work and enough money to make ends meet.

Now she had to quit her job as a social worker.

The reaction was unexpected. "The director of social work agency, where I worked, said to me, I'm glad, Marie, because I have to tell you, social work isn't for you.' But he told me, 'Communications *is* your strength. You're a natural and I'm really encouraging you to go to Radio-Canada and to stay there.'"

The response was both a shock and a relief to Marie.

It was September of 1973 and Marie's first job with Radio-Canada was with the Ottawa TV station, helping put together a local French television magazine on people doing different types of work in the Ottawa/Hull area. Marie was responsible for researching the segments and conducting the interviews in the field. One of the first jobs was a field trip, doing interviews outside Ottawa. Marie found a babysitter for Elaine—Dorothy, her former roommate—and headed out with the producer, the

> "Communications *is* your strength. You're a natural and I'm really encouraging you to go to Radio-Canada and to stay there."

man who had hired her, along with the camera operator, all travelling in the SRC van.

The interviews and filming went well, but then came a shocking incident, which Marie has told few people about over the years.

"We were in the motel after working all day. I was in my bedroom and there was a knock on the door. It was the producer. I told him that I was already in my pajamas, and he said, 'Marie, can I come in, I would like to discuss our work for tomorrow.'"

"'I'm so sorry,' I told him, 'I'm already in bed and I'm very tired. Why don't we have breakfast in the morning to discuss it?'" "He insisted on discussing it that night, saying it was too important. He was very pushy. I was trying to remain calm, saying I was really too tired. He kept insisting, but I held out and then he left," remembers Marie.

The next day, the producer acted as if nothing had happened, and they went about shooting interviews and visuals. On Friday afternoon, the crew dropped Marie off at her apartment. When she went to work on Monday there was an envelope on her desk.

"I opened the envelope and found a letter saying I was fired. It was signed by the producer. There I was, a single mother with no other income, and I had just been fired, because I had said no to him. I went into the washroom and started sobbing. All of a sudden, someone put their hand on my back. It was the assistant producer. She told me, 'You're not the first and you won't be the last. He asked you to sleep with him, didn't he?' I said yes, to which she responded, 'And you said no? I'm really impressed, Marie. Good for you, because even if you had said yes, he would still have fired you. He does it to every researcher/interviewer.'"

Marie grabbed her things, picked up Elaine from the babysitter, and went home. The following morning, she went to the unemployment office, but looking around she found the experience depressing and left. When she got home, she found out that word had spread about the sleazy producer firing her for not giving in to his demands.

"I think his assistant spoke to someone. It had reached Aurélien Bouchard, Director of CBOF, the Radio-Canada regional radio station. I knew Aurélien from our days together at Laurentian. He called and said that he had an opening for a researcher for the morning show and would I be interested? I went in for the interview and that's when I fell in love with public radio."

Marie started work, not in the same building as the television producer, but in the radio offices on the seventh floor of the Château Laurier Hotel next to Parliament Hill, where she would be working as a senator more than twenty years later.

"I walked into the room where the morning show producer and the other two researchers were, and there was an empty desk there for me. Four desks in one

Marie as Producer of a weekend radio show at CBOF, the Radio-Canada station in Ottawa (the National Capital Region). She had suggested that the show, titled "Radioactif," be aired in a public space—it became one of the first live radio shows aired by CBC/Radio-Canada, 1974.
*Source*: Radio-Canada Archives.

room. I fell in love with the sounds, the smell, and people talking to each other about the next show."

Marie was in heaven.

The Director of Human Resources at Radio-Canada, Pierre Racicot, had gotten wind of the sexual harassment issue and met with Marie to discuss it. She did not want to make an issue of it, adding: "Pierre, if I file a complaint, I'm finished."

This was in 1973, a long time before #MeToo.

Still, Pierre Racicot says though Marie might not have been aware, they had investigated other complaints against the producer. "This guy was known for trying things like that. In the end, he was let go."

Marie thrived in radio. Soon she was working as a full-time researcher for the morning show, preparing material for the announcer and three interviews a day.

"I reported to the producer, whose name was Jean-Pierre Ricard. They were outstanding professionals. Anyway, I went to the other two producers—one of them ran the afternoon show and the other looked after the weekend show—and said to them, 'If ever you want me to do research for you, it's not a problem.'"

Marie was working on freelance contracts for them. That meant each producer was paying her, which would not have happened if she had been on full-time staff.

"During the day, I would prepare interviews for the morning show, and at night, after Elaine was in bed, I would prepare interviews for the afternoon show. I was working seven days a week, twelve hours a day, preparing interviews for the three shows.

"One day, I was called into the office of the administrator. He said to me, 'You have three contracts with us?'

"I said, 'Yes.'

"Then he said to me, 'It's unacceptable, you cannot have three contracts at the same time.' I asked if there was a policy. He said no but that he didn't accept it, and he was the administrator, and it wasn't appropriate.

"I said, 'But everybody is happy with the interviews, so what's the problem?'

"He said, 'It's not appropriate.'

"My other contracts were quickly cancelled. I gave him names of people I knew would be good researchers, and everybody was happy. I couldn't complain; I already had a contract, but I wasn't making much money."

Marie learned broadcasting from the ground up: research, interviewing, and story editing. She then made a move to producing a daily program.

"One day I was called into the office of Aurélien Bouchard, who told me he needed a producer for the weekend show. He told me that I would have to work from Wednesday through Sunday, because I would be producing Saturday mornings and Sunday mornings. Saturday mornings were from six to twelve, non-stop, and Sunday mornings were from nine to twelve. He asked if I would be interested—he knew that I was a single mother. Right away, I said, 'Absolutely.'

"Aurélien was a very good radio man; he had all kinds of good ideas for radio. I kept writing and writing. I told him I'd prepare a business plan and get back to him and I was definitely interested.

"The next day I got a call from Aurélien's boss, whom I had never met. He was the big boss of the Ottawa area, English and French, radio and television. His name was Georges Huard. His office was in a building near the Champlain Bridge in Ottawa. I drove over to the building went to Mr. Huard's office, and introduced myself saying, 'Bonjour, my name is Marie Quirion, *avez-vous demandé à me voir?*'

"He said, being very formal with me, 'Is it true that you are sleeping with Mr. Aurélien Bouchard?'

"I burst out laughing, and I said, no, that's a ridiculous suggestion.

"All of a sudden, there's a person standing behind me at the door. I didn't know who he was. He said, 'Mr. Huard, I told you it wasn't true.'

"It was Pierre Racicot, the Director of Human Resources, who was the only one who knew what had happened to me in television. What Pierre told me later was that there had been a formal complaint lodged by a production assistant who wanted that job. She had tabled a formal complaint with her union, saying that I had benefitted from favourable discrimination because I was sleeping with the director. He even gave me the name of the person. It was public knowledge within the union.

"I always pretended I didn't know what she had done, because I was still working with her. I just made sure that she never became my production assistant. In those days, production assistants were usually the first ones considered to become producers. I understand her reaction: this blonde single mother had been promoted all of a sudden. I had been there only a year, and I was being promoted to producer. I can understand her thinking, 'Ah-ha, she must be sleeping with the boss.' But I wasn't.

"Talk about turning points. Becoming the producer of the weekend program was a very important project for me because it was my opportunity to create something totally new. I started working with a production assistant, and we would call each other 24/7, asking each other what we thought of this or that. I decided that it was going to be a participatory show. I made sure that it was organized in such a way that we had to question the announcer, Serge Arsenault, who became very well-known at Radio-Canada as a sports commentator nationally and internationally. He went on to become founding president of the International Marathon of Montréal in 1979 as well as the founding CEO of the Grand Prix des Amériques a few years later. His influence in the worlds of running and cycling is still greatly felt.

"I had to find a title for the show, so I looked up words related to radio and related to participation, and that's when I came up with *Radioactif*. Now, that title in French and in English was picked up over the years by several shows, and that confirms the adage, 'Imitation is the sincerest form of flattery.' I found it in the French dictionary, and I was so excited when I read it. I said, 'That's it, that's the title.' I wanted to give listeners the sense that they were part of the show. So, we would have people calling in, we would ask questions and play games with them, like remembering a song or have them try to identify who the next guest was, because we did interviews of guests from every walk of life.

"Here's an example: One day I was walking to lunch on Rideau Street and noticed Toller Cranston [figure skater winner of Olympic bronze medal in 1976]. I went up to him, introduced myself, and congratulated him for making us so proud as Canadians. He answered me in French! I said to him, 'I didn't know you spoke French; would you be willing to do an interview?' And that's how I got most of my interviews. People around me just couldn't believe that we had Toller Cranston on air speaking in French on a Saturday morning at Radio-Canada.

> "One of the most important things I learned from doing *Radioactif* was the importance of listening to people. We pick up so many ideas by listening. I would also check up on what was going on at radio stations in other countries to get other ideas."

"We tried to do interviews by phone, and I would always try to make sure the guest was on a what was then called a broadband line so that the interview would be clearer, without the poor sound that came over a regular phone line. With time, I came to realize that many of our interviewees liked to come to the studio, so I would give them the choice.

"One of the most important things I learned from doing *Radioactif* was the importance of listening to people. We pick up so many ideas by listening. I would also check up on what was going on at radio stations in other countries to get other ideas.

"I looked at what was going on both at the BBC and in France. I found them to be very ahead of their times. There was also public radio in Italy, but I found that England and France were the countries that applied the concept of public radio best. It was also what distinguished the CBC from all the private radio stations. To me, CBC was there to serve, and I found that they were doing that extremely well in England and in France. But then, in France, public radio became private, and it changed the tone of the radio stations."

One of Marie's ideas was to do live broadcasts. The Ottawa area had done programs on site before, but they were always recorded and rebroadcast. Live radio was tricky because there were so many technical things that could go wrong. But Marie talked her boss into it. They chose les Galeries de Hull, to attract as many Francophones as possible.

The public loved it. People swarmed to the shopping mall on Saturday morning to see *Radioactif* from six to noon. Serge Arsenault, the host, was popular, and people wanted to see what he looked like. The live broadcast was a huge success, doubling the program's ratings. It was also a launching pad for the next step in Marie's career.

Serge was an inspired pick as host of the program. A staunch Quebec nationalist, he had had to leave Quebec to escape political problems. He settled in Vancouver, where he started working for the new French-language station there, CBU-FM. "I started as a morning man doing radio in Vancouver, and after that, because of my (political) studies, Montréal asked me to be a correspondent, for TV and radio for the network," says Arsenault. "Three years later, Ottawa asked me to be the anchor man for the news and everything else."

That was a five-day-a-week job. Serge was a new father and wanted to stay at home during the week while his wife worked. *Radioactif* was a weekend show and the perfect fit for him.

"It seems irrelevant now or kind of stupid, but it was the first time that I had had a woman as my boss," says Arsenault. "One of Marie's wonderful qualities is listening; many producers don't even look at the content, but Marie was quite precise and would concentrate on everything I was saying. She gave me lots of liberty. I respected that very much and, because of that, I knew what lines not to cross. We also had lots of discussions about 'do we do this or that,' or what do you think of that guest. Then the communication was correct, even though off air we were two completely different people. On air, we were like brother and sister."

He says he learned a lot from Marie, and it helped him later in his career. "I learned from Marie: be stubborn, believe in yourself, balance everything, and be honest."

Serge Arsenault went on to a brilliant career, first at Radio-Canada, where he was a major sports announcer, then as an entrepreneur. Since leaving the SRC at the age of forty, he has become a wildly successful independent television producer. He has pursued numerous other interests, including serving as the founder of the Grand Prix Cycliste de Montréal. "Serge is worth a book in himself," says Marie.

"I did the weekend show until the station was given four hours a day to do a regional program every afternoon. That was big, because in those days, every regional station could have forty hours that could be done with regional shows, and the rest of the time was national shows. But Ottawa negotiated one year with Montréal that there would be more than forty hours a week. Aurélien negotiated a four-hour regional radio show produced in Ottawa for the listeners of the National Capital Region. He was very astute. The program was to run from two in the afternoon

"It seems irrelevant now or kind of stupid, but it was the first time that I had had a woman as my boss," says Arsenault. "One of Marie's wonderful qualities is listening; many producers don't even look at the content, but Marie was quite precise and would concentrate on everything I was saying. She gave me lots of liberty."

"I learned from Marie: be stubborn, believe in yourself, balance everything, and be honest."

Marie makes the cover of the December 1974 television guide of *Le Droit* newspaper (with a two-page story inside).
*Source*: Photograph by François Roy, *Le Droit*.

to six every weekday. It takes a lot of work to produce twenty hours of airtime a week.

"I proceeded in a different way: I presented my business plan to Aurélien Bouchard. It was accepted, the budget was accepted. We were trying to choose a name for the show. We brainstormed a lot. Finally, the title that was given was "Place Douze-Cinquante". Because 1250 was the station's position on the radio dial and *Place* in French really means a place where people come together and share. I was trying to create an audio magazine.

"I hired the team two weeks before the show went on air," says Marie. She says she tried to strike a balance between gender, cultural interests, and age. The youngest researcher was twenty-one, the oldest sixty-five.

"I had one announcer, and four researchers. Bernard Poulin, who, of course, I later married, was one of the four researchers I hired. I separated the portfolios among the four: one had entertainment and sports, another one had current affairs, another one had community life—Bernard had that one—and the fourth had arts and culture. It was interesting that Bernard didn't have arts and culture; it was a woman who had that portfolio. I didn't even know that he was a painter. I knew him as a community worker who had been very involved with the Children's Aid Society and who was extremely well respected for his community work in Ottawa. He was, among other things, very active with Big Brothers[1]. He was a teacher of special education at the M.F. McHugh School, which was affiliated with the Royal Ottawa Hospital. He had also founded the first French teaching services for children with emotional disturbances in Ontario.

"The show came out, the ratings were good, the team was motivated, and it seemed we weren't working because we were enjoying ourselves so much. We were in the Château Laurier. We had two rooms: one large, in which the four researchers worked, each with their own desk, and a lot of noise with typewriters going and the teletype bringing in news stories. I loved those noises, those smells—it was fantastic.

"My office was across the hall. We were on a floor in the Château Laurier where you had mansard windows. When you look at the Château Laurier, you see them—windows that have a sloping ceiling inside. It creates a very nice atmosphere in a room. My desk faced the door, and the hotel had given me a single bed that I had put at the bottom under that sloping roof. I could take a nap there. It was very practical for me because I came in so early and worked long hours.

"One morning, the director of all the radio technical services for both CBC and Radio-Canada came to see me. 'Marie,' he asked, 'can I see you in my office, please?'

---

1. Translator's note: Today this organization is called Big Brothers Big Sisters of Canada: https://bigbrothersbigsisters.ca/find-agency-near/

> "He told me he had been called by the Château at midnight and that he had to come in because there had been a serious incident.
> "I said, 'Wow, what happened?'
> "He said, 'I was brought to your office, and there was shit on your desk.'
> "I burst out laughing. 'What do you mean, there was shit on my desk?'
> "'Marie, I'm not kidding,' he said. 'There was one hell of a pile of shit on your desk.'"

"He had never done that before. I didn't really know him—we just said hello every morning. We went to his office. He closed the door and sat at his desk. He said, 'Marie, I guess you've heard about what happened last night?' I said no, I hadn't, and asked what he was talking about. He told me he had been called by the Château at midnight and that he had to come in because there had been a serious incident.

"I said, 'Wow, what happened?'

"He said, 'I was brought to your office, and there was shit on your desk.'

"I burst out laughing. 'What do you mean, there was shit on my desk?'

"'Marie, I'm not kidding,' he said. 'There was one hell of a pile of shit on your desk. Marie, your show is doing really well, really well; we're even talking about it on the English side. There's somebody somewhere who is extremely envious of you. To take the trouble to take a shit on your desk!'

"He told me that he had cleaned it all up with the help of the staff of the Château. 'There's only one person at the Château who knows about this.' He had asked him not to discuss it with anybody.

'Now,' he said to me, 'we're going to have some fun. I'd like to suggest something. Do you trust me?'

"I said, 'Absolutely, I trust you.'

"'Okay,' he said, 'You're going to get up from that chair, open the door, and you're going to burst out laughing the same way you always do in the corridor and pretend as though nothing happened every day from now on, and you will not tell a soul. They're just waiting for you to get upset; trying to get you to react and complain to the director. But we're going to outwit them and pretend nothing ever happened.'

"I laughed and laughed, saying it was the most fun I'd had in a long time. We never found out who did it. I never even looked into it. But, boy, did we ever keep that secret.

"There was a going away party when that technical director retired a few months later, and he made a coded reference to the incident. 'I know we're not supposed to name anyone, but I wanted to take advantage of this opportunity to say to you that I have worked with a lot of people, and I discovered what dignity is in working with one particular producer. I'd like to congratulate Marie Quirion for what and who she is.' He knew that somewhere in that room were those who had played the trick, and he was getting back at them. Later, when I thanked him for that, he said, 'We got them, Marie, we got them.'

"I learned that the best revenge is success," says Marie.

> **"I learned that the best revenge is success."**

★ ★ ★

Marie's life during the period with Radio-Canada in Ottawa was exciting professionally and kept her very busy. That meant that she was not able to spend as much time with Elaine as she wanted.

While working at Radio-Canada, Marie was balancing work life and taking care of her young daughter, Elaine. She found a mother of three grown children who took in babies and toddlers for the day. This was daycare before the name even existed.

"Monique Benoît was exceptional," says Marie. "When I picked up Elaine at the end of the day, she insisted that I stay for coffee. Elaine was three or four years old at the time, and Monique would tell me how she did and then ask about my day. I had no one to unload on, so Monique played a huge role in my life."

A few years later, when Elaine was in kindergarten, Marie encountered a problem specific to single mothers. With Father's Day fast approaching, Marie worried about Elaine, since she was the only child of a single parent. Soon all the children in class would be asked about their fathers; it would be awkward for Elaine.

"I explained to the teacher that my daughter Elaine is the only child in class who lives with a single mother. I said, "On Father's Day you're going to ask the children to prepare a card for their father, recalls Marie. She replied, 'Absolutely that's the tradition.'"

"Would you do me a favour?" Marie asked the teacher. "Could you ask the children to prepare a card for their father, or their grandfather, or their favourite uncle, or

> "Could you ask the children to prepare a card for their father, or their grandfather, or their favourite uncle, or their favourite neighbour? That way, Elaine won't feel different," says Marie. The teacher agreed. It certainly did her a favour as the number of single-parent families was starting to grow year over year.

their favourite neighbour? That way, Elaine won't feel different," says Marie.

The teacher agreed. It certainly did her a favour as the number of single-parent families was starting to grow year over year.

For Marie's daughter, this was a difficult period. "There was a lot of loneliness and isolation before the age of six or seven, when Bernard came around. I had a father who wasn't present, and my mother was working. She would go to work in the early mornings so I would sleep at the neighbour's house. I didn't have siblings, so I felt often alone," says Elaine. "I guess my mother was more in survival mode at that time.

"You don't realize it when you are a child. And yet, I recognized the shift that happened in her life when Bernard came into the picture. Things changed. Those were joyful years."

# Bernard and Family Life

BERNARD POULIN decided to marry Marie almost as soon as he met her.

Remembering their first meeting, he recalls, "I went home and did a sketch of her the first day I met her." (It's still on her desk.)

Marie, however, was not immediately sure of what to make of this guy.

They first met in 1976, when he had left his job at the Royal Ottawa Psychiatric Hospital and applied to work as a researcher for a new daily afternoon radio show that Marie was producing.

★ ★ ★

Bernard Poulin was born into a Francophone family in Windsor, Ontario. He speaks fluent French and totally unaccented English. Later, the family moved to Montréal, living in Ahuntsic. Only seventeen at the time, he moved to Ottawa, preferring to live on his own. After high school, he got a job and went to teacher's college.

"I began teaching in 1964 when I was nineteen. At first, I taught in a regular school in Cornwall. The kids were wonderful, but I got a little bit bored with the standard classroom routines. On weekends, I would volunteer in an ex-orphanage that had been turned into a treatment home for kids who could not fit into traditional foster homes. They were from the foster care system. The home was run by the Grey Nuns. Most of them were fairly old; the nuns couldn't handle the boys. These weren't just boys who had lost their parents, they were roughneck kids. In 1965 the nuns called me and said, 'If you don't take over the boy's section of this treatment home, we're closing the doors of this school.' So, I took the job. I lived in a boiler room for a year and a half. Once we got the treatment centre rolling, I started a school at the centre and was eventually asked by the school boards to open the first French classes for kids with emotional disturbances in Ontario. I worked at Mont-Saint-Joseph until 1968."

"It was quite an extraordinarily busy life; I was working 365 days a year with children who felt unwanted. At that time, kids were still being sent off to reform school. Basically, if you were twelve and reacted to the fact that your home situation was bad, then you got a new title: delinquent. That was the only way the

> "I was working 365 days a year with children who felt unwanted. At that time, kids were still being sent off to reform school. Basically, if you were twelve and reacted to the fact that your home situation was bad, then you got a new title: delinquent. That was the only way the system treated them. But in the 1960s, the doors opened to special education and mental health treatments, so I was there at the right time."

system treated them. But in the 1960s, the doors opened to special education and mental health treatments, so I was there at the right time. I went into it and loved it. I worked in a field that attracted few people.

"Reform schools closed eventually in the 1960s, and that's when group homes started and treatment programs at the Children's Aid Society were launched. Organizations throughout the world were finally being much more efficiently organized in the area of mental health.

"The success ratio? It's still an iffy situation. I would say about 40 to 50 percent do okay and the rest continue to struggle, not so much because of their initial problems but rather because of those caused by the system.

"Still today, some of my kids in their forties, fifties, and sixties call me. I'm the only father they've ever known, even though when I started that I was only nineteen. It's not a great social work philosophy we have in the West; we don't place kids permanently and we take way too many away from their family homes. We're something of a self-righteous society. But I was young and too stupid to know that I wouldn't be able to change the system.

"I worked as a teacher in special education until 1975. Part of my work was to establish classrooms for kids who were in psychiatric hospitals or treatment homes. These kids needed to fit into society. But by 1975, I was exhausted. I never got involved with anyone because I was too damn busy.

"In 1976 I met a friend of mine for lunch one day. I told her that I was looking for a job, so she introduced me to Marie at the SRC. Marie hired me. She was my boss. I passed my three-month probation period, and she thought I was very good."

"I asked her on a date; I had bought tickets for a concert at the National Arts Centre. But she refused, saying that it was unethical to date anyone on staff."

That was a Friday. The next Monday, when Marie arrived at the office, there was an envelope on her desk. It was Bernard's resignation. "I knew I could go back and teach at the hospital, and that would allow me to go out with her. She was quite angry with me when I quit. I told her she couldn't change my mind. 'I'm going to marry you one day.' Eleven months later we were married. That's how it happened," says Bernard.

Marie gave in and went on a date. Bernard knew from working with Marie and watching her choose music for the morning show what she would like to see. The singer was Jacques Michel. Bernard was right; it was a big hit.

"I started living with Marie and Elaine in Aylmer. They lived in the small house Marie had bought. We were married at St. Mark's, an English Catholic church in Aylmer, but they allowed a French priest to marry us there. Eventually, we moved to Touraine, just outside of Hull," says Bernard.

"When we moved to Touraine," remembers Bernard, "I had to rent a fifteen-ton truck, but I couldn't drive it because it was a standard shift." Marie, however, does. "I sat at the wheel of the truck. I drive very fast, and Bernard doesn't like me to drive when he is in the car. I knew he was watching, so I lit a cigarette and let it dangle from the side of my mouth, like a real tough guy. I put a cap on and drove

> "It's not a great social work philosophy we have in the West; we don't place kids permanently and we take way too many away from their family homes. We're something of a self-righteous society. But I was young and too stupid to know that I wouldn't be able to change the system."

In August 1976, Bernard is interviewed by Marie who is seeking researcher-interviewers for her new four-hour daily magazine show, "Place 1250." Bernard sketched it from memory after the interview.
Source: Bernard Poulin.

> When Marie arrived at the office, there was an envelope on her desk. It was Bernard's resignation. "I knew I could go back and teach at the hospital, and that would allow me to go out with her. She was quite angry with me when I quit. I told her she couldn't change my mind. 'I'm going to marry you one day.' Eleven months later we were married."

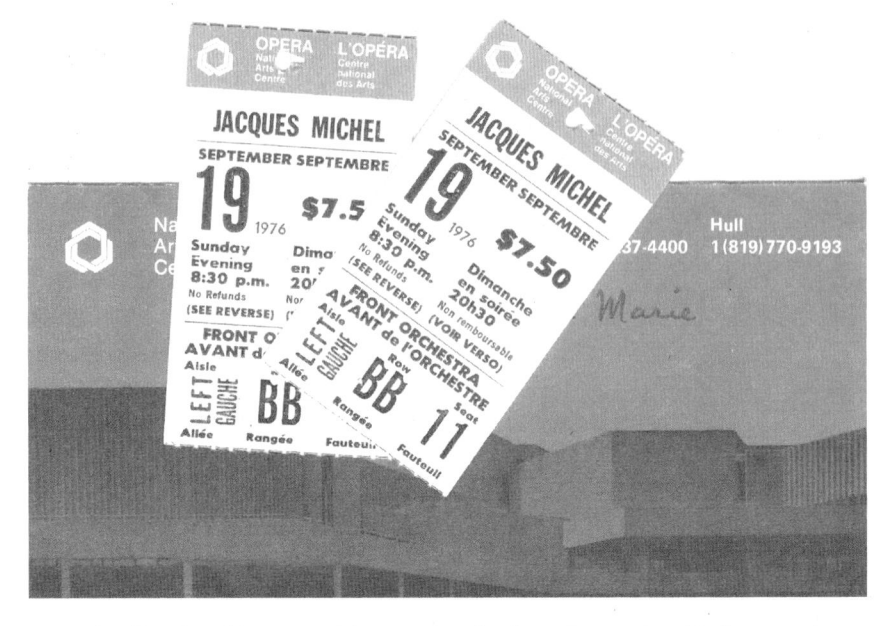

Bernard resigns from his new position as researcher-interviewer when Marie states she did not date employees. The National Arts Centre tickets for the date on which they went after Bernard's resignation.
Source: Family Collection.

off. You should've seen his face! I thought, 'He's going to follow me to make sure I don't drive too fast.' And he did."

It was around this time Bernard decided to adopt Elaine. Bernard and Marie went through the entire adoption process. Although Marie was the biological mother, Quebec law demanded that she, too, complete the full adoption process. Marie had to write a history of her life, her marriage, the breakup, Hugues's rejection of her and Elaine, the struggles she experienced, her marriage to Bernard, and their decision to give Elaine the name Poulin. Marie and Bernard felt it would be better for Elaine to have the same name as her parents and her as-yet unborn sister.

No one knew where the biological father was living. Advertisements were placed in newspapers and Hugues was found. He informed the social worker that he would challenge the adoption application by Bernard and Marie. The case had to go to court. What should have been a simple procedure turned into a dramatic event.

The morning of the court appearance, Hugues walked over to where Marie and Bernard were sitting. He ignored Bernard and said to Marie: "May I speak to you alone?"

Wedding Portrait, 1977.
*Source*: Family Collection.

Marie remembers one of the most dramatic conversations in her life. "Listen Marie," said Hugues, "We have never had any confrontation; why don't we just agree that Elaine will keep my name? We don't have to go to court today."

Marie responded, "Hugues, you kept all the furniture, all the pictures, never sent any money, and never visited. And in this case, we aren't talking about material things; we are talking about a child. I think it should be an objective third person who makes the decision about what is in the best interests of the child." They entered the court. The judge heard from three witnesses, who all knew of Hugues's rejection of his wife and child in Berkeley. The judge then

> The ruling from the judge came in December 1977. Marie was told it was the first time in Canada that a child was adopted despite the biological father's objection.

asked questions of Hugues. He answered the judge's questions even though his lawyer had told him to let her do the talking.

"Why did you never give any money for the raising of your child?" asked the judge.

Marie remembers Hugues's response: "She didn't need any money. She comes from a well-to-do family. Look at her now. She is an executive at Radio-Canada!"

At this point, the judge took the information on file, which he had read before the hearing, and slammed it on his desk.

"Hugues Quirion. Do you take me for a fool?" Marie remembers the judge saying. "I read that file. Your ex-wife had two part-time jobs to make ends meet, and still you never gave her any money."

The judge then asked Hugues why he objected to the adoption. Hugues' only response was that he wanted Elaine to keep his family name. The judge then asked Marie why she wanted the adoption to go through.

"I told him that I wanted Elaine to have the same name as the rest of the family. I had taken Bernard's name. I was three months pregnant at the time. And I felt Bernard was, in fact, Elaine's real father," recalls Marie.

The ruling from the judge came in December 1977. Marie was told it was the first time in Canada that a child was adopted despite the biological father's objection.

★ ★ ★

The issue of the relationship between Elaine and Hugues is a delicate one. Speaking as an adult, Elaine admits that her feelings toward her biological father are complex. Elaine first contacted her biological father at the age of twenty-four. "Now that is a whole chapter in itself. I don't have any contact with him at the moment. We had a close relationship for seven years or so, but I ended that in 2001, I think. I did see him again this year to kind of make peace, which I thought was an important thing to do since he is in his eighties now, but it hasn't gone any further."

One might expect Elaine to feel resentment and anger toward her biological father. "I'm not one to carry resentment. Besides, my life was full: that void had been replaced by Bernard. I didn't carry animosity. I wanted to meet him because I was curious; it was something that was lingering. I wanted to see who this person was, and I discovered that through a relationship."

★ ★ ★

Some people find it tough being married to a high-powered successful woman. Bernard Poulin is comfortable in his own skin.

"I was thirty-three when I married. I had been living my own life until then. When I met Marie, I knew I had met a firebrand. She had so many creative thoughts. She was such an organized, intelligent woman, and a great leader. People followed her right into the fire and came out smelling like a rose. She would bring people into some difficult situations where it was all brand new and difficult, but she did it all, and everyone benefitted from the adventure.

"When I met Marie, I was enamoured with her.

"Naturally, she had thoughts of her own and I have thoughts of my own too. We are two hard-headed individuals who respect the fact that we are married to someone with conviction. Here was a woman who had her own strengths and capabilities, who could say yes or no and move on and try stuff and be creative."

Bernard grew up with strong women. "I must thank my mother for that: she was a feminist woman when there was no such thing. We were eight children and there was no way in hell that our sisters were going to shine our shoes, or clean anything for us. The boys were never to treat the girls as anything less than they were—equal.

"And so, we were creative. My studio was at home; I could stay with the kids because I didn't want keys around their necks, and her travelling all the time, it was mandatory that one of us should be at home to greet the girls at the end of their school day. As a result, the girls and I have a great relationship."

Marie recalls an anecdote that illustrates this creativity within their marriage and family. "Bernard was raised by a feminist mother. The girls in the family never ironed the boys' clothes; they each did their own. Bernard is more experienced in ironing because prior to being a student at l'École normale, he worked in a men's clothing shop where he learned the art of ironing from the store's tailor. When we were newly married, I took out the ironing board one day to do the ironing. I never liked ironing."

Bernard told me, 'That's not how you iron, Marie.' He took the ironing board and turned it around the proper way. I have never ironed since. To this day, Bernard does the ironing. It's an ongoing joke between us."

# CBON (C'EST BON): The Birth of Public French Radio in Northern Ontario

MARIE AND BERNARD had only been married a year when they would experience another big change in their lives. Marie tells the story. "In January 1978, I was informed that Radio-Canada was opening a regional production centre in Sudbury, and it was suggested to me that I should apply for the job. I was seven months pregnant with Valérie at the time, so I told them that I was not interested in applying. But I said that I wanted to meet the selection committee to talk to them about Northern Ontario and Sudbury. People think that this is a mining town where people sit and drink all night. I wanted to tell them that it's so much more than that. I wanted to tell them what type of radio station was needed. I wanted one that people would appreciate and listen to. They agreed to meet with me.

"Getting to the meeting was difficult, though. I was so pregnant I couldn't fly; I had to take the train to Montréal. As well as not being able to fly, I didn't have the right clothes. Bernard took me shopping the evening before the interview because I always wore old shirts of his that were big enough to cover my bulge. He found me a blue tunic for a pregnant woman, and bought me a beautiful shirt with a bow and long sleeves, something like the outfit I wore at boarding school, and reminiscent of the outfit my mother had chosen for me when I was a toddler. The next morning, I looked completely different. I wore high heels, nylons instead of slacks, that shirt with the bow, and the sleeveless tunic. I looked quite nice."

On a crisp sunny morning in January 1978, a pregnant Marie Poulin took the morning train from Ottawa to Montréal. Maison Radio-Canada, located on René-Lévesque Boulevard across from two churches that once served the parishes of the people who lived in the area. It was the most impressive headquarters of that public corporation in the country, the home of the French network. Marie, who usually went to work in Ottawa wearing jeans and a shirt, was in the power outfit chosen by Bernard. Now, she was a grown, confident woman, but she was a little uncomfortable about meeting people while pregnant.

Marie took the elevator to the twelfth floor, where the executives who ran the network had their offices looking out over Molson's brewery and the frozen St.

Lawrence River. One of the executives, the man in charge of Human Resources, met her at the elevator and escorted her into the meeting room. There were five men in white shirts, ties, and navy-blue suits. It was a far cry from the casual office attire worn by those in the Radio-Canada offices in Ottawa.

"Messieurs, I don't usually look like this," said Marie, in obvious reference to her pregnant state. That broke the ice; they laughed, Marie laughed, and they got down to the job at hand: finding someone to open the French-language station in Sudbury.

Marie could not know it at the time, but she had already been the subject of high-level discussions at Radio-Canada—not just in Montréal, but at head office in Ottawa as well.

"We had no radio stations up north. Marie was from Northern Ontario, so when they decided to open a station in Sudbury, they hired her, which was only normal," says Pierre Racicot, who was head of Human Resources for the French network in Ottawa. "I remember being in some of the discussions where we agreed that if we were going to open a station, we should get someone who at least knew the territory. She had shown very good judgment and was a very good producer.

"We sat at a round table and began talking about Northern Ontario. I hadn't brought any notes. I was only going there, in my mind, to give them a briefing. The first thing I touched on was the importance of French culture in Northern Ontario and how Francophones there had to have a voice," says Marie.

She told them about the Jesuits and the nuns who kept the French culture alive from the very beginning. "I spoke to them about how education was encouraged in all French-Canadian families, even though at that time, there was no public education at the secondary school level. Then we talked about how many French-Canadian businesspeople are successful, giving them names and examples. I mentioned how Paul Desmarais encouraged successful businesses. I talked about the developer Robert Campeau and the communications guru from Timmins, Conrad Lavigne. I also mentioned Baxter Ricard and the radio stations in Northern Ontario he had established, and the fact that he owned both English and French private radio stations."

Then the men in the room asked a question that today would have sent them to a sexist re-education class. "If you're a successful producer, would you throw away the men on the team, like a praying mantis, who eats her mate once her goals are achieved?" one of them asked.

Quick-witted, Marie came back with a raunchy response that made them all laugh. It was bold, but it kept her in control of the meeting and showed in an instant that she could not be pushed around, that she would not fold when challenged.

"I told them that I strongly believe in the success of a well-balanced team of men and women," said Marie, who went on to describe how she ran a four-hour magazine show. The broadcast executives were amazed at the efficiency of her system for her program in Ottawa.

The interview went on for about an hour and a half. At the end, Marie shook hands and headed for the elevator to grab a cab back to Central Station and get back home and to work in Ottawa.

As she was leaving, one of the blue-suited men from the meeting called out to her. "Madame Poulin!" (Back in that era, by the way, it would always be Madame Poulin, never Marie, at least on the French side.) The elevator arrived, but she waited, heard it close and listened.

"Madame Poulin, don't leave right away," he said. "I have a question to ask you. I don't want you to respond right away, but Mr. Blais and the team would like you to accept an offer to open all the French services in Northern Ontario."

Marie burst out laughing, as she often does when she is nervous. "Look at me," she said, touching her bump. "I don't think this is a good time."

He said, "You won't always be pregnant, you know. Just think about it."

When she arrived at Central Station, Marie went to the payphone and called Bernard, collect. "You'll never believe this," she told him. "They actually offered me the job."

Bernard asked Marie to wait a minute. It was a little frustrating given the situation's drama, but Bernard had his own drama going on.

"Where were you?" asked Marie; she was worried their daughter Elaine might be ill.

Bernard answered: "I went looking for boxes because I want to start packing today." That was it. Bernard was in.

Until she gave birth, Marie would work in Ottawa. Her appointment to start a new French-language station in Ontario was of great interest in the French-language press, and she had been asked to give an interview on the topic by Edgar Demers, a journalist with *LeDroit*, Ottawa's French-language newspaper. Demers, the media columnist for the paper, had written a number of articles about Marie's programming at Radio-Canada, articles that were not always glowing. But Marie still made time for him.

As an aside, journalists who cover Radio-Canada and the CBC are feared—and not always loved—by staff; what they write can make or break careers or end a program. Sometimes a column can even raise questions in Parliament. Demers had written some texts about Marie's program at Radio-Canada, not always complimentary, but Marie allowed him constant time for interviews.

On the morning on March 21, 1978, Marie was in her office in Ottawa, sitting across the desk from Edgar Demers. She had decided to accept the interview despite the fact that her waters had broken earlier that morning. Marie had already begun to have contractions, but she carried on with the interview.

Marie's executive assistant was aware of the situation and would pop in every five minutes saying the hospital would like to see her. Finally, the journalist exclaims, "Do you mean to say you're having contractions and you're still talking to me?" Marie admits, "I didn't want to cancel our appointment."

When the assistant brought in Marie's coat and boots and told her that she had to leave for the hospital, Demers helped Marie put on her boots and later called the hospital every hour or so to enquire about Marie's condition.

His article—a positive piece about the opening of the Sudbury radio station—was filed before Valérie was born; the piece ended saying he did not know whether Marie had given birth to a boy or a girl.

Apart from the cold shoulder he sometimes experienced for being a broadcasting critic, Demers felt a coldness from colleagues and the people he covered because he was gay.

"When I heard his mother had died, I called to the presbytery and found out when the funeral was. I asked my colleagues if they wanted to go, but they just laughed," says Marie, still emotional years later. "So, I went to the church. When Edgar walked in with the coffin, there was almost no one there. I will never forget it. Everybody knew he was homosexual, and some just laughed at him. It was just so awful.

"When we walked out of the church, he looked me in the eye and said, 'I will never forget you, Marie.' That's when I realized gay people were rejected for their personal lives." Years later, in June 2005, when a federal act to recognize same-sex marriages came before the Senate, Marie voted in favour of it.

★★★

Until the baby was born, Marie was to work in Ottawa, though she had to attend meetings in Montréal. One February evening, she came home to a deeply troubled Bernard.

"I have troubling news," said Bernard. "I got a letter from school today: there is rubella in the class." Rubella, commonly known as German measles, is worrisome because it can cause serious problems to unborn babies.

Bernard had already called their obstetrician, Dr. Francis Conklin, who wanted to see Marie at his office as soon as she got home. They met Dr. Conklin at eleven that night and he injected Marie with a special drug to help protect the baby.

"I asked if there was anything I had to do after the injection and he said, 'Yes, we will all pray.'" Dr. Conklin was a religious Irish Catholic.

Two days later, Marie came down with a serious case of rubella, and her mother came from Toronto to take care of her.

"My whole body was covered in red spots. And I was pregnant. It was terribly uncomfortable. Nobody could come into our house because both Elaine and I

Family Portrait, 1980.
*Source*: Galardo & Miron Photographers.

were carrying rubella. My mother took care of me like I was a little girl," says Marie.

"When I went to the hospital to give birth in March, Dr. Conklin made sure I was put in isolation. They had to protect all the other babies in the hospital. Valérie was in a small bed next to me. Three days later they sent me home."

Despite the circumstances, Marie remembers the first thing she said when Valérie was born.

"Ah, *chou*, she doesn't have curly hair like you," speaking to Bernard.

Dr. Conklin burst out laughing, along with them both.

★ ★ ★

The Poulin family moved to Sudbury in June of 1978.

Setting up a new station in Sudbury involved a great deal of work. One of the first things to be dealt with was the call letters for the station. The first suggestions for the call letters that the SRC brass sent seemed, in Marie's mind, like they had spilled out of a Scrabble bag; they did not display any kind of thought at all. Needless to say, Marie was not happy with the suggestions.

"One day I was sitting at my desk in the living room. The SRC had registered the call letters CBJX with the federal government. I hated those call letters. I was concerned because they did not relate to all the work that the community had done to put pressure on the CBC and the CRTC [Canadian Radio-television and Telecommunications Commission, the government body mandated with regulating all forms of telecommunications in Canada] for French services in Northern Ontario," says Marie.

"There had been a movement in Northern Ontario to get Radio-Canada to set up French services. It was led by Monique Cousineau from the Centre des Jeunes. She was working on a petition with one of the employees of ACFO [Association canadienne-française de l'Ontario], which was then the provincial francophone organization. They went to Ottawa and made a presentation to the CRTC to secure services. I wanted the call letters to represent all their commitment and their hard work.

"So, there I was, sitting at the desk scribbling different options, like CBNO or CBON. Bernard looked over my shoulder and said, 'Hey, that's fun! [...] C'est bon [...] CBON.' It was a Eureka moment.

"I called the director of Planning right away and suggested we change the call letters. He said, 'No, Marie. It's so complicated to change the call letters; they're going to say no.'

"I said, 'What have we got to lose? Could you just try, explain to him why, about Ontario Nord and the fact that it's a new station and the fact that it's the first time Radio-Canada is opening a real station from nothing, and they are not buying somebody out. Also, the fact that it's *c'est bon* and I want to use it as a theme.'

"He agreed to defend the proposal. I told him: 'When I'm in Montréal tomorrow and we get those call letters, I'll buy you flowers.' The next day, in Montréal, he was waiting for me at the elevator, and had the biggest smile on his face. He said, 'Marie, I've worked twenty-four hours on this. They have accepted CBON; they were having so much fun with the new name.' I went to the florist and bought him a dozen roses. And that's how those call letters were chosen."

As well as getting the call letters she wanted for the station, Marie wanted to handpick the people to come to Sudbury. One of them was Daniel Mathieu, a twenty-something announcer with a great voice and a quick mind.

He was reluctant to go, but Marie made it work for him. Daniel had been working as a casual employee, but in trying to lure him to Sudbury, Marie offered to hire him as permanent staff, which is a big deal in Radio-Canada terms. "I didn't want to leave Ottawa, but she convinced me to go to Sudbury. When she believed in something, she'd go the distance to make it happen," says Mathieu.

"Marie is a creative person, but she likes to surround herself with strong people—I'll exclude myself here," says Mathieu with some modesty. "She said to me: 'I like to work with people more intelligent than I am, because the stronger the people around me, the stronger I'll be.' It's a good philosophy. There are

Valérie wearing her CBON sweater, 1980.
Source: Family collection.

some managers or presidents at Radio-Canada who haven't always shared that point of view, but that's a different story."

Daniel was worried about living in Sudbury. Like many people, he had heard the story of the astronauts testing their moon vehicle on the lunar like landscape of the slag heaps of Sudbury. He was a convert on the drive to Sudbury.

"Moonscape? It was quite beautiful going up [Highway] 17. Lots of forests. It wasn't grey at all; there was lots of greenery. I lived in an apartment overlooking the lake, facing Laurentian University."

The radio station gave the Franco-Ontarian community the standing and status it did not have before. Michel Morin, who worked with Marie at CBON, explains the importance of the station: "Northern Ontario, as you know, is quite big [...] it's a country! To have CBC/Radio-Canada cover the collective territory that speaks to all Francophones the same way as the Anglophones [...] Radio-Canada gave this unique opportunity to Francophones of Northern Ontario. Radio-Canada gave them the opportunity to see each other, to hear each other, to live together in their language and in their culture by having cultural programming—and to have 'an opening' to the French majority in Quebec."

Ronald Caza was a student at Collège Notre-Dame, a French-language high school in Sudbury. Thanks to Radio-Canada, he felt connected to the culture he knew at home and at school.

"I was president of my high school; as a result, I was interviewed once a week on CBON by a guy called Serge Fleyfel, who, at the time, was a very popular DJ with the younger francophone community," says Caza, now a successful litigator in Ottawa, and a lawyer who later worked with Marie when she was a senator.

"CBON was wonderful. It was a breath of fresh air; there were two English radio stations, which were quite popular. Living in Northern Ontario at the time, radio was a big deal. Everybody listened to the radio. You spent a lot of time in your car because everywhere you went was far, so radio was quite important. CBON was a class act of a radio station; it had people who were colourful, it had a lot of energy, and it was important to attract Francophones who obviously also listened to English-language media. There was a lot of wonderful music going on, and one of the ways Marie wanted to ensure CBON was relevant was to engage high schools. Basically, the whole community was involved with the radio station."

The show Ron Caza is talking about was called TNT, short for *Tout le Nord en tremble*. Michel Morin remembers Marie's approach to attracting a diverse audience for the station's programs. "From the outset, she created programming for different age groups: TNT for younger listeners, *Souvenir* for adults, and a newsroom by and for Francophones."

"She hired Quebeckers like me and hired people from Northern Ontario. That made a huge difference because it brought people who knew the country, who were sensitive to the various interests of the populations we wanted to serve."

The music on the program was only French-language rock or instrumental music. No English-language rock, since that is what the private competition was playing. As Ron Caza can attest, it was a huge success, so much so that one of the competing stations complained when CBON ratings skyrocketed in that time slot to number one in the market. As an aside, the owner, Baxter Ricard, offered Marie an important position within his own network. She turned it down, preferring to remain with public broadcasting.

It was not only the music selection that produced these stellar ratings. Marie and producer Nicole Beauchamp came up with the idea of getting every French-language secondary school in Northern Ontario involved. They would have reporters from every school feeding information about what was going on in Timmins, for example. No pay, but business cards. A status symbol at school.

At least thirty Francophone schools in Northern Ontario had students contributing to the radio show. Every day, school representatives reported on the show from a different school, which aired from three to six every weekday afternoon. It was a huge success.

"We even went to Kapuskasing [461 kilometres north of Sudbury] one week to do a remote show from the high-school gym there," says Marie. "There was an older man sitting in the audience in the front row. He must have been ninety years old. I introduced myself as Marie Poulin from Sudbury. The man—Monsieur Guénette—told me he was from Saint-André-Avellin and had moved to Kapuskasing as a young man," recalls Marie.

"He then went on to say, 'When I was a little boy, my best friend moved to Sudbury.' He said that his friend's name was Ludger Ménard. I never heard back from him.' I don't know who was more shocked when I told him Ludger Ménard

The CBON afternoon show "TNT" becomes a favourite of high-school students throughout Northern Ontario—here, in Kapuskasing in 1980.
*Source*: CBON Archives.

was my grandfather." Her grandfather was still alive, and the two men reconnected through that chance meeting.

★ ★ ★

"Serge and Nicole did a terrific job. We wanted to get francophone youth listening to French radio, and it worked," says Marie.

Marie went to a marketing agency, 50 Carleton, run by Réal Fortin. She says Réal and the agency were crucial to the branding edge that CBON had. They came up with a number of ways to promote the program. One of the most popular was the poster of Serge Fleyfel in a black leather jacket. The kids loved it.

That same marketing agent helped promote the morning show, *C'bon l'matin*.

There were two hosts, which was a first on the network, and it was a woman and a man: Dominique Lemieux and Denis St-Jules. The idea for a morning show was to offer listeners everything they needed to know to start their day, from weather to news to local events. The two hosts bought humour to the broadcast. "We used the model of George Burns and Gracie Allen," says Marie, the American comedians who played off one another in radio and television programs.

When it came to a rehearsal, Marie listened from home, over the phone, so she could be a typical listener rather than the station manager. She took notes and the team fine-tuned the program led by producer Jean Lalonde. There was a model at Radio-Canada of what a morning show should be: how much weather, the type of music, and rules for the host, almost always a man back then. CBON in Sudbury broke the mould.

A year after it aired, *C'bon l'matin* won the Prix Marcel Blouin for best morning show on Radio-Canada. It was also making a real impact in Sudbury and Northern Ontario.

Jim Gordon was Mayor of Sudbury at the time. An Irish Catholic, he kept close to the French-speaking electorate. He appreciated Marie's efforts in bringing CBON to his city. "Marie was successful at getting that station up and running. For the francophone community, it provided an additional platform for maintaining their culture and their way of life and their language, so it was important. Remember that the francophone community in Sudbury is significant, at about one third; they needed that voice," says Mayor Gordon.

"The thing about the francophone community in Sudbury is that they are very family oriented; they have a [...] closeness [...] that you don't see in other cultural groups. So, having a radio station really helped. Marie always had an excellent grasp of what was going on in the city and she understood the roots of the issues in the community itself. She understood, of course, the francophone side but the anglophone side as well."

Marie and her team celebrate the fifth anniversary of the CBON radio station as well as the fact that its morning show is recognized as the best morning radio show in Canada (Prix Marcel Blouin), 1983.
*Source*: CBC/Radio-Canada Collection.

Raymond Bonin was a school trustee at the time, and on his way to becoming a federal member of Parliament. He says having the Radio-Canada outlet changed the community, both French and English.

"We had a French radio station in Sudbury, but it didn't go beyond Sudbury. I understand that instead of opening offices throughout the North, Marie built (repeater) towers. To this day, when you drive from Timmins to Sudbury the only station that we can receive is Radio-Canada French.

"When the station first opened we were all excited and amazed, because as a trustee in education, you like to include the people who are so far away that they don't get the benefits of the city stuff so this really opened up the North and that's when we became able to promote our heroes, athletes, and achievers, and to show the francophone community that we were able and capable, which was a well-kept secret until that time.

"In an odd way, having a French-language station bridged the gap between the English and French communities in Sudbury. [CBON] was well accepted by the anglophone community. I give much credit for the harmony that now exists to sports.

"For example, as a child I played hockey for the city league. I was the only Francophone there. During the first few games, nobody would speak to me, but eventually, the parents were giving me rides. I saw that as I was growing up. When I ran in politics, the guys who I had played basketball or hockey or what have you with would call me up and say, 'Ray, I'll vote for you.'

"I give a lot of the credit to that [sports], and I give credit to our parents, who met together and built institutions. Without institutions, you don't survive, and in Ontario, all our institutions are in place. I meet Quebecers who ask, 'Is there any French in Sudbury?' I tell them within a half-hour's drive from downtown Sudbury there are twenty-five Caisses populaires Desjardins. We have a French teacher's college, and we have a bilingual medical school. We have our French school boards, both Catholic and public, administered by Francophones. So, if you look at our institutions, I give a lot of credit to our ancestors, Marie's father, and mine, and others. Having French radio throughout Northern Ontario, going beyond Sudbury, really made French culture stronger. We got to know who the leaders were in Timmins, North Bay, and what not.

"Another thing [Marie] did when she was at CBON was [to promote the] Fête Saint-Jean-Baptiste. [She] held a big [outdoor] concert every year, which was taped and shown across the country. One year, she had Édith Butler and other artists that we never saw in Sudbury. That did a lot to promote Sudbury and to confirm that there were [...] Francophones surviving outside Quebec," says Ray.

It was not only Marie's work with CBON that Ray appreciated. He also admired the volunteer work she did. "I judge people and politicians by the groups that they volunteer for. I've seen a lot of people in Sudbury promote something and then end up creating a job for themselves. The things that Marie always volunteered for, to my knowledge, didn't come with any monetary or other advantages. She worked for the good of the community. Sometimes, you would have a lawyer volunteering in a credit union, and all the contracts for the mortgages ended up going to his office. That type of volunteering I have no respect for."

# 8

## Going Home

THE MOVE TO SUDBURY had a huge impact on the lives of Marie, Bernard, and Elaine. Valérie was far too young, of course, to notice the move at all.

Moving to Sudbury pushed Bernard to take up painting full time. "Marie often travelled for work. I had dealt with many kids who had keys around their necks and were going home to nothing. I didn't want that for our girls. I said, 'No, our kids will come home to me being there if Marie isn't there.' So, I chose to start my studio at home. I thought that if later there was a change of pace, I could rent a space. I took one of the basement rooms with big windows, and I worked from home."

Although it took a little time, Elaine embraced life in Sudbury. "When we moved to Sudbury, Elaine didn't speak any English. Until then, her entire world was in French, because we always lived in Quebec," says Marie. "It was a huge adaptation for her. At first, we had to force her to play with the English kids in the street. Luckily, the street was filled with friendly children, particularly the Simond and Hinton kids living across the street."

In the end, Elaine loved living in Sudbury. It was not the wilderness she remembered but the culture. "I was happy to live in those years when we were in Sudbury and Mum was head of a radio station. We went to concerts and other events," says Elaine. "It was such an amazing cultural scene and setting to be growing up in. I loved those five years in Sudbury."

The move resulted in a reconnection with Marie and Bernard's extended family.

The Sudbury station opened on June 19, 1978. By August, Marie was exhausted. Bernard decided on a two-week vacation, without the children. Marie called her aunt Germaine, who agreed to move into the house and take care of Elaine and Valérie. By the time Bernard and Marie returned from their time off, they found Germaine was in love with Elaine and the new baby, and Elaine was in love with her. Aunt Germaine moved in and lived with the Poulin family.

At the time, Marie's parents lived in Toronto. It was a four-hour drive to Sudbury, but they made the trip often—to see Marie and her family, as well as her brother Claude and his wife, Connie, and their girls. Bernard's parents lived in

The family with Aunt Germaine, 1995.

Amos, in northern Quebec, a five-hour drive from Sudbury, so Bernard and Marie went to visit them whenever they could.

Bernard rarely accompanied Marie when she travelled on business. The first of the few trips he was able to make was when Marie went to Chicoutimi for its radio station's anniversary. Marie recalls: "The Montréal bosses were going to be there, of course, but all the regional directors and station managers from across the country would be in Chicoutimi also. So, we drove from Sudbury. It was a good opportunity for Bernard to meet the people I worked with."

Ray Bonin is not just a fan of Marie, he is also a big fan of Bernard Poulin: "People like to say: 'Behind every great man there's a great woman,' but I don't want to use it that way. In this case, Bernard Poulin is and was exceptional. You can't ask for stronger support than what he gives her. It made a difference in what she has been able to accomplish. And he does it with complete humility; he doesn't mind being in the back seat. It always impressed me."

Bernard certainly helped Marie a great deal when they moved to Sudbury. Having never lived there himself, he did not know what to expect. He only knew Sudbury had the reputation of being a tough mining town, not what he was used to.

"I fell in love with the city. It was perfect. Everyone had told me I would be lost in the art world, that it was a bad decision to go to Sudbury. I'm sure they had never been there. What a world filled with culture," says Bernard.

"Northern Ontario people are far from everybody else. I met Hagood Hardy [the composer and pianist] there. We enjoyed theatre, orchestras, and singers from the rest of Canada and beyond," says Bernard.

"Most people think that Sudbury is nothing but a mining town. In fact, it offers great cultural opportunities that are often taken for granted elsewhere. And the people are wonderful. The best thing we could ever have done was to go to Northern Ontario for five years."

Although Bernard enjoyed the cultural events, painting was the most important part of his life. "Before we moved to Sudbury, I worked part-time on creating artwork because I was teaching at the Royal Ottawa Hospital. I didn't have time to do everything that I wanted to do. But within a year [of our arrival in Sudbury] I was earning a living [by painting]," says Bernard. "The first year, I kind of just disappeared to create a show that would announce to the world I was there. An exhibition either sets you up or it destroys you—it's one or the other. The show opened in 1979, and it sold out."

The exhibition was at Laurentian University's Bell Museum, which is now the Sudbury Art Gallery. His friends Mitch and Donna Spiegel were there; they worked the entire evening as bartenders and bought the iconic piece from the show.

Because of that exhibition, Bernard received many commissions for portraits, particularly portraits of children. "When I began securing commissions for portraits of kids, I knew that many of my subjects had busier schedules than I did. They had hockey, violin, piano. I had to fit into their schedules. Parents would say: 'You only have half an hour because they have to go to their violin lesson.' So, I began simplifying the portrait sessions. I just decided that I wasn't just going to do posing sessions; I let them be who they were. That worked wonders; my portraits came alive."

As Marie's career went from strength to strength, Bernard's portrait business took off. "One of my clients was a teacher. Léonne Ducharme had several sons, and every time one of them turned thirteen, she had their portrait painted. I told her that because I would be painting so many portraits I'd give her a discount, but she insisted on being treated like anybody else. 'I'll have the money once the boys turn thirteen,' she told me. And she did," recalls Bernard.

When Bernard presented his first show, there were almost fifty pieces. "It was a mixed bag: still life, landscapes, portraits; there was almost everything there. And a lot of what I call 'genre' paintings are story paintings. It was a huge show that took up two floors of the gallery," remembers Bernard.

Paintings of nature also formed an important part of the show. Sudbury is an urban island in a sea of forests and lakes. This is ideal for an artist. "In Northern Ontario, all you can see are birch forests. It was just the beginning of the greening of Sudbury; birch trees were the first trees that grew. The other thing you see are

*Blueberries* by Bernard Poulin.
*Source*: Bernard Poulin.

blueberries. Those are the two symbolic things that are reminiscent of Northern Ontario; the one painting that stood out and became the icon of the show was a painting called *Blueberries*," says Bernard.

Bernard did more than stay home and paint. He became involved in the community. He served on the board of the Big Brothers Association. Mitch Spiegel got Bernard involved with the Sudbury Algoma Hospital once he discovered Bernard's unique background.

Bernard's arrival in Marie's life changed both their lives. Bernard was able to paint full time and take his artistic career to a new level. Marie was able to devote more time to her career at Radio-Canada, because Bernard was there to look after the girls and the household. Many people outside the family comment on what a perfect marriage they have, on many levels. The proof of its success is the love both Elaine and Valérie have for Bernard and Marie.

Bernard was painting but he also started doing a cartoon—with the character MiG—for a local newspaper, the *Northern Life*. The paper was owned by Michael Atkins, who had moved to Sudbury after running another paper on Manitoulin Island.

It was the late 1970s and a lot of things were coming together in Sudbury, but few of these were good news. On September 15, 1978, 11,600 Inco workers went on strike until June 1979. At the time, it was the longest strike in Canadian history, and it almost destroyed Sudbury. The Inco strike had a spill-on effect, meaning it hit families, and directly touched the lives of forty-three thousand people—more than a quarter of Sudbury's population.

Michael Atkins and others got together to rescue the city.

"A group of us got together and started an organization called Sudbury 2001. The idea was to stand up for Sudbury because we were on our knees. At that time Marie was a player in the community, she was important in the media, and the SRC as always has been influential in a place the size of Sudbury. She worked with us to animate it and to amplify the ideas and the urgency," recalls Michael, who was co-chair of the reform group along with the head of the local labour council.

"Marie played a big role of changing the mindset of the community from that of a mining camp to a more diverse community," says Michael. "Think about it, in a community of a hundred and fifty thousand we lost twenty thousand jobs. People are beside themselves because we are losing a hundred jobs at Laurentian University, but we lost twenty thousand jobs over ten years. We have them with intellectual capital of mining solutions, new products, and Sudbury has become a brilliant research cluster attracting the best mining techniques from around the world. So, from that moment began the evolution of a city from a mining camp to an exporter of intellectual capital. Marie was a big part of that."

Marie would soon be facing a strike of her own at the CBC.

# The NABET Strike

IT IS TOUGH, BUT NOT IMPOSSIBLE, to run a broadcast network like the CBC/Radio-Canada without the technicians who perform the magic to get words and pictures on the air. The technicians outside Quebec, such as the announcer-operator Daniel Mathieu, belonged to the National Association of Broadcast Employees and Technicians (NABET). Technicians in Quebec belonged to a separate union, though if the technicians worked outside Quebec for the French network, they were a NABET member. Geography ruled, not language.

The technicians went on strike on May 21, 1978, and the strike lasted for 102 days, into early September.

"I received a call at four in the morning informing me that the strike was effective immediately. I had to get up and hurry to the radio station to make sure that we would get on air anyway, with music coming in from the network and with an appropriate message from the network announcing that, unfortunately, we couldn't serve our listeners because of the NABET strike," says Marie.

Daniel Mathieu, the young announcer she had brought from Ottawa to Sudbury, was already at work. He was a member of NABET, but did not know he was supposed to be on strike. He heard about it from his boss.

"I arrived at the station as usual at 4:30 a.m. and proceeded to open up, settle in, and read the wires—the usual. Marie arrived around 5:00 a.m. and asked what I was doing there. She told me I was on strike," recalls Daniel.

Marie told Daniel to shut everything down.

"I did as she asked. I shut everything down, including the transmitters, and I left. I waited outside for the others who arrived around 6:30 a.m. I went home and came back later. That's when Marie came to see me on the picket line and asked in a low voice. 'Daniel, what do we do to go on air?'"

Marie wanted to put on some music and explain to listeners that there was a strike. Daniel told Marie which switches and buttons to push, and an hour later there was music, though not the regular morning program.

There was a more dramatic incident: the transmitter, located on a hill in Sudbury, was hit by lightning and CBON went off the air. The only way to fix it was to go to the transmitter and restart it.

Cartoon gift—depicting Marie as quite capable of running the radio station all on her own if need be—given to Marie by radio announcer Christiane St-Pierre during the NABET Strike of 1981.
*Source*: Cartoon by Oryst Sawchuk.

Bernard and Marie drove in the storm, going up a hill to the transmitter. It was behind a barrier that they had to climb over because they could not drive past it. Bernard and Marie, dressed in rain gear and boots, trudged up the muddy hill in a lightning storm; they used the key Marie had remembered to bring, and got inside.

Now, what?

There was a telephone inside with a direct connection to a technician in Toronto with a sign over it reading: *Use Only in an Emergency*.

"How do I fix this?" Marie asked the technician at the other end of the line.

"Did you walk up there in a thunderstorm?" he asked. "You've got more guts than any guy I know."

It was a simple fix. The equivalent of flipping a breaker switch at home—bingo, CBON was back on the air.

The CBC's Sudbury operation was small, about twenty employees on the French side and maybe thirty on the English side. There were always some of them on the picket line. Marie might have been the manager, but she wanted to make sure things ran smoothly.

"I contacted all our employees on the French side individually and asked the non-union employees to respect the picket line, not to come in through the back door, to be gracious and respectful to their colleagues who were on strike. I wanted to make sure that friendships would not break down," says Marie.

"My office was facing Main Street, which was where the picket lines were. I wanted to hear what was being said on the picket lines, so I moved my desk in such a way that my chair was positioned near the window. I wanted to make sure that everything was calm. Whenever I felt things were getting a little bit tense, even between employees who were picketing together, or between employees who were coming in and crossing the picket line, I would go outside. The picketers had put a small table out and were playing cards. I went and asked if I could play cards with them even if there was a strike. 'Sure, Marie.' So, I would sit down and play cards with them and chat. I knew this was unusual, but it was important to keep an ongoing open relationship between everyone.

"One day I got a call from the editor-in-chief of the *Sudbury Star*, whose offices were kitty-corner to ours at CBC/Radio-Canada, and he said to me, 'Marie, this is totally inappropriate. We live in a union town. You cannot publicly be seen to be approving a strike that is hurting your services'."

"I said, 'I'm sorry, but I think that the relationships between striking employees and non-striking employees and management are more important than what people will think about me. I don't want to upset the protocol of striking, but I think this is very important. So, if you want to come over and play cards come over anytime. That ended that discussion.'

"Another morning, I was listening to what was going on with strikers. Things were not going well. It was hot outside; it was mid-July. Because it was so hot, the strikers didn't want to be there; they wanted to be at their cottage or at Ramsey Lake having a good swim. Bernard and I had just installed a pool in our yard, and I had an idea that I thought might help things.

"I went downstairs and I asked to speak to the union representative. He was a key technician, and he was the official representative in Sudbury for NABET. I asked him if we could meet alone in my office. He came in, and I served him a coffee and said, 'Jim, I'd like to discuss something just between you and me. It's really hot outside and people are antsy and unhappy right now. I'm talking about your people on the picket line and my employees in the office now. I'd like to throw a party today at my house where everybody is invited. I'm offering free beer and hot dogs, and I'm not asking you to bring anything. I'm asking you not to inform Toronto and I will not inform Montréal. This is between us: we take one day off from the strike, that's all. We don't discuss the strike at all until tomorrow morning when you come back on strike. Give it some thought.' So, he went outside, and he came back in fifteen minutes later and, smiling, he said, 'Marie, it's a deal. I take it you will not talk to Montréal, and we will not talk to Toronto.' I confirmed that it was a local understanding."

★ ★ ★

A brief aside about that pool before continuing with the story. The reason Bernard and Marie had just installed the pool is related to Marie's smoking.

Marie did not start smoking until her early twenties. She had read enough about the dangers of smoking that she did not smoke when she was pregnant with Elaine. But when Hugues left her, she took up smoking with a vengeance.

Marie quit when she was thirty-five after a trip to Dr. Chan, her family physician in Sudbury. He was astounded when Marie told him she had a four-pack-a-day habit.

"You have to find a way to quit," he told her.

"I confess that I enjoyed every cigarette. I hardly ate, so I was very thin. What I discovered later was that I was getting my energy from the nicotine. The last thing I did before turning off the light at night, was to smoke a cigarette. I would get up twice in the night to go out to the living room to smoke. I would ponder problems from the office, smoke two or three cigarettes, then go back to bed. Everybody knew that I was a smoker," says Marie.

"In May of 1980, I had gone to Timmins to open our new newsroom. I came back late that night. Bernard was at the dining room table; his arms were crossed and on the table were all kinds of papers. He looked at me and he said, 'Dr. Chan called me and told me about your smoking. What is it that you've always wanted, Marie, that you don't have yet?'

"I replied, 'An in-ground pool.'

"Bernard said, 'I will build you an in-ground pool if you stop smoking.' He had all these different pamphlets for pools. He said, 'Choose your pool tonight; we are not going to bed until you choose your pool.' He was serious. I picked one from the pamphlets.

"He said, 'Okay, it will be opening on July 1. We are currently mid-May. I know if you give your word that you will have stopped smoking [by July 1].'

"On June 30, at midnight, I was alone in the living room, smoking. I put out my last cigarette, went to the washroom, threw my last cigarettes in the toilet, and flushed."

It was not that easy. There were rituals of smoking that are hard to kick.

"I was convinced that I could not be happy and content working hard without smoking," says Marie. A doctor taught her self-hypnosis. A few times a day, Marie would close her eyes and see herself in a mirror in her mind's eye. "I would see myself in that mirror, smoking and happy. Then I would take a big black marker and put an 'X' on it in my mind, and I would see myself without a cigarette in the mirror of my mind, happy and content."

There are two certainties here: it's hard to stop smoking, but once you've succeeded, you save a lot of money.

*   *   *

Back to the strike and the pool party.

"I called Bernard and said, 'I hope you can take the day off; we're having about fifty people over today to swim in the pool.' He burst out laughing. I said, 'Can you go to the beer store right away? We need beer, hot dogs, buns, and mustard and relish.'

"I told him to expect them at about eleven thirty. It was about nine thirty when I called. I told him the conditions of the local understanding. By the time I got home, the beer was cold, and everything was organized. I still don't know how Bernard did it. He had prepared a huge sign, which was already on the front door of the house in both English and French: 'When you cross this threshold, you will not discuss the strike or production; you will only be with family and friends.' So, people knew not to discuss anything like that.

"I must tell you, it was such a touching party. All of a sudden, I looked into the pool and I saw all these young men playing ball in the pool and giving themselves elbow punches. There were union and non-union guys, but they were all in the pool together, and I could see the friendships rekindling. They left at midnight. It was a wonderful experience.

"The next morning, everyone had a straight face. Those on the picket line and the others crossing the picket line. No one said a word. No one ever found out. I thought it was a healthy way to continue the strike. It was a long strike; it only finished in the fall. Despite this, there were no ill feelings. It was very comfortable."

Daniel Mathieu remembers the strike well. "During the strike, she would come and talk with us because, clearly, she wanted to maintain good relations between CBC/Radio-Canada and the employees. It meant a lot to her.

"For instance, as there were few Francophones on the picket line, she wanted to make sure there was always one of us. Toward the end, though, I was the only one left; the others had gone, discouraged. It depended on one's situation. I didn't have a family to feed; I wasn't out of money yet. But others had to find alternatives.

"It was at that time that my union leader said I could have a break. 'Go visit your parents in the Laurentians and come back in a week.'

"Three days later, I received a call from Marie. 'Why aren't you on the picket line?'—always speaking in a low voice.

"'Because I was given time off.'

"'When are you coming back? It's important,' she said.

"I explained that I'd be back at the end of my break and asked her if she realized that, as my boss, she was calling me at home to ask when I'd be back on the picket line. Something weird there," says Daniel.

★ ★ ★

"Employee relationships were important to her. She wanted things to be good when we returned, that there would be no unhappiness, bitterness, or hard feelings. She would do things for us, like collect funds, bring us coffee and donuts. She also arranged for a cable to connect a radio. There was also a phone line with a number for emergencies—because back then there were no iPhones.

"One day, the employees received a letter from Radio-Canada at their home telling them that the corporation's last offer was final and pointing out how stressful it must be for families. In fact, they were trying to get the spouses to put pressure on the employees so they'd vote for a return to work. It angered many employees, who felt it showed a lack of respect. The employees were very upset and so was Marie. While she won't say so, I'm convinced she intervened and told management that this was unacceptable—like throwing oil on a fire.

"One day, the Inco people came calling. It was the Teamsters and their union boss. He asked, not me, but our representative, if we wanted a few of his men on our picket line for support.

"'How many men?'

"'We could send you one thousand.'

"There were five of us on the picket line and the Inco group wanted to send one thousand men by noon to show their support for NABET.

"Marie didn't like that at all. If she hadn't gotten involved, there probably would have been one thousand Inco men on the line.

"Radio-Canada probably didn't realize what a big mistake they had made. It could have turned badly with all those people wanting to help. Other people were also offering their support—the *Sudbury Star*, which was just in front, came to demonstrate with us at lunchtime; some politicians showed up. For Marie, it was very important, and that's probably why later on she did such a great job as VP Human Resources."

# 10

# Head Office

MARIE'S SUCCESS IN SUDBURY led to an unusual promotion for an executive running a regional station; in 1983 she was offered a job at the head office of the CBC in Ottawa.

Bernard remembers the move well. "After five years, Marie was called back to Ottawa to the headquarters of CBC/Radio-Canada to become Associate Vice-President of regional broadcasting for French radio and television. So that brought us back to Ottawa.

"As for me, I was already working full time and making a living as a portrait painter," says Bernard. "For me there were no changes except for geography.

"We moved to Alta Vista on Heath Street, right near the CBC headquarters. We didn't like long commutes, and both liked living downtown. When we moved to Alta Vista, Elaine was twelve and Valérie was five."

Bernard had stayed behind in Sudbury to deal with closing the house there. Marie had done all the work on buying the new house, securing the mortgage and reviewing the legal papers, but when it came time to actually move in, she was taken aback. The real estate agent would not give her the key. "'I can't give you the key, Marie. Bernard is not with you.' I said you must be kidding. He said only the husband could accept the key. This was as recent as 1983. Shocking," says Marie.

The move was not only good for Marie, but also for Bernard. Ottawa in 1983 was eight times the size of Sudbury. And richer. Ottawa is the wealthiest city in Canada measured by family income; Sudbury is no slouch, but is number ten.

"My business just moved forward," Bernard continues. "I carried it over and kept promoting myself. For me, it was first and foremost a business. My father had trained me to not starve. But I had to stop advertising because I was getting too many orders. I guess I was at the right place at the right time. Through an agent I was still selling in Sudbury. In Ottawa, I just opened doors in a lot of ways. I would, for example, exhibit in church basements, which was sort of sacrilegious in the art world. I would announce to the people gathered at the church that there was an exhibition downstairs with free coffee, and I started selling that way. I was selling to the average Joe, and my prices were not that high because I was still just beginning, only five or six years in.

"I was always involved in social organizations like Big Brothers, and I was on the board of the Children's Hospital, so all that kept me out there. I did work for the hospital to raise funds for them. The more I got involved, the more I met people: lawyers, corporate people, and everyone and anyone who was interested in art at that time."

Bernard and Marie's partnership followed the same pattern they had developed in Sudbury. She had a steady income, with benefits and a pension plan, while Bernard worked as a successful painter.

"That was pretty much our set-up. Marie travelled a hell of a lot, from one end of the country to the other, visiting all the radio and television stations. That meant there had to be somebody at home because we had two kids. So, I went against the grain again. I didn't get a loft with a monstrous window somewhere. I was in a basement which was where I earned 90 percent of my living.

"We stayed in Alta Vista for seven or eight years before we moved downtown to the Glebe on Pretoria Avenue. We had seen a house that we wanted to buy on a small lake. But we lost the bid. Our house was already sold, so we went looking for something else. We found an old Victorian house, which we grabbed. We completely restored it. It even had paintings on the ceiling. It was a beautiful restoration."

At that stage, Elaine graduated at the age of nineteen and was immediately off on a year-long trip, backpacking around the world. Elaine had been working part-time since she was fourteen and had money set aside for travel. Valérie was starting high school.

The Poulin family eventually sold that house and moved back to Alta Vista.

Marie's promotion and the resulting move to Ottawa were the result of a combination of luck, hard work, and family support.

★★★

To understand the turn of events that led to the family's move to Ottawa, it is necessary to back up a bit.

The story begins with the arrival of Pierre Juneau in Ottawa. Juneau was a giant in the Canadian cultural world. The Juno Awards are named after him. The year 2021 marked the fiftieth anniversary of the Canadian content rules that mandated that a certain amount of music played on radio had to be Canadian and that movies and television programs had to have a minimum number of Canadian writers and performers. Pierre Juneau was the father of that policy, one that helped many Canadian recording artists gain national and then international appeal.

There is a reason the Juno Awards are named after him.

A boy from Verdun, a working-class neighbourhood in southwestern Montréal, Juneau graduated from the Université de Montréal and then studied in Paris, where he met Pierre Elliott Trudeau. The two men became lifelong friends.

Trudeau Sr. trusted Juneau's judgment and named him to key cultural posts: The National Film Board; vice-chairman and the last chairman of the Board of Broadcast Governors, which morphed into the CRTC, where Juneau was the first chairman from 1968 to 1975; the minister of communications; and then, since 1982 until 1989, president of the Société Radio-Canada.

Juneau set out to shake things up.

Pierre Racicot, who was in the head office of the SRC at the time, remembers that one of the first things Juneau wanted to do was to better balance the power structure within the corporation. Marie feels that Juneau was not there to take away power from Montréal and Toronto. She remembers discussing the issue with him and him telling her that he felt it was unbalanced.

Racicot, though, believes that Juneau had a quite radical restructuring in mind. "Juneau decided that to better enable him to manage the corporation he had to [take away some of the power from the offices in] Toronto and Montréal. Juneau was experiencing difficulties with the people who were heading the networks. [He] decided to [...] reorganize the structure of the management of the corporation [...]. He created regional broadcasting or recreated it since it had existed at one time.

"They appointed Doug Ward as Vice-President of regional broadcasting. He had been working in Northern Service in Thunder Bay before, and then became Director of the service. I was seconded to the project of creating regional broadcasting, working with Doug. We set up a structure, and then it came time to recruit people," recalls Pierre.

"In those days, we were in the 'equity days.' We had to have a better balance of male/female managers at Radio-Canada. So, we started looking [for female candidates] to fill the new positions. I proposed Marie as Associate Vice-President. Doug interviewed her, and they promoted her to that job, which was due [to the] fact that she was from the region and the job was for French programming. She also had all the prerequisites for the job, the education, and the experience."

It was June of 1983 when Marie and Bernard moved back to Ottawa. These relocations did not bother Bernard. "I never thought about it. It was just a fact of life. Marie went from position to position, and I just stood there in awe of the career advancements that she was making. Every time she spoke at gatherings and played the role of boss in whatever position she was in—it was incredible because she was so talented in whatever she did. She wasn't stopping me from doing what I wanted to do. We were just there being each other's best friend and greatest fan."

Marie began work at the CBC head office on Bronson Avenue. She came to love the building, and not just because of her many interesting years there. "It was purpose-built as the head office. It was an ultra-modern structure, emblazoned with the words 'CBC/Radio-Canada.' When you walked up those steps, it was so

> "The French production centres around the country weren't very big, except for the one in Moncton, so they didn't have network programs. If you were a CBC person in Winnipeg or Vancouver, on the other hand, you had network programs, and there were area heads if you needed to talk to someone. The French production centres were delighted that Marie was now at the big table. She was in Ottawa and had direct access to the president and could do political things there. They knew that her job was to keep Franco-Canada alive and thriving in the CBC."

impressive. There was a simple but huge entrance, and on both walls, you had the history of the building: who had been the architect; which prime minister of Canada had come to the official opening. "Years later, long after I left, I remember the CBC decided to sell the building. You can't imagine how upset I was," recalls Marie.

But on that first day, she met with the man who had reached out to hire her. Doug Ward oversaw the regions, which in CBC parlance meant the whole country, apart from the two network head offices, and he needed Marie to help him, in particular on the French side, Radio-Canada. It meant Doug Ward was responsible for all English-language regional broadcasting while Marie was responsible for all French-language regional broadcasting except that in Montréal.

"Juneau realized he didn't control the CBC because all the power was in Toronto and Montréal. He wanted power in Ottawa, so he set up this regional vice-presidency," says Ward.

"I am not fluently bilingual," Ward continued. "I can get along but for me to listen to a subtle debate in French and know whether it was the real goods or not would have been a lie. I hired Marie as Associate Vice-President for the French. I talked to her, having known her from her Sudbury days when I was in Thunder Bay. She understood broadcasting and was passionate about French Canada, both inside and outside Quebec, so I hired her."

Ward appreciated Marie's knowledge of the French language and of French culture in Canada, and he respected her experience in regional broadcasting. But what really impressed Ward was her enthusiasm and the fact that she was almost addicted to hard work.

"She is all energy and has a passion for Franco-Ontarian culture, and the French reality in New Brunswick and across the country outside Quebec. That passion was exactly what I was looking for," says Ward.

That passion was needed, Ward recalls, because there were problems setting things up. "The French production centres around the country weren't very big, except for the one in Moncton, so they didn't have network programs. If you were a CBC person in Winnipeg or Vancouver, on the other hand, you had network programs, and there were area heads if you needed to talk to someone. The French production centres were delighted that Marie was now at the big table. She was in Ottawa and had direct access to the president and could do political things there. They knew that her job was to keep Franco-Canada alive and thriving in the CBC. I think she was very much appreciated in that role."

It was a tough job, Marie remembers, one that demanded a lot of her. "For five years, I oversaw French-language radio and television across the country. We increased the contribution of radio and television programs to the networks, which was my key objective. It was my job to ensure that the network increased its regional presence. It was the objective that had been given to me by Mr. Juneau, and it was one of the objectives that had come out in the communications report under [Communications Minister] Francis Fox.

"We were going through difficult budget cuts and were trying to find ways to spare the regions, but couldn't. One of the things Mr. Juneau did with the board was to protect the stations located in areas where French was the minority language. His theory was that Radio-Canada was more than essential in those areas; it was the *raison d'être* of the public broadcaster. So cuts were made, but they were not big compared to any other network services or English regional radio and television."

Though Pierre Juneau did not, in the end, wrest power from Montréal and Toronto, the effort was more successful on the French side, with Marie on the road for five years, travelling to stations across Canada. It was a job she loved: "To have the opportunity as the associate vice-president of all French language regional broadcasting across Canada—radio and television—to travel to Rimouski one week, to Edmonton the following week, to Winnipeg, then to Moncton [...]. It really enabled me to discover how each area of the country is unique and is a culture within itself. I really hadn't had the opportunity to discover the uniqueness of Quebec City or Vancouver before."

Marie was struck by the unique qualities of the different cities she visited. "When I was in Saskatoon, I was looking out the window of the hotel room. I thought, *The urban planner who designed this was brilliant.* And Quebec City. I had never been there as often as I was during those five years when I was responsible for the radio and television stations."

She loved the people she met when travelling. "I was visiting with staffers, not only the senior managers who ran each station. I made sure to say hello to everyone. I knew what everybody was doing, and I spent a lot of time in the newsroom because that's where I gathered information on how it was all working with the journalists and the latest news in Matane, Sept-Îles, or Vancouver."

On one trip to Rimouski, Marie started chatting with a television technician. He explained that the future was in videotape, not film. Video cameras were

Marie on the cover of *Liaison* magazine following her appointment as Associate Vice-President responsible for French regional broadcasting in Canada, 1984. *Source*: Cédéric Michaud.

expensive, but film had to be developed: that took time and money. And once an editor was used to video, it was faster to edit than film, where each shot had to be attached to the other shot.

When Marie got back to head office, she began a campaign to introduce video shooting and editing in every French-language regional station in the country. When her counterpart in the English network objected that the French network was leapfrogging his English stations, Marie was uncharacteristically blunt. "When was the last time you spoke to a technician in a local station?" asked Marie.

Of course, Marie's business travels made her life as a mother and a wife difficult. It helped she had an understanding husband, who worked from home.

When Marie was away, Bernard would begin the day by making sure the kids got up, had breakfast, got off to school. Then, he would have a full day in the studio. "When the kids came home," he remembers, "they generally came to the studio and started their homework on the floor. We would talk like a bunch of magpies for a good two hours."

Dinner was always an important part of their daily lives. Bernard comments: "When Marie travelled, she would always have the freezer loaded up with food." Marie also planned the meals, Bernard notes. "We knew what we had to do and which meals we would have. If there were any leftovers, Elaine, who was old enough at the time, and I would start mixing up food, trying to figure out what kind of a meal we could make out of the mess we created from food left over from Marie's recipes."

Having at least one parent at home all the time was something that both Marie and Bernard felt strongly about. Bernard comments, "There's one thing I was adamant about, and we both agreed on it. Our kids were going to have someone at home. I didn't need to rent a studio. I had a space in the house where I could be alone during the day, so I was fine."

Marie adds, "Elaine was a young teenager by that time, and technically, she would have been old enough to come home alone and babysit Valérie. But we never wanted Elaine to feel responsible for her sister, so we never asked her to do that."

When Marie had to travel, she was always careful to let her daughters know when she would be home. "I felt it was important that the girls knew way ahead of time that

> Bernard would begin the day by making sure the kids got up, had breakfast, got off to school. Then, he would have a full day in the studio. "When the kids came home," he remembers, "they generally came to the studio and started their homework on the floor. We would talk like a bunch of magpies for a good two hours."

> "Every week, I left home on Monday morning and came home on Wednesday—I was never away for more than two nights. We would talk on the phone at seven every night. The girls knew that they could talk to me then."

I would be leaving 'that' afternoon and would be coming back on 'this' afternoon.

"Every week, I left home on Monday morning and came home on Wednesday—I was never away for more than two nights. We would talk on the phone at seven every night. The girls knew that they could talk to me then."

When asked how the girls felt about Marie's absences, Bernard has this to say, "The kids were very adaptable. They understood that that was how we lived. Of course, they missed their mother. But if they were frustrated, they didn't show it.

Marie, Bernard, and Maô, their chow-chow, 1996.
*Source*: Family Collection.

"I decided that a sense-of-humour attitude was the best one to have with them. I also flat out told them that, 'Hey, this is your mother's job, and this is my job.'

"There were other working women at that time," Marie adds, "I was maybe on the edge, but I wasn't unique. I was very lucky, though, in that my husband was able to work from home. I was very aware of it."

Though Bernard was usually able to work from home, he did, occasionally have to make some out of town trips himself. "I was there more than their mother, but sometimes I'd go down to the States to teach courses or complete a portrait commission," remembers Bernard.

Marie adds, "We coordinated to make sure that our trips would never be during the same week. We never discussed it; we just did it."

***

Marie's job on the road was not all meet and greet. Tough decisions had to be made. One of the problems in an organization based on performance and writing talent is that succeeding as an announcer, reporter, or producer does not mean

As Associate Vice-President of French Regional Broadcasting and guest of honour of the Junior Hockey Tournament opening game in Matane and Rimouski, (Québec), Marie is asked to drop the puck. Alongside her is Maurice "The Rocket" Richard, 1985.
*Source*: R. Bélanger, Mont-Joli photographer.

> "I want you to be the person between the board and me. I'm very busy overseeing CBC. The board members need a person they can deal with on a daily basis, someone they can talk to about any issue concerning CBC/Radio-Canada. You now know our organization so well that I know if you don't have an answer to a question, you'll know where to find it."

that person will succeed as a manager. That was the case at one Radio-Canada station in Quebec.

"There are so many toxic workplaces. People seem to be afraid to make tough decisions. People want to be liked. And if you want to be liked, you can't be a leader," says Marie.

Marie had noticed unhappiness and chaos at the Quebec station. She went and sat in to see first-hand what was happening. It turned out the manager of the station was not coming into work every day. The place was in chaos. He was replaced—he went back to being an announcer, so it was not a hardship, but suddenly, the station turned around.

After five years, Marie was well known at head office and the president asked her to take on a new position. In 1988, Gordon Bruce, the Secretary General to the Board of Directors, was leaving the CBC to head a Canadian Museum.

"Mr. Juneau asked me to become Secretary General. Remember I was Associate VP of Regional Broadcasting. I reported to Doug Ward, who was Vice-President, and he reported to the Executive Vice-President, Bill Armstrong, and Bill Armstrong reported to Mr. Juneau. So, when Mr. Juneau called me to his office one day and asked me to become Secretary General, it was a huge surprise. I said to him, 'I'm not a lawyer, and I've always been told that it's easier for someone in that position to be a trained lawyer.'

"He said, 'No, I'm giving you a specific responsibility.'

"I was looking forward to a change since it had been five years and I had been on the road so much. I found it difficult to be away from Bernard and the girls.

"He said, 'I want you to be the person between the board and me. I'm very busy overseeing CBC. The board members need a person they can deal with on a daily basis, someone they can talk to about any issue concerning CBC/Radio-Canada. You now know our organization so well that I know if you don't have an answer to a question, you'll know where to find it. I know that you'll always have very open and transparent information coming from the operational level.'

"'You've been giving reports to the board now for five years,' he told me, 'and they have developed a great deal of respect for you because you have made them feel responsible for regional operations.' Suddenly, I went from reporting to Doug Ward to reporting directly to the President. That was a huge step for me. I was only forty-three years old.

"For two years, I worked closely with Mr. Juneau. I received so much mentoring from him. I learned a lot from this great man.

"You could nearly always predict what he was going to say because he was so logical. I asked him about that one day and he said, 'Don't forget, I was raised by Jesuits.'

"I told him that I was taught by Jesuits in Sudbury, and he said, 'Oh, that's what it is.' He felt that the logical approach to life was important. And we agreed that it was important to balance logic with feelings. Today, my conviction that mentoring is key in every person's life is probably due to Mr. Juneau. I probably would not have agreed to lead CSARN [Canadian Senior Artists Resource Network] today, which offers mentoring in the cultural industry, if it had not been for Mr. Juneau."

Pierre Juneau mentored Marie. He told her of the importance of good governance, and of having courage. He led by example. The other thing that was important to him was language and using it well.

"Mr. Juneau spoke French beautifully, and I purposefully began to improve my spoken French and my written French. I came to understand the importance of the quality of the language that you speak.

"I appreciated the way he dealt with people. He always treated every VP who reported to him as an equal. Everyone was shown respect. He never spoke about one VP to another. He hated rumours and gossip.

"Also, he was a kind man who had a beautiful relationship with his wife, Fernande. He had all these success stories behind him, and yet he was, above all, a very good man. He treated everyone very fairly."

After being appointed, Marie got to work. "The first thing I did was submit a twenty-four-month business plan to Mr. Juneau. As part of that plan, I outlined where I wanted the board to meet; instead of meeting in Toronto, Montréal, or Ottawa, as they usually did, I suggested they

> Pierre Juneau mentored Marie. He told her of the importance of good governance, and of having courage. He led by example. The other thing that was important to him was language and using it well.

meet in all different parts of the country. My idea was accepted.

"The board's visit to Iqaluit in Nunavut was applauded by employees across the country. They loved it. At that time, we had—and still have— a well-functioning radio station in Iqaluit. A great if small CBC team. We were taken by the station to the village to let us discover how people lived in that territory. The board members were extremely touched. It made us all realize that CBC is the key thread that keeps the country together; it provides contact with people on a daily basis and it's alive and it's extremely flexible."

It was through such initiatives that Marie was able to further contribute to the CBC.

***

While Marie was Vice-President and Secretary to the CBC's Board of Directors, Pierre Juneau asked Marie to work with Erik Peters on a project.

Peters, a former member of the Auditor General's Office, joined the CBC in 1984. He was hired following a devastating report the Auditor General published on the finances at the CBC. Pierre Juneau wanted to ensure that did not happen again, so he reached out to Peters.

"The report was somewhat devastating," says Peters, "but I managed to significantly reduce its impact and then put the CBC on a course to financial stability. At the time, CBC was considering selling their properties in Toronto to build the Broadcast Centre. Without financial credibility, the CBC would not have been able to do this. We engaged a team, among them Denis Desautels—who later became AG of Canada—and formed a specialized committee to restore financial credibility to the CBC," says Peters.

Peters next became involved with a troubling situation at CBC Enterprises, which had been set up to be the entrepreneurial arm of both the French and English networks. Among other things, its job was selling CBC programs as well as derivative products to foreign broadcasters. It was on this project that Marie and Peters worked together.

"Marie had had quite a career at the SRC/CBC. She acted on the broadcasting management side; I was on the financial side, looking into CBC Enterprises. The project involved a lot of travel to Montréal.

"I sold CBC television programs at the Cannes Festival in France," recalls Peters. "It was fun, largely because the people on the French side of CBC/Radio-Canada didn't know who the hell I was. One of the executives had rented a villa for the CBC to entertain dignitaries from the various television networks. He was somewhat extravagant." An understatement from a careful accountant.

There is a political element to every government job, and this was particularly true at the CBC at the time. The Conservatives under Prime Minister Brian Mulroney had been in power since 1984 and board members were appointed by the government. Many of them were people who did not trust the CBC, who saw it as a permanently Liberal-left organization or, in the case of the French network, a nest of separatists. Marie had her work cut out for her.

"It was 1988, and those were challenging times for Mr. Juneau: the board members were trying to find fault with him because he was a well-known Liberal, and the board members, by then, were Conservatives," says Marie.

She had a small team of three or four people, and she found being the go-between was more work than she anticipated.

"Number one: there was a relationship between the board and the government, and they all had government contacts. Then there was the relationship between the board and Mr. Juneau, the board and the executive and the regional stations.

The Conservative government changed the rules governing the top job at the CBC. Following Pierre Juneau's departure in 1989, the position was split in two. Gérard Veilleux became the new president, while a separate chairman was appointed. The inaugural chairman was Patrick Watson, a brilliant broadcaster who had been part of the team that invented the revolutionary 1960s program, *This Hour Has Seven Days*. He has a beautiful voice and a calm delivery that is the essence of Marshall McLuhan's cool.

Producers and journalists had high hopes for Patrick Watson. But while he was a brilliant broadcaster, he was

> The Conservatives under Prime Minister Brian Mulroney had been in power since 1984 and board members were appointed by the government. Many of them were people who did not trust the CBC, who saw it as a permanently Liberal-left organization or, in the case of the French network, a nest of separatists. Marie had her work cut out for her.

Marie and Pierre Juneau, president of CBC/Radio-Canada, receiving a medal of recognition from the Conseil de la vie française en Amérique. Alongside them are Raymond Marcotte, Director of the Saskatchewan Radio Station and Jean Hubert, President of the Conseil de la vie française en Amérique, 1987.
Source: CBC Archives.

at sea in the bureaucratic world of Ottawa, up against Gérard Veilleux, a skilled political practitioner who had risen through the ranks of the bureaucracy. When it came to the running of the CBC, the president had much more impact on operations than the chairman did. Watson had little success defending the CBC from the political forces buffeting it at the time, but he remained a popular figure among staff.

Marie admired the fact that he was such an outspoken supporter of public broadcasting in Canada. She also got along with him on a personal level. She remembers a personal incident with the likeable chairman. "One day, I said to him, 'I love your pen.'" It was one of those new rollerballs. "About a month later, I was in his office meeting with him. There was a little package, all wrapped up, on his desk. He gave it to me and told me to open it. It was a pen exactly like his. He gave it to me as a gift to thank me for the support that I was giving him," says Marie.

# Vice-President, Human Resources and Industrial Relations

DURING THIS PERIOD, the union situation at the SRC/CBC was a Byzantine mess. CBC staff were represented by a number of different unions, and people who did similar jobs, such as announcers and journalists, were sometimes represented by different unions. As a result of this crazy situation, jobs that could have been done simply by one person required the input of several people—each aspect of a given job was assigned to someone from a different union. For example, an announcer was not allowed to change the copy he was given to read. This situation prompted Lloyd Robertson to resign as the anchor of CBC's National News and move to CTV in 1976. Technicians were frustrated with technical changes they felt threatened their jobs. There were separate unions for technicians in Quebec and journalists in Quebec, which meant there were different pay scales from their counterparts in the rest of Canada.

In short, it was an industrial relations disaster.

In 1990, the position of Vice-President of Human Resources and Industrial Relations became vacant. When Marie did not apply for the job, Gérard Veilleux spoke to her about it.

"I don't know anything about human resources," said Marie. However, her track record in Sudbury and in dealing with people in the regions clearly showed that she had a talent for it.

The President was adamant.

"No, I'd like you to apply because negotiations with the thirty-three unions are coming up and I know that you know so many of the presidents because you have worked with them somewhere, somehow in some city," Gérard Veilleux told Marie. "You know them all and I think it will make negotiations easier if they are negotiating with someone they know."

He was right. Marie applied for the job, went through all the proper interview rituals, but in reality, the fix was in—the President of the CBC knew precisely who he wanted for this position.

She was particularly needed in industrial relations. As she learned while running CBON in Sudbury, the CBC had a long record of strikes. Indeed, at another time and place, it was the producers' strike in 1958 that had influenced the young René Lévesque, then host of a popular Radio-Canada TV program, *Point de mire*. The strike lasted sixty-eight days, was historically significant, and had long-lasting effects.

Marie reported to Tony Manera, who would go on to become president of the CBC after her departure. But the person she really enjoyed working with was Roy Heenan, the CBC's external labour lawyer, co-founder and managing partner of Heenan Blaikie.

"We worked very closely to establish the strategy for each union," Marie says. "I also worked closely with the vice-president responsible for the operations of those workers. We really enjoyed ourselves. Roy Heenan kept asking me, 'Are you sure you haven't done your law, you think like a lawyer, so logical.' He is probably the one who inspired me to attend law school fifteen years later. It was such a joy working with a professional who was convinced that industrial relations didn't have to be defined by conflict all the time. We renegotiated thirty-three union agreements within ten months. It had never been done."

There was no strike. Marie Poulin and Roy Heenan had pulled it off.

★ ★ ★

An aside:
"Roy Heenan was a great Canadian art collector," Marie remembers. "One night, we worked until nine thirty. I

finally went home. As I was taking my coat off in the entrance of our home, the doorbell rang. I said, 'Holy shoot, who's coming here at nearly ten o'clock?'

"'Oh,' Bernard said, 'I forgot to tell you.'

"I opened the door and there was Roy Heenan.

"He said to me, 'What are you doing here?'

"I said, 'Roy, I live here.'

"He said, 'Oh my, I never made the connection between Bernard Poulin and Marie Poulin. I'm here to talk to Bernard about some of his artwork,'" recalls Marie.

"It was unbelievable!"

This connection helped make an already great working relationship even better. "He was a great mentor to me," says Marie. "He was very generous with advice and suggestions. He was a truthful and honest man. And an outstanding lawyer!

"One of the negotiations we worked on together was particularly interesting. I can't remember which labour union was involved. I knew the president of the union particularly well, having worked together years before at CBOF in Ottawa when I was a producer there. He was sitting in front of me, and he gave me a list of all the 'asks' of the union.

"By the way, in those days the vice-president didn't usually sit at the negotiation table—he or she would be brought in later, if necessary, as a last resort if negotiations weren't going well. But not initially. This was a change in strategy we made. Roy wanted me at every negotiation table. He knew that even if I didn't know the union president, I would know somebody on that executive who was sitting across the table.

"So, there I was, looking at the president. I said, 'Here is what we are able to give.' Then I said, 'Why don't you and I go out and have lunch. Let's let our teams discuss this. Let's come back at the end of the day and try to reach an agreement before five o'clock.'

"We got up from the table and went to a restaurant. I had a huge briefcase with me.

"He said, 'I hope that isn't full of agreements you want us to sign.'

"I said, "No, no, they are just files.'

"But they were the agreements. And at five o'clock, we actually signed them. I'll never forget that day. It was a delicate point in the negotiations."

Marie and Roy had great success renegotiating contracts, but they also had to deal with staff layoffs, which were occurring at the time as a result of budget cuts. Marie suggested a way to improve the process both for the CBC and for its employees: "Formula 85." The idea behind it was simple: if your years of service added to your age hit the number eighty-five, you were eligible for early retirement.

> Marie suggested a way to improve the process both for the CBC and for its employees: "Formula 85." The idea behind it was simple: if your years of service added to your age hit the number eighty-five, you were eligible for early retirement.

Formula 85 was not unique to the CBC. Other large corporations were using the idea of adding years of service to an employee's age to come up with a way to start their pension early. Marie dreamed up a new way to do it.

"What was different," says Marie, "was the way we implemented Formula 85. I dreamed of it one night. I called it the 'Domino Approach.'

"I went to Tony Manera early one morning and told him that I had thought of a way we could actually apply Formula 85 that would make downsizing much more humane and fair.

"A supervisor could bring his or her team together and say, 'We have two jobs to cut.' If there are two people in this team who want to take early retirement, we will organize the work and simply change the job numbers.' It worked like magic. People were not laid off; they were choosing to leave. That's all it was.

"The unions agreed with this approach. It really worked. When it came to the administration of the downsizing, the manager of that team would simply switch the job number on paper."

"Even though I was being hired for industrial relations, I did a lot of work for HR," Marie notes. "One major achievement was developing a policy regarding harassment. Everybody seemed to think that harassment was always against women and it was usually sexual. When I did my research and interviewed people, I discovered that harassment was not something that only affected women—far from it. And there wasn't only sexual harassment; there was bullying too," says Marie. "I'm sure the policy has evolved since then, but that was one of the first things I worked on."

Marie feels that bullying in the workforce remains a major problem today. She also feels that the differences in wages and opportunities are still a problem for working women today.

> "I experienced bullying, my daughter Elaine experienced bullying, and so did my daughter Valérie. Now, if three women in the same family experience bullying in the workforce, something is wrong."

"Why? It's a power struggle. I think there is more bullying going on today than there was in the past," says Marie. "I experienced bullying, my daughter Elaine experienced bullying, and so did my daughter Valérie. Now, if three women in the same family experience bullying in the workforce, something is wrong."

Marie says when you are bullied you might think it is your fault; that is just one reason people do not report it. And she says bullying is a tactic used by both men and women in equal measure.

Marie's concerns when she was VP of Human Resources and Industrial Relations also extended to mental health.

"I set up a service for CBC and Radio-Canada staffers who needed help but couldn't afford it. The service was entirely separate from the Human Resources Department. If you needed a psychologist, you could access their services, which were completely confidential. We had lists of professionals in both languages in every city across the country where we had CBC stations. We were able to offer these services at no charge to the employees; the CBC paid for the service. It was called EAP, short for Employee Assistance Program.

"The other thing I developed within Human Resources was the feminization of the French language on air. There was an office, le Bureau de la Femme, at CBC in Montréal. The woman who ran it was made decisions regarding the appropriate feminine form of a word— *avocat/avocate*, for example. If you were doing an interview, you were required to use the right term on air. We were approached about this initiative by various Quebec women's associations—I didn't think of this on my own.

"Personally, I have never believed in the feminization of titles in French. I think job titles are gender neutral. When I was at CBON, the title on my door was 'Directeur.' Later, in the Senate, I was the only woman who said 'Senator' has no gender and so my title was 'Sénateur Marie Poulin.' All the other women were called *sénatrice*, a female derivative of *senator*. They must have discussed this because whenever the Speaker of the Senate would invite me to speak, he would say 'Sénateur Poulin' with some emphasis. I had discussed it with the Speaker; he agreed with me that a title is neutral. There's a big debate right now going on in French radio—I heard it yesterday. A female author is no longer an *auteure*, she is now an *autrice*. Like really? The feminization of titles is still an ongoing debate," says Marie.

> "I set up a service for CBC and Radio-Canada staffers who needed help but couldn't afford it. The service was entirely separate from the Human Resources Department. If you needed a psychologist, you could access their services, which were completely confidential. We had lists of professionals in both languages in every city across the country where we had CBC stations."

★ ★ ★

> "When I was VP of HR and Industrial Relations, bonuses were offered to vice-presidents if they received good job reviews. My review was good and so I was expecting a bonus. One morning, I arrived at the office and found a brown envelope under my door. Inside was a piece of paper with a list of all the vice-presidents who were at the same level as me. I was the only woman in the group. All the others were getting twice the bonus I was getting."

Marie loved working at the CBC, and as is clear, she was successful and well regarded. Or so she thought. She discovered, like other women, that being good at her job did not mean that she would be rewarded commensurately.

"When I was VP of HR and Industrial Relations, bonuses were offered to vice-presidents if they received good job reviews. My review was good and so I was expecting a bonus. One morning, I arrived at the office and found a brown envelope under my door. Inside was a piece of paper with a list of all the vice-presidents who were at the same level as me. I was the only woman in the group. All the others were getting twice the bonus I was getting," recalls Marie.

"When I looked at that, I had to sit down. I was in shock. Don't forget that settling with all the unions without a strike was big news within the CBC.

"I went to Senior Vice-President Tony Manera and stated, 'I thought I had received a good evaluation for the work I did.'

"He didn't say anything at first. Finally, he said, 'All final decisions are made by the president.'

"Next, I went to see Executive Vice-President Michael McEwen because I didn't feel comfortable going to Veilleux. I explained that I was struggling to understand why I wasn't getting the same bonus as my colleagues. I told him that while I was sure that they had all done excellent jobs, I didn't think I had done less of an excellent job than they had.

"I said, 'Michael, remember, we renegotiated thirty-three union agreements within ten months.'

"He said, 'Marie, come on, we all know you're just the cheerleader. It's your people who do the work, not you.'

"I looked him straight in the eye and said, 'Thank you, Michael,' and walked out."

"He said, 'Marie, we can continue talking.'

"I said, 'No, Michael, I have to go buy myself some pom-poms.'

I walked back to my office and called my husband. I started crying. I said, 'Bernard, I have to leave Radio-Canada and find myself another job. It's like divorcing from my own family, I just love it here so much, but I can't stay. My work is not recognized.'

"Three months later, I left. I was appointed by the Clerk of the Privy Council Office [PCO] as Deputy Secretary to the Cabinet, responsible for communications and consultations."

They say you cannot go back in life. But you can certainly look back at things that were once a huge part of your life.

"I'm very proud of my accomplishments at CBC/Radio-Canada," says Marie. "The most important, perhaps, is the founding of CBON, the French-language production centre in Northern Ontario. It's still there, and I'm very happy that it's flourishing and playing an important role."

# Life after Radio-Canada

IN JUNE 1992, when Marie decided to leave CBC because of the bonus issue, she quietly put the word out to the many contacts she had made over decades to find a position that suited her experience and in which she could use her vast communications experience.

Two of her key contacts were Hugh Segal, who at the time was Chief of Staff to Prime Minister Brian Mulroney, and Alain Gourd, Deputy Clerk of the Privy Council.

Marie had met Hugh Segal when he was Chief of Staff to Bill Davis, perhaps the most famous Progressive Conservative premier of Ontario in the twentieth century. Premier Davis was in Sudbury during the 1981 provincial election, his fourth campaign since becoming premier in 1971. The Tories were known as "The Big Blue Machine," and their politics were as "centre" as you could get—their appeal to the average voter was the reason they won time and again. But they had their work cut out for them in Sudbury. Bud Germa, a union official, had won three elections as the NDP member for Sudbury. In 1981, he was up against Jim Gordon, a high school teacher, and popular mayor of Sudbury.

Hugh Segal accompanied Bill Davis on the tour with the Premier in Sudbury. It was a seat they thought they could win.

Marie remembers that meeting. "I was in Sudbury then as head of French radio and they came to the radio station for a press conference. I noticed they didn't have a place to work privately, so I offered Hugh Segal my office. He was very appreciative. He and Bill Davis sat in my office while I got coffee and cookies for them at Cecutti's, Sudbury's famous Italian bakery. They appreciated it. When they left, Hugh asked if he could ask me a question. My response, 'As long as it isn't about my age or my weight, sure.' ensured that from that day forward, we would be friends."

The trip was a success for Davis and Segal; Jim Gordon won the seat for the Progressive Conservatives and sat for two sessions in the Ontario Legislature. In many ways, it was also a success for Marie. Later, when he became Chief of Staff to Prime Minister Brian Mulroney, Segal was instrumental in helping Marie move to a top post in the Privy Council Office.

Marie made a point of keeping in touch with politicians in Sudbury and Northern Ontario. On the day Jim was to be sworn in at Queen's Park, Marie

> "As an executive of the CBC, I had regular meetings with Alain Gourd to ensure he was informed of goings-on, not only from a political perspective, which is the minister's responsibility, but also from a bureaucratic standpoint."

met him on the plane from Sudbury. "Since his wife was a teacher and couldn't take the day off, Jim asked if I might accompany him to his swearing-in. I have a photo of that occasion. A lot of people thought I was a Conservative when the picture was published in the *Sudbury Star*."

Marie also had a connection with the Gourd family from Abitibi. They owned and operated Gourd Broadcasting, which had a string of private radio stations in northern Quebec. "When I was Secretary General to the Board at CBC, Mr. Juneau asked me to make sure that the lines [of communication] were open with the minister's office. The minister at the time was Francis Fox. The deputy minister was Alain Gourd," recalls Marie. "As an executive of the CBC, I had regular meetings with Alain Gourd to ensure he was informed of goings-on, not only from a political perspective, which is the minister's responsibility, but also from a bureaucratic standpoint."

Glen Shortliffe was Clerk of the Privy Council Office (PCO) while Brian Mulroney was Prime Minister. He reached out to Marie, asking her to head the Communications Secretariat at the Privy Council Office. Three months after Marie decided to leave the CBC, she stepped into her new job.

★ ★ ★

The PCO is the engine of government and is the pinnacle of power of the civil service. "Clerk of the Privy Council" sounds like a modest position, but in fact, the Clerk is the most powerful civil servant in the federal government. All deputy ministers report to the Clerk, and the heads of Crown corporations, such as the CBC, report directly to Cabinet ministers.

Though she had spent many years in Ottawa, Marie did not fully understand the importance of the PCO to the governance of the country. She feels that her lack of understanding was something she shares with most Canadians: "I would say that 90 percent of the Canadian population is not aware of the huge responsibility of the PCO."

The PCO is not a political body; rather, it is designed to ensure the government runs properly and follows the direction set by the elected government of the day. When there is a change of government, the PCO carries on without so much as batting an eye.

Every morning, the Clerk would chair a meeting. Marie, who oversaw communications, would attend, as did the heads of every secretariat. The secretariats deal with such things as federal-provincial relations and all the other aspects of running the federal government.

Jocelyne Bourgon was named Clerk of the Privy Council in 1994, after Marie had left the PCO, though the two women met later in their careers and remain good friends to this day. Madame Bourgon worked for three very different prime ministers: Brian Mulroney, Kim Campbell, and Jean Chrétien. She exemplified the neutrality of the Clerk of the PCO.

"I worked with many prime ministers, not all of the same stripe, but I think you could say that all of them were served well (by me). I am a non-partisan," says Madame Bourgon.

"I think Canadians are vaguely aware of the importance of the PCO, but I'm not sure every citizen needs to understand the nitty-gritty of every one of the public agencies or departments and ministries," says Madame Bourgon. "Do they know it's at the centre of government? Yes."

Though the PCO is apolitical in a sense, it is not without its own internal politics, Marie observes. "There are definitely politics, as in any organization. You could feel the power struggles. At the Privy Council, those who become deputy secretaries responsible for an area are usually very experienced public servants." It was difficult for Marie, as an outsider, to fit in. "It was a huge challenge for me because I had a steep learning curve; the public service has a culture of its own."

She did find a place for herself, however, and became privy (there's that word) to all the inside secrets of the federal government. "Work at the Privy Council Office (PCO) was entirely confidential. There were always big issues to deal with. Very often, the head of the military would come and give briefings. There were also the heads of security, CSIS, who would give briefs on what was going on such as how many threats the prime minister has received."

> "Work at the Privy Council Office (PCO) was entirely confidential. There were always big issues to deal with. Very often, the head of the military would come and give briefings. There were also the heads of security, CSIS, who would give briefs on what was going on such as how many threats the prime minister has received."

> **One of the biggest issues Marie dealt with during her time at the PCO was the Charlottetown Accord. The ten provinces and the federal governments had agreed on amending the Constitution. For all those parties to agree on such an important issue was in itself a miracle and Marie was closely involved in all the discussions on the content of the Accord.**

"I immediately observed that everyone who worked at the Privy Council Office demonstrated a high level of professionalism. I learned how complex the governance of the country is, as well as the complex nature of the dialogue between the different secretariats, different departments, and between the provinces and the federal government. It is so important for the running of the country. This is how I discovered what we call in Ottawa 'the machinery of government'—how Ottawa works. To this day it serves me well.

"The Clerk of the Privy Council is, in effect, the deputy minister of the prime minister. The prime minister and his staff rely on the Privy Council for objective, researched information," says Marie.

One of Marie's key jobs was to make sure that all departments were singing from the same songbook when it came to messaging. That was sometimes a difficult proposition. Marie is convinced that her background in industrial relations at CBC/Radio-Canada was of great use during her time at the PCO.

The weekly meetings involving the deputy ministers allowed them to voice their opinions. Marie was able to see who was comfortable with a notion and who was not. "Sometimes people disagreed. These disagreements had to be discussed and resolved. You must reach consensus; the deputy ministers need to agree to move forward on an issue. So, it's very important for the senior personnel at the PCO to have negotiation and mediation experience." In the end, an agreement would be reached regarding the path forward and how to communicate that. It was Marie's task to speak with the communications directors of all departments to ensure they implemented that message.

One of the biggest issues Marie dealt with during her time at the PCO was the Charlottetown Accord. The ten provinces and the federal governments had agreed on amending the Constitution. For all those parties to agree on such an important issue was in itself a miracle and Marie was closely involved in all the discussions on the content of the Accord.

"It was difficult to get the message out about what that document contained," says Marie. "The whole issue of federal/provincial authority was very important. There was an entire team, I was not alone. The lead for all the Charlottetown agreement in the Privy Council was the Deputy Clerk, Alain Gourd. My job was dealing with the communications strategy: the formal, the informal, the messaging. It was 24/7, I have to tell you."

The Charlottetown Accord was defeated in a referendum in late 1992, which led to the 1995 Quebec referendum on independence. "It was a big disappointment to everybody when it didn't pass."

Marie also came to better understand the connection between the Prime Minister's Office and the Privy Council Office.

One of the more interesting files Marie worked on was putting together a book that chronicled the achievements of the Mulroney years.

"We were told very confidentially that Mr. Mulroney was retiring from politics. I was called to the office of Glen Shortliffe, the Clerk, who told me that the Prime Minister had informed him that he wanted a book to recognize all his accomplishments during his two terms in office. He said to me, 'Marie, as Secretary of Communication and Consultation, I would like you to take the lead for that project,' which I did.

"I really enjoyed working with Mulroney on the book. I consulted quite a few of my colleagues within the PCO on how to build such a book, the chapters, whether it should be organized chronologically or by subject. I presented a business plan

As Deputy Secretary to the Cabinet at the Privy Council Office, Marie assists in preparing the book Prime Minister Brian Mulroney was writing on his accomplishments, 1993.
*Source*: Photograph by Ken Ginn.

to the Clerk, who then took it to the Prime Minister. I worked with every deputy minister of every department, making sure that all information contained in the book was validated by a senior bureaucrat. It became the track record of the Brian Mulroney years. The project was a pleasure to manage.

"Many photos were taken during that time, but the key one for me was a picture of my meeting with Mr. Mulroney, whom I had never met in person. I was brought by the Clerk one morning to Mr. Mulroney's office in Centre Block. The Clerk informed me that the Prime Minister wanted to see what stage the project was at. I brought samples of the book cover—Bernard had found me a very good artisan who worked with leather. The picture I have is of Brian Mulroney sitting down, looking at all these things while I stand across the desk from him looking on.

"I was totally focused on my presentation. Mr. Mulroney was very positive saying he 'liked this and liked that.' He was very encouraging. Once the photos had been taken, the Clerk of the PCO told me that would be all.

"What I didn't know was that there was a journalist from the *Globe and Mail* sitting on a couch in the PMO. There was also the Prime Minister's photographer, Ken Ginn, who was the official photographer of the PMO. His family was well known in Ottawa for its photography business. I didn't know all this at the time.

"As I left, Ken Ginn asked, 'Aren't you Marie Poulin, married to Bernard Poulin the portrait artist?' I answered "yes," proudly.

He then asked: "Are you always this comfortable with people in power? You're afraid of nothing."

"He said that when he looked at someone through the lens of a camera, he could sense what they were feeling, and he said that I looked totally confident."

Part of the reason was that Marie, like many journalists, was used to meeting important people, and meeting them on an equal footing. On top of that, Prime Minister Mulroney was an open person and not the least bit stuffy.

Marie's time at the PCO was before the era of the Blackberry and cellphones. Senior PCO staff had to leave a forwarding number if there was someone important who had to speak to them. This was true for Marie too.

As it turns out, one night the most important person in Ottawa tracked her down: Prime Minister Brian Mulroney. "Bernard and I were going to visit friends of ours for dinner. I called the switchboard (of the PCO) and said I would be at such and such a number and could be reached at any time, and I should be back home around ten o'clock.

"Around eight, the phone rang. Our hostess said, 'Marie, it's for you; it's the Prime Minister on the phone.' I thought they were playing a joke on me, but the lady said, 'Marie, I recognize Mr. Mulroney's voice and he is on the phone.'

"I picked up the phone, and he said, 'Marie, I'm just looking over the book and looking at the accomplishments of one of the departments. Would you mind if I changed the wording a bit?

"I said, 'Mr. Mulroney you can make all the changes you want to my drafts, but you know that I check every one of your changes with the Deputy Minister.'

"He burst out laughing and said, 'Boy, you're a tough one to deal with but okay.'

"He was extremely accommodating."

Marie was impressed that Mulroney always remembered her when they met socially a few times over the years. He does not forget a name or an incident, something he shared with Marie.

Marie was involved with Prime Minister Mulroney's departure in another capacity, but that involvement took place after she left the PCO.

"I was called to the Office of the Clerk of the Privy Council, Glen Shortliffe; Alain Gourd, the Deputy Clerk, was there too. I was informed that I was leaving the Privy Council and that I was being appointed as founding chair and CEO of the Canadian Artists and Producers Professional Relations Tribunal; it was a quasi-judicial tribunal for all self-employed people who worked for the federal government and its agencies. The tribunal was enabled by the Status of the Artist Act [Bill 73, adopted in 1992]. But that legislation had not been enacted."

That same week, a large party was to be held for the departing prime minister. Of course, entertainment was planned for the event. At the last minute, however, the President of l'Union des artistes (UDA) of Quebec called the Prime Minister's Office to inform them that no member of the UDA would be performing at his concert because the agency had not been set up as promised.

"Alain Gourd said to me, 'Marie, you know every head of every artistic agency and union in Quebec. You've dealt with them at CBC and negotiated every agreement with them. You know them and they know you. We would like you, within the next twenty-four hours, to make a personal call to every one of them announcing confidentially that you will be the founding CEO of that tribunal according to the *Status of the Artist Act*.'

"My first call was to the President of the then UDA. After that call, word got around and everything went smoothly, including the concert.

> "Marie, you know every head of every artistic agency and union in Quebec. You've dealt with them at CBC and negotiated every agreement with them. You know them and they know you. We would like you, within the next twenty-four hours, to make a personal call to every one of them announcing confidentially that you will be the founding CEO of that tribunal according to the *Status of the Artist Act*."

"So, that's how I ended up leaving the Privy Council. That move was very difficult for me because I was enjoying myself. To feel that you are at the centre of governance and to have access to such privileged information and access to analysis of it was a privilege for the brief time I was there."

Brian Mulroney remembers the work Marie Poulin did on his book. "Ms. Poulin was with the PCO, and she prepared the book that gave an account of our government from 1984 to 1993," said Brian Mulroney in an interview in December of 2020. "Marie did very good work for us, and I have fond memories of her." But more to the point, Mr. Mulroney could not recall the issue with the performing unions and the gala. Marie had ironed out the issues, and everything had gone off without a hitch. That is what members of the Privy Council are supposed to do: solve minor, annoying problems before the prime minister even knows about them. The union glitch at the concert is a perfect example.

## Called to the Senate

THERE ARE PEOPLE who lobby hard to become senators. Marie Poulin was not one of them. It was childhood friend Ray Bonin who helped make her one.

Raymond Bonin had vaulted from local to federal politics when he was elected to Parliament as the MP for Nickel Belt in the Liberal landslide of 1993. That election made Jean Chrétien Prime Minster while the Progressive Conservatives, who had been in power since 1984, were reduced to two seats.

Bonin saw something in Marie that he liked. He had been impressed when she brought French-language radio to Northern Ontario. He was reminded of her commitment to Northern Ontario when she received an honorary doctorate from Laurentian University in June 1995.

And so, he began the campaign to have her named to the Senate. The plan was so low key that Marie was not even aware of it until the last minute.

"I don't even know if Marie knows it," Bonin told me, "but I was the first person to recommend her as a senator. I made that request directly to Jean Chrétien by letter. Then I lobbied his chief of staff, and it happened. She was living in Ottawa then, but I considered her as a Northern Ontarian. She was always loyal to that duty to look out for Northern Ontario. So, when she received her honorary degree [in June 1995], I hosted a number of receptions in Ottawa, and I was really happy to do so."

Twenty-five years later, Marie speaks appreciatively of all that Ray Bonin did for her and for their mutual childhood friend Bob Del Frate. "Bernard was given an honorary doctorate by Laurentian University in June of 2019. There were two people sitting near me: Ray Bonin and Judge Bob Del Frate. After the ceremony, as we were walking out, I asked Valérie to take a picture of Bob, Ray, and me. I asked the men to stand on either side of me."

"Only we knew that we were where we were because of Ray Bonin. I knew how hard Ray had worked to get Del Frate appointed judge because we had worked at it together. That's how I recognized the importance of Ray's role in my being called to the Senate."

★ ★ ★

> "Only we knew that we were where we were because of Ray Bonin. I knew how hard Ray had worked to get Del Frate appointed judge because we had worked at it together. That's how I recognized the importance of Ray's role in my being called to the Senate."

Let us dial back to September 1995. Marie was sitting in her office at the tribunal when she received a call from Ray Bonin.

"Marie, I have a very confidential question to ask you," said Ray.

"What is it?" asked Marie.

"I'd like to submit your name to represent Northern Ontario in the Senate to replace Dr. Desmarais." Dr. Jean Desmarais had died a few weeks earlier, before his retirement age.

Marie burst out laughing saying, "Are you out of your mind? Me?"

"Leave it with me, Marie. You've got the experience, the training; you've got a master's degree and an honorary doctorate, and your work has been recognized. You would be fantastic. But you can't tell anyone about this call."

He then asked Marie if she knew anyone at the PMO.

She replied the only person she had met was Jean Pelletier, Chief of Staff to Prime Minister Chrétien.

"You know Mr. Pelletier?" Ray asked.

"He wouldn't remember me," Marie replied, "but when I was the regional vice-president at CBC, I met him. Whenever I travelled to one of our stations across Canada, I would always do a courtesy visit with the mayors of those cities. On one of my visits, I met with Jean Pelletier, who was mayor of Québec City at the time. He used to work for Radio-Canada, and we so enjoyed discussing public radio and what it means for Canada. So, maybe he will remember and maybe he won't, but we always got along very well."

About a week later, Marie got a call from Jean Pelletier. He remembered her.

"This is highly confidential. I've been asked to call you to see if you would agree to have your name put on a short list for an appointment to the Senate. There has always been a Francophone from Northern Ontario and that would be you."

Marie was flattered, but she immediately thought of the practical aspects. She and Bernard were a two-income family, and she knew what they needed.

Marie receiving an honorary doctorate from Laurentian University, 1995. *Source*: Family Collection.

"I can't say yes, and I can't say no because I don't know the conditions of the work. How much does it pay per year?" she asked.

He said, "A little bit over seventy thousand dollars."

> "I told him I would have to discuss it with Bernard and that I would call him back in the morning. Until his dying day, the joke between Jean Pelletier and me was: 'You're the only one who ever said they had to discuss a possible Senate appointment with their spouse.'"

"I burst out laughing. I said, 'Mr. Pelletier, I'm currently making $140,000 a year, so that would be a reduction of more than 50 percent. I'll have to discuss this with Bernard. Do I get to keep my chauffeur?"

It was Pelletier's turn to burst out laughing.

"Senators don't get a chauffeur, Marie."

He started with the argument that it was an honour to serve your country and the opportunity to influence legislation. Then came the money side.

"Marie, you are fifty years old, and you will be sitting as a senator for twenty-five years. Multiply seventy thousand by twenty-five years. You are currently making $140,000 a year, and your appointment as chair of the tribunal is for seven years. You've got five years left. Multiply $140,000 by five. Financially, you'll be better off at the Senate."

It was a pretty dicey financial argument.

"I told him I would have to discuss it with Bernard and that I would call him back in the morning. Until his dying day, the joke between Jean Pelletier and me was: 'You're the only one who ever said they had to discuss a possible Senate appointment with their spouse.' We became good friends, and he became one of my key mentors in politics."

Bernard was supportive, as usual. The two of them figured they could scale back on expenses.

While they awaited developments on the Senate front, they got on with life. Marie had just turned fifty, and Bernard was planning an art show in Italy the following year; he had already sold the entire exhibition of his Italian paintings sight unseen. The celebration of Marie's birthday tied in nicely with Bernard's show, so they planned a one-month working holiday in Italy.

They had been gone for two weeks when the concierge in their hotel delivered a fax. This was before the widespread use of email. The fax was from Nathalie Grimard, Marie's executive assistant back in Ottawa.

The message: Please call. URGENT!

Marie made the call. Long-distance was expensive in 1995, so they made it short. Nathalie got straight to the point. "I just heard from the PMO. The Prime Minister would like to talk to you as soon as possible. Would you be available tonight?" asked Nathalie.

They were not staying at the Ritz, but at a small, two-star hotel in Venice. Telecommunications were still quite primitive back then, but the owner was a gracious Italian. The Poulin charm was successfully put to work: the switchboard usually closed at eleven, but the owner put the call through at midnight, or 6 p.m. Ottawa time.

"'Madame Poulin, this is Jean Chrétien,' said the familiar voice every Canadian knows. 'I'm calling to see if you would accept to serve in the Senate of Canada.'

"I was just so taken aback. It felt as though the carpet had been pulled from under my feet. I laughed and said, 'Are you sure you want to do this?'

Prime Minister Jean Chrétien tried to reach Marie to invite her to represent Northern Ontario in the Senate; this was the fax received by Marie, in Italy, 1995.
*Source*: Family Collection.

**Marie had just turned fifty, and Bernard was planning an art show in Italy the following year; he had already sold the entire exhibition of his Italian paintings sight unseen. The celebration of Marie's birthday tied in nicely with Bernard's show, so they planned a one-month working holiday in Italy.**

**"'Madame Poulin, this is Jean Chrétien,' said the familiar voice every Canadian knows. 'I'm calling to see if you would accept to serve in the Senate of Canada.'
"I was just so taken aback. It felt as though the carpet had been pulled from under my feet. I laughed and said, 'Are you sure you want to do this?'"**

> Marie told Prime Minister Chrétien that they would be back in Canada in two weeks. But that option was not on the table. Canada was in the middle of a referendum campaign for Quebec independence, and it was all-hands-on-deck.

"He burst out laughing and said, 'You do realize that I've never appointed a person as young as you to the Senate.'

"He didn't believe in appointing someone for such a long mandate.

"'I appoint older people, but you come highly recommended from so many sources. I want you to work hard. I want you to represent Northern Ontario, women, the Francophones of Ontario, and your profession, communications.'

"'My mother, Marie Boisvert, was from Saskatchewan, so I have a very strong admiration for minority languages. I know what people went through; my mother told me all about it. I want you to be on the road, out there meeting groups, meeting people, and I want people to better respect the Senate. I'm told that you are a hard worker and I'm expecting you to work hard.'"

The answer?

"I said yes, that I would be honoured, and thanked him profusely for the privilege of representing not only Northern Ontario but Francophones of Ontario but also women. I immediately knew that I was the first francophone woman from Ontario named to the Senate. Monsieur Chrétien was giving me a mandate, which I respected for the twenty years that I sat in the Senate," says Marie.

Marie told Prime Minister Chrétien that they would be back in Canada in two weeks. But that option was not on the table. Canada was in the middle of a referendum campaign for Quebec independence, and it was all-hands-on-deck.

"I want you sworn in as soon as possible," said the Prime Minister.

"Natalie was brought in on the secret. She had to manage all the organization for the swearing-in while still under a cone of silence. Bernard and I went to the travel agency and booked a flight for the next day.

"I'll always remember what Bernard said to me, 'Mr. Chrétien owes us a two-week vacation in Italy.'

"Natalie met us at the airport. Our daughters were there too. They didn't know; we were told not to discuss this with anyone.

"The date of the swearing in was to be the September 21, 1995, at two o'clock. A press release went out a few days before. The morning it was released, Bernard told both girls and I called my parents.

"It was announced that the Prime Minister was appointing four senators, three women and one man. There was Bill Rompkey from Newfoundland, Lorna Milne from Toronto, Doris Margaret Anderson from Prince Edward Island, and myself.

"I informed Elizabeth MacPherson from the tribunal of the appointment and that a replacement would be appointed by the government in the coming days. I recommended David Silcox, one of the board members, to replace me as CEO of the tribunal. He had written quite a few books on well-known Canadian painters. He replaced me. I wanted to be sure that I wasn't leaving any loose ends."

The indispensable Nathalie Grimard went with Marie to the Senate.

Marie was told that for the swearing-in she could have only fifteen guests. She chose the following people to attend this important ceremony: Bernard, of course, as well as Elaine and Valérie, and their boyfriends; Marie's parents; Bernard's mother; Monsignor Audet; Marie's brother Claude from Sudbury and his wife Connie; her sister-in-law Yvette Charette from Montréal; long-time friend Don Mitchell; Natalie and her husband Gaétan; her researcher Michel Lamoureux; and Jean Pelletier, the Chief of Staff to Jean Chrétien.

The actual ceremony took place in the Senate Chamber in the Centre Block of Parliament and was held at 2 p.m., at the start of that day's Senate session.

Marie with Monseigneur René Audet, celebrating their forty-five-year friendship as well as his spiritual guidance and mentoring, 2003.
*Source*: Family Collection.

Marie, in the Senate Chamber, being escorted to her swearing-in ceremony by her sponsor, Senator Leo Kolber, and Senator Joyce Fairburn, Leader of the Government in the Senate.
*Source*: Senate Archives.

> "I wanted to show that minorities were extremely important in Canada, so as the first Franco-Ontarian woman appointed to the Senate, I chose an anglophone minority from Quebec to be my sponsor."

This particular swearing-in ceremony was unusual in that there were three women and one man joining the Senate.

A new senator is allowed to choose their sponsor in the Senate, and Marie decided on Senator Leo Kolber from Montréal. She made the decision to send a message—remember this was at the height of the Quebec referendum campaign.

"I wanted to show that minorities were extremely important in Canada, so as the first Franco-Ontarian woman appointed to the Senate, I chose an anglophone minority from Quebec to be my sponsor."

This was contrary to Senate culture—the usual thing is to choose a sponsor from your own province. Right off the bat, the new senator rubbed some of the old senators the wrong way.

On the day of her swearing in, Marie was welcomed to the Senate by Speaker Gil Molgat. Present for this occasion (from left to right): Paul Belisle, Clerk of the Senate, Raymond Bonin MP for Nickel Belt, Marie, Natalie Grimard, Marie's executive assistant, Michel Lamoureux researcher, and Jean Pelletier, Chief of Staff to Prime Minister Jean Chrétien, 1995.
Source: The Senate of Canada Archives.

On the day Marie was sworn in, she gave a moving speech. Don Mitchell remembers that day well: "Marie was a very powerful speaker in the Senate. I was there when she was sworn in in September of 1995. The swearing-in ceremony was followed by tributes to Senator Dr. Jean Desmarais. Marie wanted to pay tribute to him as she was replacing him in the Senate."

His brother Judge Robert Desmarais, who knew Marie from childhood in Sudbury, approved of her nomination. "Marie, of course, being from the same area, was a prime candidate. She was a very enthusiastic Sudburian, and as far as I'm concerned, she was an excellent replacement for my brother," says Judge Desmarais.

"She made her maiden speech on the day of her swearing-in. People were amazed at her fluency in both languages. All senators, especially the Conservative benches, looked shocked. I was sitting in the Senate Chamber, in the gallery, and could see the individual faces of the senators, even their emotions," says Don Mitchell.

After the excitement of the swearing-in, Marie slept soundly.

"That night," she recalls, "I dreamt I was in a big concert hall; there was live music. A grand waltz was playing. Lester B. Pearson came over to me and invited me to dance. I danced the grand waltz with him."

Who knows what makes people dream the things they do? There was the obvious Liberal Party link. Marie told Bernard about her dream and said maybe she had dreamed about Lester Pearson because he was the member for Algoma East, a riding in Northern Ontario. The Liberal prime minister and winner of the Nobel Peace Prize had represented the riding through eight elections from 1948 until he left politics in 1968.

Who to tell about that dream? As it happened, when Marie arrived at the Senate, there was a senator named Pearson: Landon Pearson, who was married to Geoffrey Pearson, the late prime minister's son. The two women sat near one another in the Red Chamber, but that was not the place to bring up something as personal as a dream.

On a fall day in mid-October, a few weeks after Marie was sworn in, she was walking outside when she ran into Landon Pearson. Though she was worried it might sound odd, she decided to tell her about the dream.

"I asked her, 'Did your father-in-law like to dance?'

"She replied, 'Oh, absolutely not.' Then, as she was walking away, she turned and said, 'Wait a minute, there was one dance he loved to dance, and it was the grand waltz.'

"My eyes swelled with tears. 'I have to tell you a story,' and I told her about my dream.

"This brought tears to her eyes as well. She said, 'I actually believe that you danced with my father-in-law, and he must be very proud to see you in the Senate today.'"

★ ★ ★

Marie was never a member of the Liberal Party of Canada before her appointment to the Senate. She never discussed how she voted. Indeed at the CBC/SRC in those days, it was a rule that you kept your politics to yourself; putting an election sign on your lawn was a no-no.

But Marie had met Jean Chrétien, briefly, when she was in charge of Radio-Canada in Northern Ontario.

"Mr. Chrétien received an honorary doctorate from Laurentian University in 1980," says Marie. "At the time, I was the director of Radio-Canada in Northern Ontario, and the university had invited me to give a short speech at convocation in the name of the Laurentian University alumni. So, I gave my speech, congratulated Mr. Chrétien, and sat down.

"I have a wonderful picture of that occasion, by the way. There's Dr. Best, the President of Laurentian, Father Michaud, who was the president of Sudbury University, me, Mr. Chrétien, and Paul Desmarais, who had also received an honorary doctorate.

Paul Desmarais, of Power Corporation, and Jean Chrétien, then Minister of Justice, receive honorary doctorates from Laurentian University. Marie was then the managing director of the CBON radio station in Sudbury, 1980. Left to right: Father Lucien Michaud, President of the University of Sudbury, Henry Best, President of Laurentian University, Paul Desmarais, Marie, and Jean Chrétien.
Source: Laurentian University Archives.

"Mr. Chrétien, who was Minister of Justice at the time, spoke to the graduates after receiving his honorary degree. His speech was about Canada and the importance of Canadian unity.

"While he was speaking, I was thinking to myself, 'My God, I would love to work with this man one day.' I had never heard such passion for our country. I never forgot that."

Jean Chrétien was equally impressed with Marie, and did remember meeting her in Sudbury.

"I had met her socially; when you're in Ottawa you meet a lot of people, and she was involved in public affairs. I think I met her sometime when I was visiting Sudbury too," said the former prime minister. "She had a good reputation in Ottawa. We were looking for a senator, and I wanted to name a francophone senator and a woman. So, it was a good occasion. I named her, and I was happy with my appointment."

> "She had a good reputation in Ottawa. We were looking for a senator, and I wanted to name a francophone senator and a woman. So, it was a good occasion. I named her, and I was happy with my appointment."

Since Jean Chrétien retired in 2003, he and Marie have continued to see each other from time to time; she has coffee with him, and after his beloved wife, Aline, died in 2020, the former prime minister has had quiet dinners with Bernard and Marie.

"I am always learning from him. When time allows, I make an appointment at Dentons [the law firm at which Mr. Chrétien serves as counsel] and we catch up. And I continue to ask him about good governance, balanced politics, factual reporting. You name it, I ask it."

Marie has a great deal of respect and admiration for Jean Chrétien, and had enormous respect for Aline Chrétien, as the following anecdote demonstrates.

"One day, I received a call from the president of Laurentian University who said that the Board of Governors of Laurentian had decided to appoint its first chancellor and wondered if it would be a good idea to approach Mr. Chrétien to become that chancellor," recalls Marie.

She had to think of an honest but diplomatic answer, since she knew Mr. Chrétien's answer would be no. "I said that I was sure that he would be honoured to serve as chancellor but that he would probably decline the offer.

"One of the things he has told me is that he is not accepting any appointments outside of his own region. Since his retirement from politics, he is flooded with invitations, and he didn't like having to decide who to say yes to and who to say no to," says Marie.

She nonetheless came up with an idea.

"Have you thought of Madame Chrétien? She is an outstanding woman. She is the honorary chair of the Royal Conservatory of Music's Advisory Board. She speaks four languages fluently. She strongly believes in training and education. She is a pianist, and she is also well-read; you can discuss anything with her. She knows history, geography." Marie could tell right away the suggestion won the day.

"I offered to give the name and phone number of a person whom I knew Aline trusted implicitly and told him that he would have to go from there. That if it was meant to be, it would happen.

"A few days later, Madame Chrétien (that was always the way Marie addressed the Prime Minister's wife, even

Marie and Bernard accompany the Right Honourable Jean Chrétien and Madame Aline Chrétien during her first official function as Chancellor of Laurentian University.
*Source*: Laurentian University Archives.

though she came to know her well) called me saying she was so touched by my referring her to Laurentian University. She asked me to come with her to Sudbury when the announcement was made. I told her that I would be honoured."

"Madame, treat me like your executive assistant, I am there to serve you.'

"I travelled with her, and we stayed in Sudbury one night. There was a lot of work to do, as she was getting briefings from Laurentian University, meeting a lot of people, and doing a lot of media interviews. I accompanied her throughout."

"After giving her speech, Chancellor Aline Chrétien was surrounded by about twenty-five journalists because this was big. It was on the national news. She handled that scrum as though she had been doing them for years. I admired her for handling it like a pro. She said, 'Senator, I have been observing for forty years. Do you think I learned nothing?' She had a great sense of humour."

The first chancellor of Laurentian University, Aline Chrétien, took up the position on September 22, 2010, and held it for three years.

"I was invited to her funeral. Very few people were allowed to attend due to the pandemic; in all, there were possibly thirty people who were not family at the service.

"When her daughter, France Chrétien-Desmarais, rose to give her tribute, the first thing she said was, 'My mother always felt that education was a priority in her life. When she was appointed chancellor at Laurentian University, we teased her saying, "Maman, you've always wanted to attend university; now you are entering by the front door."'"

# Work and Life in the Senate

CANADIANS ARE SOMETIMES CYNICAL about the Upper House.

Marie disagrees. She was very proud of the Senate and her role in it.

"The honour of being named a senator struck me when I thought about the appointments to the Order of Canada. The Senate has been operational since 1867. It is 154 years old, and there are, at this time, fewer than a thousand Canadians who have been called to the Senate; according to the count it's 941 over those 154 years," says Marie. "By comparison, the Order of Canada has been operational since 1967, which is 54 years, one hundred years less than the Senate. And, up to now, more than 7,000 Canadians have been invested into the Order of Canada. That difference underscores the unbelievable privilege it is to be called to the Senate. That's why I felt the honour so deeply."

Marie also felt great satisfaction in the Senate because, for the first time, she was receiving the same financial reward as her male colleagues. Equal pay for work of equal value was not just a throwaway line in Ottawa, at least on Parliament Hill. "All my working life, I had been paid less than men, including at Radio-Canada. For the first time, I was receiving the same pay as them."

She also feels the Prime Minister's Office, at least under Jean Chrétien, was not entirely driven by politics.

"Mr. Chrétien used to say, 'Good policy doesn't always make good politics.' Sometimes you must make decisions based on good policy; I think the best example of that was Chrétien's decision not to join the United States in the Iraqi War," says Marie.

Marie and Bernard wishing Prime Minister Chrétien a Happy New Year, December 1997. *Source*: Photograph by Jean-Marc Carisse.

> **Marie also felt great satisfaction in the Senate because, for the first time, she was receiving the same financial reward as her male colleagues. Equal pay for work of equal value was not just a throwaway line in Ottawa, at least on Parliament Hill.**

She also feels that when it came to fighting the budget deficit, it was Jean Chrétien, a former finance minister, who was driving the bus.

"Jean Chrétien led the review of all programs and had great respect for the public service. He knew the quality and dependability of their work. Mr. Chrétien set up the program review committee chaired not by Minister of Finance, Paul Martin, but by a former senior public servant, who was minister federal and provincial, a member of the Cabinet, Marcel Massé. That seasoned politician, appointed as minister in charge of federal public service renewal, knew the names of every department head, every governmental agency, where to go and who to call to meet the deficit reduction objectives the prime minister had set out. The real goal was to balance the budget. It was not an easy task, and some tough decisions were made."

★ ★ ★

As a senator, Marie enjoyed honour and (finally) equal pay. However, being named to the Senate produced an unpleasant break in Marie's relationships with a group of her women friends. Upon hearing that the newly named Senator Charette-Poulin was sitting in the Liberal caucus, some women cut ties with Marie. They never spoke to her again.

Marie recalls running into one of these women. They came face to face over a vegetable stand in an Ottawa supermarket.

"I looked up, saw her, and said, 'Bonjour, how are you?'

"She gave me a look of contempt, quickly turned away, and stalked off with her cart."

"In the same aisle was a man in a wheelchair who had observed this incident. He came up to me and said, 'Madame?'

"I asked if I could help him.

"He said, 'No, I'd like to help you. I saw what just happened; that woman is evil. I am very, very upset; I strongly recommend that you keep away from her.'

"It was such an intense moment. I still feel a little sick when I think of it."

Shirley Westeinde was one friend who stuck by Marie despite her political leanings. As often happens in these cases, the friction that developed with others created a stronger bond between Shirley and Marie. Both were prominent women, were successful in their respective fields, and achieved firsts. They never met a glass ceiling that they did not want to smash.

Elaine on the water, 1986.
*Source*: Family collection.

> "When Marie was appointed to the Senate, Shirley recalls, I sent her flowers and congratulations. Some time later, she mentioned that some women had stopped speaking to her because she had accepted the position. I was flabbergasted. I didn't know if they had done that because they were jealous; I couldn't believe that it could be purely political, that they would end their friendships with her because her appointment came from Jean Chrétien."

As well as serving as an honorary colonel in the Canadian Armed Forces, Shirley was the first female chair of the Canadian Construction Association and the first female president of the Building Owners and Managers Association of Ottawa. Shirley chaired the Board of the Children's International Summer Village (CISV), which her own children attended, along with both Poulin girls, Elaine and Valérie.

"The original concept of CISV, which goes back to the 1950s, was to get eleven-year-olds from approximately fifteen countries to meet someplace in the world in a so-called village. Four eleven-year-olds from Ottawa would go with a leader to Germany and four eleven-year-olds from Japan, Korea, China, and South America," says Shirley. "The idea was that eleven-year-olds had not yet formed malicious opinions about other countries; it didn't matter what colour their skin was; they were just eleven-year-olds having fun together. The concept was that as they grew up, should there be a conflict with China, for instance, they'd remember it's not the kids who were in the village who are responsible."

Though Marie and Shirley remained close after Marie's Senate appointment, Shirley was initially unaware of the estrangement with the other women. "When Marie was appointed to the Senate, Shirley recalls, I sent her flowers and congratulations. Some time later, she mentioned that some women had stopped speaking to her because she had accepted the position. I was flabbergasted. I didn't know if they had done that because they were jealous; I couldn't believe that it could be purely political, that they would end their friendships with her because her appointment came from Jean Chrétien. I'm still astounded by it. But it did happen. I never spoke to them about it, but I thought, 'If that's what they were really like, I didn't want to continue to be friends.'"

Marie's daughter Valérie never doubted that it was politics that caused her supposed friends to pull away. "I'd witnessed my mother deal with all of that, all the way back to the Mulroney days when she was at PCO. When my mother was appointed to the Senate, she had these two best friends; they were inseparable. We were at their houses all the time. It was a super tight-knit friendship. Then, she was appointed to the Senate by Chrétien and from then on, we never saw them again. So, I witnessed the meanest of mean-girl things. Overnight, they just totally shut her out and their entire network just disappeared. My parents weren't hyper-social people to begin with when I was a kid, so this was a big change. But, through it all, my mother always acted like everything was fine."

Others, though, thought that Marie deserved to be in the Senate and were happy about her appointment. Marie had never been involved in politics, but people who worked with her at Radio-Canada thought she was a natural politician, even if she always adhered to the institution's rule of being non-partisan.

"I wasn't surprised when she was named to the Senate because I know Marie Poulin," says Doug Ward, the CBC vice-president who first brought Marie to the head office in Ottawa.

"She's ambitious with a capital 'A,' and she delivers. I remember when she got her office. She invited me to have a look at it—it was like going into the office of some major politicist. The anteroom was full of signed pictures of every politician who had anything to do with Franco-Canada. I think there was even a picture of the Pope there. You knew that you were in the presence of someone who was a political animal, someone who just lived and breathed that and who saw the CBC as a crucial vehicle for her constituents.

"Walking into that office, I just knew that this wasn't me; it wasn't what my background was. I was in radio production, and I loved production. I also loved management, but I had been heavily involved in student politics and that had been enough for me.

"I remember Marie telling me one day, 'You know, your office isn't big enough; you have to get a bigger office.' I asked why.

"She said, 'When I bring the regional director from Moncton to Ottawa and I want them to meet my boss, I want you in a big office.'

"She's probably like that to this day; she's a very out-there person and ambitious. With reason, she wants that her physical environment reflects her achievements."

> "I remember when she got her office. She invited me to have a look at it—it was like going into the office of some major politicist. The anteroom was full of signed pictures of every politician who had anything to do with Franco-Canada. I think there was even a picture of the Pope there."

> "Marie exudes enthusiasm and grows her contact list, which is probably a mile long. She cultivates those contacts; she takes good care of them—she does all the things that good politicians do."

"Marie exudes enthusiasm and grows her contact list, which is probably a mile long. She cultivates those contacts; she takes good care of them—she does all the things that good politicians do," says Pierre Racicot, with whom Marie is still friendly today and who is a fellow governor of the Actra Fraternal Benefit Society (AFBS), insurer installed in Toronto.

★ ★ ★

When Marie-Paule Charette-Poulin was sworn in as a senator, she had to take an oath of allegiance to the Queen, who served as the head of state of Canada from 1952 to 2022. As Marie is Francophone, you may think she would have some objection to swearing allegiance to the monarch of Great Britain. You would be wrong. Since she was a little girl, Marie-Paule loved the Queen; one reason is that as a young child she and the Queen looked alike.

Marie has a great anecdote relating to this: "A few years ago, when our granddaughter Claire was five years old, she

Marie welcomes Governor General Michaëlle Jean to the Senate, 2005.
*Source*: Government of Canada Archives.

gave me a little battery-operated bobble-head doll. The doll was dressed in the Queen's usual dress, with a coat and hat. Whenever the button was pushed, the Queen waved. I told Claire it was a fun gift and she responded, 'You really look like her; that's why I bought it.'

"If you look at a picture of Princess Elizabeth when she was five years old and compare it to my picture at five, we look like sisters. When I was a little girl, we wore our hair the same way; it was the same colour: light brown."

Welcoming the Prince of Wales to Canada, 1996.
*Source*: The Senate of Canada Archives.

Given Marie's long-time fascination with Queen Elizabeth, it is no surprise that she was delighted to learn she would be meeting her at a royal dinner in Toronto. Marie remembers the moment well: "I was introduced to her at the Royal York Hotel. It was such an honour. She was such a beautiful woman in person. Her eyes were of a blue colour that I had never seen before. They were full of life and humour. What struck me was her genuine interest in every person she spoke to. As many others around the world, I cried when I heard the news of her passing in September 2022. I am convinced that she knew she was leaving the monarchy in good hands. King Charles III sees far and wide: he was one of the first individuals in the public realm to raise awareness of the environmental challenges we face. When I met him in 1996, I was impressed by his warmth, graciousness, and respect towards others," says Marie.

"The Queen's passing reminded me that she had appointed former Prime Minister Jean Chrétien to the Order of Merit, the highest honour granted to twenty-four outstanding individuals from around the world, and from different walks of life. She then commissioned his portrait and Bernard had the honour to be chosen. When we were invited by the curator, Lady Jane Roberts, to visit the Print Room at Windsor Castle, it was a privilege to see original works by Leonardo da Vinci, John Singer Sargent, and many others. Bernard's portrait of *The Right Honourable Jean Chrétien* is in good company."

Of course, life at the Senate is more than gala functions with dignitaries. The workload is quite heavy, as Marie explains. "The responsibilities of a senator include a) the parliamentary sittings; b) the review of legislation that is tabled before those sittings; c) committee work—senators typically serve on three standing committees—; d) the work for the region we represent; and e) the work we do for groups, be they from educational, cultural, business, or whatever constituency. As part of all of this, we're always receiving requests for meetings, information, and speeches.

"When you are first called to the Senate, you're overwhelmed by the number of requests that you receive from

*The Right Honourable Jean Chrétien* by Bernard Poulin, 2010.
Source: Royal Collection Trust / © His Majesty King Charles III, 2022.

people. You suddenly become their go-to person. The first day I arrived, I couldn't get off the phone; it was unbelievable," says Marie.

Marie points out that when a member of Parliament is elected and first comes to the House of Commons, they are given extended training on the rules governing

> "When you are first called to the Senate, you're overwhelmed by the number of requests that you receive from people. You suddenly become their go-to person. The first day I arrived, I couldn't get off the phone; it was unbelievable."

parliamentarians. When senators are appointed, there is no such instruction. It is sink or swim. It is difficult for new senators to learn the formal rules as well as the informal, unwritten culture, when there is such an instant demand for a new senator's time and attention.

"Natalie [Grimard, who came with her from the tribunal] and I were both overwhelmed. She received no training on the administrative rules and regulations; I was simply given books to read, and I mean books. The regulations for the Chamber, for Parliament, and all the administrative rules," says Marie.

Another woman on Parliament Hill, the Honourable Sheila Copps, former Deputy Prime Minister, agrees. "I had a slightly different situation because when you're an elected person, there's a whole learning process that you go through," says Copps. "I gained a lot of inside political insights, from the time I went from being an MPP in Ontario to a federal MP in the House of Commons in Ottawa. People who are appointed senator are not usually part of the political process, so the learning curve is a lot

Marie visiting an underground mine in Sudbury, 1997.
*Source*: Laurentian University Archives.

steeper. You don't get a lot of that time that you would normally have gotten if you were in a political situation."

One of Marie's first major accomplishments involved what was known as the *Wired to Win* study, which focused on the future of telecommunications. "That was really a huge commitment." The idea for the study came to Marie in 1997 when she was waiting for a plane at the Sudbury airport. A man was deep in concentration, fingers flying across a small keyboard. Always curious, Marie asked the man what he was doing.

What he was doing was working, sitting in an airport, far away from his law office in downtown Toronto. He was working on a Blackberry, a Canadian invention years ahead of its time. The man she spoke to was a Sudbury native, and the managing partner of the renowned Toronto law firm Wildeboer Dellelce. Perry was one of the first users of the advanced Blackberry with a keyboard, the RIM 900. Perry's young firm scored a major coup when it landed the legal work for the Blackberry initial stock offering in 1996.

What you had at the airport were two people born and raised in the mining town of Sudbury who were both on the cutting edge of the digital revolution: one a lawyer who saw the potential of a small company from Waterloo, Ontario; the other a senator whose bold curiosity was about to launch a major study on how Canada could hitch a ride on the internet.

"Think about it," says Marie. "The Senate, an institution considered so behind the times, filled with dinosaurs, approved an international review of Canada's position in the new world of communications in 1997, providing an interim report in 1998 and a final report in 1999. All this because I saw a man at the Sudbury airport sending an email on a hand-held device. It just lit up my curiosity."

The *Wired to Win* report was released in 1999. It was produced in conjunction with John Manley, then Minister of Industry in Jean Chrétien's Cabinet, and written at a time when ordinary Canadians were joining the internet. In 1998, 36 percent of Canadians households were online; one year later, this had jumped to 42 percent.

"Industry Canada collaborated with the Senate because we were engaged with everything to do with telecom and

> "People who are appointed senator are not usually part of the political process, so the learning curve is a lot steeper. You don't get a lot of that time that you would normally have gotten if you were in a political situation."

> "The Senate, an institution considered so behind the times, filled with dinosaurs, approved an international review of Canada's position in the new world of communications in 1997, providing an interim report in 1998 and a final report in 1999. All this because I saw a man at the Sudbury airport sending an email on a hand-held device."

> "It's actually quite difficult to have a special study funded by the Senate. I had to sell the idea to the committee and then had to sell the idea to the full Senate because if you're going to do a well-researched study, you need funding."

> At the end of the meeting, the Senator asked Negroponte: "Years from now when the internet is more developed, what will people be looking for? He had a one-word answer: Simplicity."

the internet. At the time, there was no Google, there was Netscape and there was Alta Vista; it was quite primitive," says John Manley. "There was a lot going on then; it was the beginning phases of the internet."

"It's actually quite difficult to have a special study funded by the Senate. I had to sell the idea to the committee and then had to sell the idea to the full Senate because if you're going to do a well-researched study, you need funding," says Marie.

Part of the Senate budget covered international travel to see how other countries were moving into the Internet Age. The researchers attached to the study, including Marie, first visited the Massachusetts Institute of Technology (MIT), where there were brilliant thinkers such as Nicholas Negroponte, who wrote the prophetic book *Being Digital* in 1995 and had a column on the back page of *Wired Magazine*, a must-read in its day.

Marie met with the internet superstar at MIT, where he and his students operated something called The Media Lab. At the end of the meeting, the Senator asked Negroponte: "Years from now when the internet is more developed, what will people be looking for? He had a one-word answer: Simplicity." The study team then went to Silicon Valley to take a closer look at the internet and the digital revolution.

One of the principal researchers of the Senate study was Matthew Fraser, who went on to write several books on internet-related subjects, as well as hosting a media program on the CBC and becoming editor of the *National Post*. He notes, "The background to the Senate report in the mid-1990s was the hype, at that time, about the 'information superhighway' and 'convergence' between telephone and cable TV companies. Satellite [communications] were also threatening to destabilize the Canadian television landscape. Canada is a country that was built on infrastructure—first the railway, then electronic communications. So, this was an important subject at the time."

Senator Charette-Poulin and the team also visited France and Belgium to see how the European Union was handling the newly wired world. Other countries were faltering on the internet. France tried to jumpstart a home communications service, but it was complicated and was washed away by the simpler World Wide Web. Britain was another story. "In the UK, we met with the head of the BBC and their regulator. In the UK, the government spent a lot of money investing in public broadcasting and offering public services. It was not entirely controlled by private companies, like in Canada, where private companies manage all online services. I am convinced that the cost of equipment and of the services are a big chunk in a family budget in our country," says Marie. "We know that the UK doesn't have Canada's geography and that the challenges aren't the same, but it was the policy that struck me; the fact that everyone had to have access."

★ ★ ★

Since one of Marie's mandates was to represent Northern Ontario, she worked closely with members of Parliament from the area, in particular Ray Bonin. He remembers that time: "I was Chair of the Northern Ontario caucus at the time, and with every project that we undertook, Marie was always 'all in.' She always contributed. What helped was every time we needed to talk to someone, she said she knew someone, and she would call them to get to the person we needed to talk to. She always knew somebody, and she was a very good lobbyist for our caucus."

As she did throughout her long working life, Marie made new contacts and kept in touch with old ones. One of these was Jim Gordon, who was the mayor of Sudbury again after having served two terms in the Ontario Legislature. She had first met him when she opened the Radio-Canada French services for Northern Ontario, in Sudbury. Marie made another courtesy call to Mayor Gordon's office in 1997, this time as a senator.

"Oh! You're in my bedroom," said Marie to a shocked Jim Gordon. Seeing his expression, she quickly explained herself. "What I meant, Mr. Mayor, is that your offices are exactly where our family home was. When I look out this window, I see exactly what I saw as a little girl looking out my window every night. My bedroom was facing the street just as your office is. It's the same view: looking at Helvi's

> "I was coming to work one morning at 55 Metcalfe, and as I turned the corner there was this man and this woman hugging and kissing each other right in front of the building. It was Marie and Bernard. That symbolizes what Marie is: she is in these organizations, and she gives these organizations a big hug."

Flower Shop. I remember so many evenings as a little girl when I would look out the window and watch people going by in the evening."

★ ★ ★

Marie's job meant she was on the road a lot. Not only did she have to travel frequently to see her constituents in Northern Ontario, she also had to travel elsewhere in Canada and, not infrequently, she had to travel abroad. She was away from home a great deal, and she relied heavily on Bernard to be there for Elaine and Valérie.

Marie tells a story of sharing her parenting experiences with Jean Monty, who was then CEO of Bell Canada Enterprises (BCE), after having led Nortel, Canada's most successful communications company at the time. She was visiting him as a senator because she was chairing the Senate's *Wired to Win* committee. The conversation changed to personal things. "We were discussing our families, and I was telling him about the amount of travel I had to do, even when the kids were small, and how lucky I was that my husband worked from home," Marie says.

"He asked me, 'How are your kids doing without a mother?'

"I said, 'They are doing so well. Could you imagine, if I had stayed home, how screwed up they'd be?'

"He said, 'I can see you don't feel guilty.'

"It was a choice that Bernard and I made together. He could easily have rented studio space."

Ronald Caza thinks Marie's relationship with her family mirrors the relationships she has with the organizations she is involved with. "I was coming to work one morning at 55 Metcalfe, and as I turned the corner there was this man and this woman hugging and kissing each other right in front of the building. It was Marie and Bernard. That symbolizes what Marie is: she is in these organizations, and she gives these organizations a big hug."

"At the Senate, she was giving all the projects she was involved in a big hug. It's love, it's caring, and it's energy. She has so much care and love for other people, for her community, and for these projects. I've seen that more than once and that's who she is and that's what she's like. I have all day for that. We do not have enough of that in the world, and it's so important that we have that."

As a sitting senator, Marie Poulin was also involved in passing legislation, work that has had long-lasting impact.

As one example, Marie helped to have the federal government declare June 21 Aboriginal Day. "It was one of my first files in the Senate in 1996," Marie remembers. "Ron Irwin was then Minister of Aboriginal Affairs[1], which was a position Mr. Chrétien once held. Ron represented the riding of Sault Ste. Marie. He and I would travel from Northern Ontario to Ottawa, but we'd always go through Toronto. One day during the winter of 1996, I was coming in from Sudbury and Ron was with his executive assistant

**She has so much care and love for other people, for her community, and for these projects.**

Celebrating the first National Aboriginal Day in Canada on June 21, 1996 [now referred to as National Indigenous Peoples Day]. Depicted: Speaker Gil Molgat, and parliamentary team and chiefs who worked with Marie.
*Source*: Senate of Canada Archives.

---

1. At the time, this department was officially called the Department of Indian Affairs and Northern Development.

> Ron Irwin, the Minister of Indian Affairs and Northern Development, sent Marie a hand-written note: "I wanted to thank you for your work and enthusiasm in relation to the recognition of Aboriginal people."

coming in from the Soo [Sault Ste. Marie]. When we met at the Toronto airport, he said, 'Hey, Marie, you're just the person I wanted to see.'"

Irwin told Marie that the government wanted to create something to celebrate the Indigenous people of Canada. He wanted to create a "National Aboriginal Day," but he did not want the bill to be a government bill. He wanted it to be tabled as a private member's bill. Irwin also thought it had a better chance of passing if it came from the Senate, not from the House of Commons.

"Ron said he wanted me to lead that file. I hadn't even been in the Senate a year when he asked me to do that. I said I'd love to, but that I would only do it on one condition: that Aboriginal Day be on June 21. He asked why. I said, 'It's my birthday.' That was the reason that day was picked," Marie says, laughing. "Actually, it was chosen at the request of the Assembly of First Nations, I think. As we know, the summer solstice is a significant time of year in Indigenous cultures," says Marie.

"When I returned to the Senate, I consulted with the Speaker of the Senate at the time, Gildas Molgat. He told me to call a meeting of the Indigenous senators to outline exactly what I was proposing to ensure their buy-in. I didn't think it would be appropriate for me to sponsor the bill. Leading the project wasn't a problem, but I really felt it should be sponsored by one of our colleagues. He agreed, saying it should be the one with the most seniority.

"We started meeting each week to iron out the objective and content. Meanwhile, I had introduced all this to Irwin's chief of staff to make sure we were all on the same page, and also with the Department's deputy minister. I thought we should get it done now and not wait a year. 'Let's get this through,' I said. I was sure we would get unanimous consent. It all worked out well, and we had our first Aboriginal Day on June 21, 1996. It was my first experience with a private member's bill."

Ron Irwin, the Minister of Indian Affairs and Northern Development, sent Marie a hand-written note: "I wanted to thank you for your work and enthusiasm in relation to the recognition of Aboriginal people. Considering how low our budget was, the day went well right across Canada."

Over the twenty years Marie was in the Senate, she sponsored two other private members' bills.

"On another bill dealing with commemoration, I helped pass the International Holocaust Memorial Day. It seemed touching to me that, as a Christian, I was sponsoring this bill. Senator Jerry Grafstein from Toronto asked me to do it. It was a more complex undertaking, but it all worked out well. It seems that private members' bills that start in the Senate advance slightly faster than those that begin in the House of Commons. I think that's simply because there are more members in the House than in the Senate. In the end, Bill C-459 was passed in 2003; it established the National Holocaust Memorial Day," says Marie.

"The other bill I sponsored was for the establishment of Vimy Ridge Day, which is now observed on April 9. That project began in the House of Commons; it was sponsored by a member from Northern Ontario, Brent St. Denis, the member for Algoma—Manitoulin—Kapuskasing. Brent came to see me because I was from Northern Ontario also," says Marie.

There was a real Northern Ontario connection with the Vimy Ridge Day Bill. It was originally suggested by

> "On another bill dealing with commemoration, I helped pass the International Holocaust Memorial Day. It seemed touching to me that, as a Christian, I was sponsoring this bill."

> "The other bill I sponsored was for the establishment of Vimy Ridge Day, which is now observed on April 9."

Marie and some of her colleagues welcome a delegation of parliamentarians from Japan in the Chamber of the Speaker of the Senate, 1996.
*Source*: The Senate of Canada Archives.

> "My experience working on those three private members' bills allowed me to learn a lot about our history. But it also made me realize the importance of legal training. It greatly contributed to my motivation to go back to school."

Robert Manuel of Elliot Lake—in Northern Ontario. Manuel was a veteran of the Korean War. He worked underground in the mines as an electrician and was active in the Royal Canadian Legion. Along with Vimy Ridge Day, Manuel also initiated the recognition of National Peacekeepers Day in Ontario.

"From the beginning, we wanted to give credit to Robert Manuel, who had suggested the bill. In the end, it was received by both Houses with a lot of enthusiasm. That bill was also introduced in 2003.

"My experience working on those three private members' bills allowed me to learn a lot about our history. But it also made me realize the importance of legal training. It greatly contributed to my motivation to go back to school."

# 15

# A Franco-Ontarian Fights for Canada

MARIE'S WORK on National Aboriginal Day and National Holocaust Memorial Day would strengthen her connection to the Indigenous and Jewish communities, but as a Franco-Ontarian, her strongest connection has always been with the French constituency in Canada.

As a little girl, Marie spoke only French. It was not until she was five or six that she learned English. Her parents were proud of their language and culture and made sure to pass these on to their children. They also worked hard to preserve them in the Sudbury community—not always an easy task. The use of French was not encouraged in Ontario at the time. Indeed, the use of French in education was actively discouraged by the Ontario government for many decades.

Things began to change for the better in the 1960s. Franco-Ontarians, and French speakers from New Brunswick and other parts of the country saw their rights protected first by Lester Pearson, and then his successor Pierre Elliot Trudeau, who introduced bilingualism across the country. Signage at the Sudbury airport was updated to include both English and French. It was a point of pride in Franco-Ontario when the provincial government began providing services in both languages.

While official bilingualism is welcomed in Ontario, it was much less so in Quebec, where it is perceived by some as part of a risk of encouraging assimilation.

When Marie attended university in Montréal, she discovered Quebec nationalism; Hugues, her first husband, was unilingual and a staunch nationalist.

She remembers her own experience and observations. "There were quite a few demonstrations by students.

> Marie's work on National Aboriginal Day and National Holocaust Memorial Day would strengthen her connection to the Indigenous and Jewish communities, but as a Franco-Ontarian, her strongest connection has always been with the French constituency in Canada.

Marie and her parents, Alphonse and Lucille Charette, on the tenth anniversary of CBON, 1988.
*Source*: CBON Archives.

I attended one but never did again. We were demonstrating on rue Sainte-Catherine. People were chanting, 'more French, more French.' Someone yelled, 'The horses are here; the police horses are here.' Right in front of me, horses were galloping. Just in time, I managed to jump onto the sidewalk. I held on to a telephone pole while the horse galloped by. That fright is still fresh in my mind.

"There's something else I particularly remember. There used to be a meeting once a year of the representatives of all Canadian francophone associations, including those in Quebec. It was called *États généraux du Canada français*. One was held in 1969 in Montréal. One meeting was at the Université de Montréal's sports facility on Édouard-Montpetit. My father was attending because he was very involved in the Northern Ontario francophone groups.

"I was coming back from one of my classes at the university, and suddenly, I could see all these adults walking down the street. I spotted my father. As he passed me, I said, 'Papa, what's going on?'

"'This is a historic moment, Marie-Paule,' he told me. 'We were informed during discussions with the leaders from here that they were busy taking care of Quebec and weren't interested in francophone matters outside the province.' He said that this was a very sad day as it highlighted the division of the Francophonie in Canada. Every Francophone from outside of Quebec had risen from their seat, left the meeting, and came out to the street to slowly walk away from it all."

Marie and Hugues were living in California during the October Crisis, the name given to events that took place in October 1970. In response to the kidnapping and murder of Quebec Labour Minister Pierre Laporte and the kidnapping of British diplomat James Richard Cross by the Front de libération du Québec (FLQ), Prime Minister Pierre Trudeau invoked the *War Measures Act*. During the crisis, police rounded up 497 people, including singer Pauline Julien and her partner, poet and future Quebec cabinet minister Gérald Godin, poet, union activist Michel Chartrand, and journalist Nick Auf der Maur.

Hugues, a staunch separatist, was outraged. "Some of Hugues's friends had their apartments searched by police; some were even jailed. He was very upset. I still remember saying to Hugues, 'We are so lucky to be in Berkeley because you probably would have been questioned.'

"I did not want Quebec to separate because that province was important to Francophones living in other parts of Canada. Our families come from there. *Ce sont nos racines.* They are our roots."

Marie never judged individuals because of their political views. An excellent example of that is the announcer Serge Arsenault, the host of *Radioactif*, the weekend show she produced in Ottawa early in her Radio-Canada career.

"Marie was incredible. We had great respect for each other even though politically, culturally, and socially speaking, we were black and white," says Arsenault. "She was a federalist from Northern Ontario, and I was a sovereigntist from Quebec. She knew it; I never used it on the air."

But once he was off air, he would go back to working for the cause of the Parti Québécois. René Lévesque and he lived in Gaspesia some time and in his house in Knowlton, Eastern Townships, a picture of himself and the former Quebec premier hang on the wall.

Marie, meanwhile, worked for the federalist cause, especially during the second referendum on Quebec sovereignty project.

> "'This is a historic moment, Marie-Paule,' he told me. 'We were informed during discussions with the leaders from here that they were busy taking care of Quebec and weren't interested in francophone matters outside the province.' He said that this was a very sad day as it highlighted the division of the Francophonie in Canada. Every Francophone from outside of Quebec had risen from their seat, left the meeting, and came out to the street to slowly walk away from it all."

> "'I notice you're planting a tree,' I said, 'and I also notice that you're using ten fingers to grip the shovel.' I told him that if he lost the thumb on his right hand, he wouldn't be able to plant that tree. He wouldn't be able to grip the shovel properly. 'If we lose Quebec,' I said, 'Canada would lose, and that's why I'm here.'"

"When I was called to the Senate, it was just before the 1995 referendum. I informed the PMO that I was available if they wanted me to get involved in the campaign for unity. I was invited to a huge rally in Montréal that Mr. Chrétien was chairing. He made a point of introducing me as someone from Sudbury and of saying how important Quebec was for all francophone communities in Ontario.

"I was also sent door to door in areas of Montréal that were identified as extremely separatist. No one wanted to come with me because they were afraid of getting doors slammed in their faces, but that didn't bother me. In fact, I was looking forward to it.

"I think the riding I was sent to was Hochelaga-Maisonneuve. So, off I went with all these pamphlets in my arms. I came to a house where a man was planting a tree. I introduced myself, telling him I would like to convince him to vote 'No' in the referendum. "He looked at me and asked where I was from, saying I didn't have a Montréal accent. I said I was from Sudbury, in Northern Ontario. He asked why, then, I would be concerned about a Quebec issue.

"I told him it was important to me. 'I notice you're planting a tree,' I said, 'and I also notice that you're using ten fingers to grip the shovel.' I told him that if he lost the thumb on his right hand, he wouldn't be able to plant that tree. He wouldn't be able to grip the shovel properly. 'If we lose Quebec,' I said, 'Canada would lose, and that's why I'm here.'

"He looked at me and said, 'I'm moved by what you just said.'

"The referendum was close. The *sondages* [opinion polls] were saying that the *Oui* side was doing well; yes, it was tight. But we were fired up and working hard. Mr. Chrétien would say, 'Every vote counts.'

"We did win, but might not have. That's why the issue has always been an important one for me. So much so that when I was invited to chair the Fédération Canada-France, I accepted. The federation was founded in the early 1950s to enable French and Canadian soldiers to remain in contact. Over time, it included men and women who had not fought in World War II. I worked

Marie is awarded the distinction of Officier de la Légion d'honneur by the president of France, via his ambassador in Canada, Philippe Guelluy, 2003.
*Source*: Family Collection.

for five years to contribute to this connection based on culture, business, and friendship. We had no budget, so all travel was paid for personally. What a great experience!

# The Law

IN 2004, after nine years in the Senate, Marie decided to attend law school; she wanted to better understand what she and her colleagues in Parliament were doing. The first thing she had to consider was the optics: How would it look for a working senator, and she had a sterling attendance record, to be taking classes part of the day?

"The first person I consulted was the Clerk of the Senate at the time, Paul Bélisle. He was a lawyer and knew the workload of the Senate. He told me that I should go for it.

"I asked him, 'Is it reasonable to think I could do it while working full time as a parliamentarian?'

"He replied, 'Marie, I did my law school while I was working full-time in the Senate. You just simply lose a little bit of sleep for three years.'

"I also consulted Paul during those three years on what courses I should take, which would be most helpful to me as a parliamentarian," says Marie.

Others also encouraged her, including the Liberal leader of the Senate, Jack Austin. He said as long he could see her in the Senate, it did not bother him. Newly elected Liberal MP Ken Dryden told Marie: "If I could go to McGill Law School while playing hockey, you can do it while sitting full time in the Senate."

But perhaps the most supportive and practical advice came from a young law student, Myriam Beauparlant, who was working in Marie's office as a summer intern. "Myriam was a real fireball. Seeing that I was having trouble with the legislation, she said to me, 'Why don't you do law?'

"I said, 'Oh my God, I'm fifty-nine years old.'

"She said, 'So?'

"She told me that law school always seems to reserve a few places for adult students," recalls Marie. Myriam then

> "I find that discrimination against women is often subtle. A difference in salary isn't, but the lack of recognition of a duly earned title is not always noticed. If you have a PhD, you worked damn hard for it. It is the same with titles such as Honourable or Right Honourable."

told her that the law school in Ottawa was an easy walk from Parliament Hill. This was the practical advice.

"At lunch hour we walked to the university, then walked back to Parliament Hill. She showed me a shortcut. It took fifteen minutes," says Marie.

The next step was meeting with the Dean of the Law School at the University of Ottawa. "Bruce Feldthusen was so encouraging. He said there was a parliamentarian from the House of Commons who was enrolled in the civil law program; this was MP Richard Marceau. I wanted to do common law. He responded it would be interesting to have two parliamentarians doing their law at the same time while both sitting and working full-time," says Marie.

Marie wanted to study part-time. However, she was told that was not allowed. The dean suggested she try it for a semester, which she did. It worked.

And so, Marie went to school for the first time in almost forty years. The class was half women, half men. The youngest person in the class could have been her grandchild; Marie was one of two over fifty.

"About ten of the students worked full time, like I did. Two recognized me because they were Parliament Hill pages. They called me 'Senator,' but I said, 'No, here we all use our first names and mine is Marie.'" Although Marie felt it was unnecessary for her classmates to address her as "Senator," she nonetheless feels that it is important to recognize the achievements of women by using their proper titles.

Later, recalls Marie, when Joe Biden won the presidential election in November of 2020, a writer in the *Wall Street Journal*, which was rather pro-Trump during his four years in office, took a swipe at Dr. Jill Biden, criticizing, in particular, the fact that she calls herself "Dr."

"Any chance you might drop the 'Dr.' before your name? 'Dr. Jill Biden' sounds and feels fraudulent, not to say a touch comic. Your degree is, I believe, an Ed.D., a doctor of education," wrote Joseph Epstein. The reaction was immediate. Even writers from *The Atlantic* and the *Los Angeles Times* chimed in, calling his column "a sexist essay."

Marie wholeheartedly agrees with this criticism. "I agree with Dr. Biden. I find that discrimination against women is often subtle. A difference in salary isn't, but the lack of recognition of a duly earned title is not always noticed. If you have a PhD, you worked damn hard for it. It is the same with titles such as Honourable or Right Honourable," says the Honourable Senator Marie-Paule Charette-Poulin, BA, LLB, MA.

"I had an interesting experience: I was on the board of a start-up organization. The formal letterhead came out. At the bottom of the letterhead were the names of the people who sat on what they called the advisory board, which was made up of about 50 percent men and 50 percent women. Three of the members had official titles: one was a Right Honourable, one was an Honourable—me—and the other person had a doctorate. The titles of the three women were not included. I had to publicly bring the issue to the attention of the chair. I cannot believe this is still happening today."

At public events, more often than not, a male dignitary will be referred to using his title and last name; a female dignitary, on the other hand, will frequently be referred to by her first name.

Several of Marie's fellow parliamentarians had encouraged her to pursue a law degree, and the Dean of the Faculty of Law had accepted Marie as a student in the program. But there were opposition politicians who saw this as an excuse to attack her and leaked a false narrative to their favoured reporters.

"While I was doing my law [degree], I would go to the office very early in the morning to get all my correspondence done before my classes, which were at the end of the day.

"One morning, I encountered a journalist with a cameraman on Parliament Hill. As I walked to the door of my office, he said, 'You're Senator Charette-Poulin, aren't you?'

"I said yes.

"He said, 'Are you the senator who is doing her law degree on the Senate's dime?'

"I answered, 'Certain senators go to the gym at the end of the day, and they exercise their bodies; I go to university and I exercise my little grey cells every evening.' I turned around and left.

> "Certain senators go to the gym at the end of the day, and they exercise their bodies; I go to university and I exercise my little grey cells every evening."

> Marie articled at Heenan Blaikie's offices in Ottawa in 2006. She was the oldest student they had ever taken on.

"I knew this encounter had been important. I immediately called my friend Duncan Fulton, who was chairing my campaign for the presidency of the Liberal Party of Canada. He made a few calls and was informed that the 'story' came from a well-connected conservative senator. That is when I discovered, for the first time, that I was in political trouble."

Other members of the media were only too happy to attack Marie as well. *Frank Magazine* attempted to bully not only Senator Charette-Poulin, but also her husband Bernard and her daughter Valérie. *Frank*'s childish, smart-ass, frat boy "humour" labelled Marie Poulin "senator hyphen"—an obvious anti-Francophone dig, since the use of hyphens in names is almost exclusively Francophone.

At the time, *Frank* was run by Michael Bate, a British immigrant who tried to mimic the style of the muck-racking British publication *Private Eye*. Plagiarism failed. His stock-in-trade was making fun of people's names, their weight, and appearance—adolescent excess. He was fed material by members of the PMO and other Ottawa insiders with a grudge. The Senate was a favourite, easy target. While most of its victims ignored the slander and mocking directed towards them, Senator Duffy fought back. He sued *Frank* and won forty thousand dollars.

"My campaign for the presidency of the Liberal party was in full swing; this made me a target. They tried to make me abandon the leadership race as well as my law studies. Marie, however, persevered. She completed her studies and became a lawyer, while also being an engaged senator."

### Heenan Blaikie

Marie articled at Heenan Blaikie's offices in Ottawa in 2006. She was the oldest student they had ever taken on. Her introduction to the firm was through the co-founding partner of the firm, labour lawyer Roy Heenan, with whom Marie had worked at the CBC as Vice-President of Human Resources and Industrial Relations. He knew she would be a good fit and he hired her before he told his partners.

Bruce Johnson was the articling student in the office next to Marie's. He too was a bit older than the other articling students, though only twenty-eight, having worked in the film business before going back to law school. The shared film-broadcasting background was one bond. The two had also worked for former prime minister Jean Chrétien, who had joined the firm in 2004 after he left office. Bruce remembers feeling lucky to travel with Mr. Chrétien to Kazakhstan and Saudi Arabia. "Here I was a kid from Dollard-des-Ormeaux [a Montréal suburb], flying around the world with a former prime minister," says Bruce.

Senator Charette-Poulin joined Chrétien on a similar trip a year or two later. It was highly unusual then for a woman to be invited to the strict Muslim country of Saudi Arabia.

"Marie came to Saudi Arabia as an invited guest, which was a rarity when we were talking about 2007 or 2008; she was often the only woman in the room. They treated her like royalty; I'll never forget they bought her a very colourful *abaya* because of who she was as a senator," says Bruce.

"Marie put in as much time as any of us did, which was very impressive. She would split her time between being up on the Hill and yet she was in the [law] office just as much as any of us. She didn't expect to be treated differently than any other junior lawyer but, of course, she would be afforded the respect that comes with the career that she had had," states Bruce.

"It was an extraordinarily good decision to have hired Marie," says Norman Bacal, the co-managing partner of Heenan Blaikie's cross-Canada practice and the man who wrote the book on the firm, *Breakdown: The Inside Story of the Rise and Fall of Heenan Blaikie*. "Once I got word of her having started, I took her under my wing. I thought there was a fantastic opportunity to use her for other things not necessarily having to do with her legal skills."

"Apart from anything else, she is an incredible promoter. She knew everybody. Marie was an incredible source of business contacts, and I used her on various files that really had nothing to do with legal talents so much as interpersonal skills," says Bacal, who worked out of the Toronto office of Heenan Blaikie.

> "Marie put in as much time as any of us did, which was very impressive. She would split her time between being up on the Hill and yet she was in the [law] office just as much as any of us."

Marie with Premier Jennifer Smith of Bermuda, 1999.
*Source*: Family collection.

Marie remembers one of the projects she worked on. "A Toronto lawyer I'd never met told me one of his clients was an important pork farmer. The lawyer had heard that the Minister of International Trade was going to Asia and that his client would love to accompany him. He asked how we could do that. I developed, in writing, a seven-point plan for him, which clearly identified the work he had to do as a lawyer. Three months later, the guy was on the mission with the Minister. The pork farmer in Ontario was able to sign a deal in Asia; the lawyer said he'd never be able to thank me enough."

During the 2008–2009 financial crisis, one of the files involved an American insurance company. The law firm needed a connection with the company, and Norman Bacal asked Marie to help. She did not know anyone, but that did not stop her. "For Marie, it was just a matter of six degrees of separation. I don't know how many phone calls she made to find out who the in-house chief legal counsel was, but she managed. We approached him, and then the three of us went to New York and pitched them on agreeing to hire us to begin work on the mediation," says Bacal.

Marie remembers that trip well. "It was really a very interesting meeting: The guy wanted to know more than merely what Heenan Blaikie offered as litigation services; he wanted to know how the Canadian government works. He had a job as a young lawyer for a member of the Senate in Washington, so he was really interested in learning about the Canadian Senate."

Notes Bacal, "Once I tasked her how to 'get us in the door.' She spent literally months on it. When I brought her in to assist me on something, there was no question but that I could count on her. She took it all very seriously, and she was very proud of the work she was doing."

Marie was also able to use her connections in Sudbury to help the firm. Heenan Blaikie built a mining practice about the same time as she joined it. Though she had never worked in mining, she had connections in Sudbury.

One of those connections was a lawyer she worked with at Heenan Blaikie, Ronald Caza, who was also from Sudbury. As mentioned earlier, he was an admirer of hers from the days when he was a teenager listening to CBON in Sudbury when Marie ran the radio station. Ron Caza is now a litigator who handles the tough cases that usually go to court. He was amazed at how quickly Marie began contributing to the firm. Jean Chrétien was a formidable

> "For Marie, it was just a matter of six degrees of separation. I don't know how many phone calls she made to find out who the in-house chief legal counsel was, but she managed. We approached him, and then the three of us went to New York and pitched them on agreeing to hire us to begin work on the mediation."

Marie named as the Person of the Year by Richelieu International, 2008.
*Source*: Richelieu International archives.

force at Heenan, where he was involved in many international projects. "They involved Mr. Chrétien because his wisdom and experience were very useful to the people who were retaining us," says Mr. Caza. "Marie played a very important role in many of those projects. What was amazing was that although Marie was new to the practice of law when she came on board, she was so confident in her abilities to contribute to the success of a project. She always approached the right people in order to ensure that she would be involved. She also used her own connections and her own experience to start some of those projects on her own for the firm. She has got such a good presence—I'll use the word *classy*."

Norman Bacal was not only impressed with Marie Poulin's work ethic, but also by her integrity.

> "Marie had to make some very important decisions at a certain point in time, and in making those decisions, she always thought about what was in the best interests of the people she represented as a senator."

★ ★ ★

It therefore came as a shock when, one day, Bacal read of allegations being brought against her in the Senate expenses investigations.

"I thought it was an atrocity," says Bacal. "I knew how scrupulous she was from first-hand experience. I recall pointing out to the person who interviewed me just how careful she was about not mixing anything related to the Senate with anything related to the firm, including her expense accounts. We were always extraordinarily cautious about that as a firm. We did not want to take advantage of anybody's political connections to benefit the firm. We didn't need the bad press, and we didn't need what ended up dogging her in the end."

Ron Caza says Marie was never capable of the transgressions she was charged with. "Marie has always been very sensitive to the fact that she needs to be careful to make sure that everything she does is ethical. She has always been very sensitive of that, and she bent over backwards to make sure that would happen," says Mr. Caza. "At the Senate, there were a lot of things going on. I guess what was perceived as abuse by other senators—not Marie—led to a lot of overreaching and led to something akin to a witch hunt. People were trying to find fault where fault may not have existed. I'm not sure what reasons the Senate might have had to do so. What I do remember is that Marie had to make some very important decisions at a certain point in time, and in making those decisions, she always thought about what was in the best interests of the people she represented as a senator."

## Gowlings

In February 2014, Heenan Blaikie imploded. Its legal staff scattered to other law firms. Senator Charette-Poulin was recruited by Gowlings.

"Pierre Champagne, who had worked with me at Heenan Blaikie, was the one who suggested to Wayne Warren, the managing partner at Gowlings, that they hire me. I was expecting to be brought in as a senior counsel. I had also been approached by Marc-André Blanchard from McCarthy Tétrault, who became Canada's ambassador to the United Nations. He came to see me at my office in the Senate and we had a great meeting, but I told him I had decided on Gowlings," says Marie. "Some of my former colleagues from Heenan Blaikie were there. I did a lot of research about the firm too. Gowlings has always had an impeccable reputation. Not only was it a pan-Canadian firm, like Heenan Blaikie in many areas, but it also practised in many specialties that I liked. And they were thinking of going international.

"I had a meeting with Wayne Warren. I found him to be not only well informed and well connected, but also respectful and kind. I have to say that when he offered me the job, not only did he offer me a position as senior counsel, which was equivalent to the position I had held at Heenan Blaikie, he offered to make me a partner. I was quite surprised; I was not expecting that.

Wayne Warren, Managing Partner at Gowlings, remembers: "Heenan Blaikie had a good number of political actors in it, such as Jean Chrétien. Marie was also one of those people. So, I met her sometime in 2014 when I was looking at the contract that we had with her. We ended up bringing her on as an income partner in July 2014."

There were other refugees from Heenan Blaikie at Gowlings, including Bruce Johnson, who after his early experience in Saudi Arabia went to on to become a specialist of the Arab world. "Marie and I moved to Gowlings in 2014 and continued to work on some airline files. She was involved in the Qatar Airlines file to secure landing rights, so was helpful to me on those files, and we just continued to have a great relationship. Gowlings was lucky to have her," says Bruce.

Bruce Johnson recalls being appalled at the treatment Marie suffered at the hands of the Auditor General. "I had friends on both sides of the aisle. When I saw what was happening to her it angered me. She and I talked and emailed many times about it," says Bruce.

"I have a nine-year-old daughter and Marie has been there for us. She has always made us stay proud Canadians, especially with our kids. Even throughout that entire ordeal she still had time, at the height of all that, when my daughter won her class election, she was the only person who took the time to email my daughter."

Bruce also said people often underestimate Marie because of her open personality. "I think she's the kind of person who loves to work, who has much to contribute and, like her, I don't see myself ever stopping. I think she's having too much fun and she's still relevant; she evolves and stays relevant. Then you become ageless."

To this day Marie remains close to Gowlings, and continues to refer clients to them.

> "Marie and I moved to Gowlings in 2014 and continued to work on some airline files. She was involved in the Qatar Airlines file to secure landing rights, so was helpful to me on those files, and we just continued to have a great relationship. Gowlings was lucky to have her," says Bruce.

> "I think she's the kind of person who loves to work, who has much to contribute and, like her, I don't see myself ever stopping. I think she's having too much fun and she's still relevant; she evolves and stays relevant. Then you become ageless."

# President of the Party

A LAW STUDENT in Marie's class at the University of Ottawa came up with the idea. "Why don't you run for president of the Liberal Party? You'd be good at that," said the young woman. Other students agreed. Many of them had parents who were strong Liberals, and they pointed out the party had never had a Francophone woman as president. Indeed, only one other woman, Iona Campagnolo, had served as president. In 2006, Michael Eizenga, a Toronto lawyer, was stepping down from the post, which he had held since 2003.

Back in Parliament, after spending the day at law school, Marie met others who suggested she should run. She reached out to a Senate colleague, Lise Bacon. "Senator Bacon had deep political experience. She had been deputy premier of Quebec. I called her and asked her what she thought of the idea. "She said, 'It is very risky; you probably won't win, but if your instinct is telling you to run, go ahead and do it. You'll regret it if you haven't followed your instinct.'

"I decided to run, and formally announced my candidacy."

Duncan Fulton remembers Marie's decision to run: "She thought the party needed renewal, since the party had been in power since 1993. She wanted to bring in more youth, and she wanted women to play a more prominent role in the party. She thought people in Ottawa were too focused on playing politics versus growing the party at the grassroots level."

Marie's main opponent was Tony Ianno from Toronto. It would be a bitter fight.

The Liberal Party was in turmoil at the time. Paul Martin and his backers had forced Jean Chrétien from office in

> "She thought the party needed renewal, since the party had been in power since 1993. She wanted to bring in more youth, and she wanted women to play a more prominent role in the party. She thought people in Ottawa were too focused on playing politics versus growing the party at the grassroots level."

> "Tony called me and asked me not to run. He told me that if I dropped out, he would give me a job within the party; he'd create something for me."

2003, and Prime Minister Martin had initiated the Gomery Commission into the Sponsorship Program, because this program had been flagged by the Auditor General. In the end, the Gomery Commission found irregularities and one main culprit, an advertising man who profited from the plan. No parliamentarians were found to be involved.

It kept the Liberal Party on the front pages for months.

Tony Ianno, a former junior minister in Paul Martin's cabinet, was the favourite of the ruling class of the party. Marie, who had always supported Jean Chrétien, was given little chance of winning. She knew Ianno, the former member of Parliament from Trinity-Spadina. They were colleagues in the Liberal caucus. And Marie had canvassed door-to-door in his riding, one that was always a tough one for Liberal candidates. "I thought of Tony as a friend. His wife is charming and a hard worker," says Marie.

Ianno had lost his seat in the 2006 election to Olivia Chow, wife of NDP leader Jack Layton, and he wanted the presidency of the party to remain connected in Ottawa. Ianno did not simply want to win, however; he wanted to be acclaimed.

"Tony called me and asked me not to run. He told me that if I dropped out, he would give me a job within the party; he'd create something for me. He asked me why I wanted to run. I said, 'To bring financial sustainability to the party.' I refused to drop out; he was not a happy camper," says Marie.

When Marie refused to withdraw, the Ianno team asked the President of the Liberal Party of Manitoba, Bobbi Ethier, to run for the presidency as well. In any case, there were now three contenders.

Marie asked Duncan Fulton, who had worked in the PMO with Jean Chrétien in communications, to become her campaign manager. He remembers their conversation about him joining her team and her chances of winning: "When Marie called and asked if I would do this—you know, she's just such a genuinely good human being and her heart was totally in the right place—I remember meeting her and saying, 'If you do this and I help you, we have to be totally honest with each other throughout this whole thing.' And it starts with, 'There's a high likelihood that you are going to lose. Do you want to spend the money and time with an outcome that today I would weigh heavily in Ianno's favour?'

"She didn't even hesitate. She said, 'Why do you think I'm going to lose?'

"I said, 'Because the entire party apparatus is supporting Tony.'

"She replied that maybe she could go from the bottom up rather than from the top down and get enough delegates to vote for her.

"[I felt that] this kind of bewildered notion that she couldn't understand why she couldn't lose was naive, but in the end, I completely underestimated her. What I loved was that it never even occurred to her that losing might be inevitable. She just said, 'I'm going to work harder than he is.'"

And she did. Duncan describes Marie's efforts to recruit supporters: "She would go to the riding and get on the phone and call the whole riding executive, and they would recommend talking to various individuals. And every person they said she should talk to, she talked to. On top of that, she sent them all hand-written notes afterwards thanking them for their time.

"I would watch her do phone calls all day long and then write thank-you notes all night long. I would say overall that she spoke to far more people than Tony ever did, and I think that was the determining factor in her ultimately winning: she just outworked her opponent, which is the story of her life."

Of course, to set up an office and to travel across the country, Marie also needed a good deal of money. As a senator, she was entitled to fifty-two free flights a year for political business, but she did not want to use those. She also kept a strict wall between her expenses for the presidential run and those of her Senate office.

Duncan had agreed to do the job pro bono. Indeed, Duncan and all staff members who worked on Marie's campaign did so for nothing. Any money raised was used to pay for things such as flights and hotel rooms.

But where to find the money?

Enter Bernard.

> "There's a high likelihood that you are going to lose. Do you want to spend the money and time with an outcome that today I would weigh heavily in Ianno's favour?"
> "She didn't even hesitate. She said, 'Why do you think I'm going to lose?'"

Marie with the Mayor of Xi'an, visiting China's Terracotta Army, 2005.
*Source*: Government Archives.

He and Duncan came up with a plan.

"Bernard eventually emerged from his studio with a beautiful painting he had created of all former Liberal prime ministers of Canada. It was a long horizontal painting," says Marie.

"Duncan and Bernard planned to sell high-definition framed prints of the work. The painting had cost nothing, and Bernard had negotiated with a framer in Ottawa for a very reasonable price. They had a simple plan: everybody who gave a thousand dollars to the campaign would receive a framed print as a gift.

"Our house became a small manufacturer; I was campaigning while Bernard handled the reproduction and delivery of all these beautiful prints. It was a hit. I was able to raise eighty thousand dollars. It was the amount of money I needed to really have a strong cross-Canada campaign."

Although she had been involved in many election campaigns and in the Quebec referendum, Marie had never run for office herself. "It was my first experience in politics and in running for office."

Her campaign for the presidency of the Liberal Party was overshadowed by the leadership race to replace Paul Martin. Many candidates ran for the leadership. Two of the higher-profile ones were Bob Rae and Michael Ignatieff. Marie and

Duncan came up with the idea to follow these two candidates to cities where they were holding leadership debates. It was decided that this was a good way to meet Liberals across Canada.

Marie also felt it was crucial to attract the youth vote. "In every city I went to, I met with young Liberals. I targeted that vote, and to this day, I'm convinced I was elected thanks to the young Liberals," says Marie. "I have pictures of myself with Justin Trudeau, who was then very close to them. He wore one of my campaign buttons. Later, he came to me and asked me to support him as leader of the party. I worked for him during his leadership campaign."

Ultimately, Marie beat Bobbi Ethier and the establishment favourite, Tony Ianno.

As the new president of the Liberal Party, she set about reforming the financing of the party, at both the national and riding levels.

Marie came up with a unique fundraising plan, one that is still used by the Liberal Party to this day. Jean Chrétien brought in legislation that forbids political parties from taking donations from corporations and unions. Donations were restricted to individuals. Partnerships such as legal or accounting firms could only donate money in the individual names of partners. Marie's plan was simply to allow individual members, or potential party members, to donate as little as five dollars. Marie called the fundraising program, "The Five and Five." The idea was that every member was invited to donate five dollars a month to their riding and five dollars a month to the National Party. Meetings were held with the Board of the Liberal Party of Canada in the fall of 2007.

"Marie had just been elected as the president of the Liberal Party. I was asked to a meeting where Marie's proposal about how to build the membership of the Liberal Party was being tossed around," recalls Al Albania, whose marketing firm, ACART, worked on this and other Liberal Party projects. He described the fundraising idea as "a unique selling proposition," designed to not only raise money in small amounts but also attract more long-term members. "Prior to that, to become a member you had to pay something like a hundred and twenty-five dollars, so it was a fairly steep buy-in. Some people just can't afford

> "Duncan and Bernard planned to sell high-definition framed prints of the work. The painting had cost nothing, and Bernard had negotiated with a framer in Ottawa for a very reasonable price. They had a simple plan: everybody who gave a thousand dollars to the campaign would receive a framed print as a gift."

> Marie's plan was simply to allow individual members, or potential party members, to donate as little as five dollars. Marie called the fundraising program, "The Five and Five." The idea was that every member was invited to donate five dollars a month to their riding and five dollars a month to the National Party."

that, so if you're trying to initiate conversation with the grass roots, you have to allow them to get onside with very little effort. I always thought that the Five and Five was a great way to achieve that result; get them keenly interested and keep them for a long time."

"Marie told the meeting that if all the members of the ridings throughout the country donated five dollars a month to their riding and five dollars a month to the Liberal Party of Canada, the finances of the party would be in very good shape. It was the first time anyone had heard of such an idea," says John Duffy, a chartered accountant and successful entrepreneur who was chief financial officer of the Liberal Party from late 2006 until 2008.

Once the proposal was approved by the board, meetings were held with the leader, ministers, and caucus members. Some MPs bought into the idea immediately, despite the fact that it meant additional work for their riding—Marie was convinced that the fundraising proposal would only succeed if riding associations were involved.

"Today, it's the most stable fundraising vehicle for the party. In 2018, I checked their financial statements. Fundraising brought in fifteen million dollars. And it all came right out of Marie's head," says Duffy. As an aside, he added that he admired how Marie handled the post as president of the party. "Marie was very good, very much like a CEO," says John.

★ ★ ★

Before Marie ran for the leadership of the Liberal Party, she worked on the 2003 John Manley leadership campaign. Manley was up against the front runner, Paul Martin. Jean Chrétien had resigned in 2004, and the leadership of the party and the office of PM were up for grabs.

In retrospect, it might have been naive of Marie to back anyone other than the front runner in the Liberal Party leadership race, who was to become the next prime minister of Canada. Rather than welcoming competition—winning a fair fight looks better for the winner than does a coronation—the Martin team displayed intense animosity toward all who dared to contest their campaign.

"She was one of the key players in the campaign as a political advisor, but she also did a lot of fundraising for me," says Manley. "Marie paid a price for supporting me; a lot of people did. The Martin crowd were pretty vicious; they weren't interested in earning the top spot and then healing the party; they wanted dominance. So, she paid a price and others did too. She lost a board position that she had, almost certainly because of the campaign."

John Manley recalls that Marie was targeted when she ran for—and won—the presidency of the Liberal Party of Canada. "The problem was that she did it without knowing who the leader of the party was going to be. Would she have run if she knew beforehand that Stéphane [Dion] was going to become the leader? [Dion replaced Paul Martin as leader of the Liberal Party in 2006.] I don't know. Having a sympatico relationship between the leader of the party and its president is a crucial thing." Marie and the new leader of the LPC Stéphane Dion worked well together. They remain friends, even today.

Politics can be a dirty business. You would think winning the presidency of the Liberal Party of Canada would make Marie a popular figure. But that was not the case. Her long-time friend Don Mitchell says the people who supported Tony Ianno, her opponent, were not happy with the outcome of the election.

Marie welcomes Edna Bélisle, wife of the late senator, to her home.
*Source*: Photograph by Gilbert Belisle.

> You would think winning the presidency of the Liberal Party of Canada would make Marie a popular figure. But that was not the case. Her long-time friend Don Mitchell says the people who supported Tony Ianno, her opponent, were not happy with the outcome of the election.

One of those people was Senator David Smith, who backed the Liberal Party favourite. Recalls Mitchell: "Marie won because she worked bloody hard. David Smith considered himself as the replacement of Keith Davey, but he wasn't the rainmaker [the term *rainmaker* was one given to Davey because of his ability to influence things], though he thought of himself as one. He was an extremely good organizer. We always remained friends."

So, Marie ended up with enemies within the party. In considering her situation, she recalled a remark Jean Chrétien once made regarding his battle against the forces of Paul Martin within the Liberal Party. "My opponents are in front of me," said Mr. Chrétien of the Opposition Tories, Bloquistes, and NDPers facing him from his seat in the front row of the House of Commons. "But my enemies are behind me."

> "My opponents are in front of me," said Mr. Chrétien of the Opposition Tories, Bloquistes, and NDPers facing him from his seat in the front row of the House of Commons. "But my enemies are behind me."

Marie received a piece of political advice from Michel Patrice, who was the clerk of the committee looking after the special study that Marie was chairing on the internet. "A word of advice, Senator. Don't put your head above the others. Because someone will knock it back down. He said that it's like that saying about sunflowers: if one grows higher than the others, they cut it off," says Marie. "'Be careful,' he said. He was dead serious."

His advice might seem cynical, but it was realistic.

Don Mitchell feels there is little doubt that Marie's victory over the establishment favourite in the contest to become president of the Liberal Party diminished her level of support within the party. Unlike Jean Chrétien, though, Marie's real battle was not against those within the party; rather, it was against the combative and ultra-partisan leader of the Conservatives in the Senate.

That battle would come later, and would be hugely damaging.

★ ★ ★

One of Marie's closest aides at the time was her daughter Valérie. She is fiercely loyal to her parents and despised what she saw in the campaign for the presidency of the Liberal Party.

"I was on her campaign for the Liberal Party presidency; people were awful, just awful. She was running against Tony Ianno, who was a Paul Martin supporter. It was thought by some that Ianno had the Liberal presidency in the bag. They were wrong. But she beat him fair and square, and it really pissed them off.

"Marie did it the right way: she did it with a smile on her face, which is exactly the way you should do things. My mother has never engaged in the dirty politics thing, and that has actually bitten her in the butt more often than not. I love her dearly but there's a certain naïveté about her," says Valérie.

> "A word of advice, Senator. Don't put your head above the others. Because someone will knock it back down. He said that it's like that saying about sunflowers: if one grows higher than the others, they cut it off."

Marie, as candidate for the presidency of the Liberal Party of Canada, speaking at the National Convention in Montréal, 2006.
*Source*: Family Collection.

> **Valérie has a good deal of insight on the "dirty" qualities of both. "I don't know if one is dirtier than the other. One is all about power, the other about greed. I saw some pretty dirty things in both worlds."**

Valérie started her work life in politics and knows that world well. She was one of those backroom people who, armed with a Blackberry or cellphone, keep track of ministers. She worked at the federal level and later at Queen's Park in Toronto, for the provincial Liberal government. Then she went to one of the big five banks. As someone who has worked successfully in both the political and corporate worlds, Valérie has a good deal of insight on the "dirty" qualities of both. "I don't know if one is dirtier than the other. One is all about power, the other about greed. I saw some pretty dirty things in both worlds."

★ ★ ★

John Manley is certain that being president of the Liberal Party put a target on Marie's back when, later, the time came to choose which senators would be the subject of an expenses audit. "Absolutely. She paid a huge price for it. The vindication that she finally got was a little bit of cold comfort. She had to go through hell," said Manley.

"I might have the sequence wrong but, in my mind, when Prime Minister Stephen Harper went ahead and decided that he couldn't reform the Senate, he decided that he was going to use it. He put Mike Duffy and Pamela Wallin into the Senate. But they got into trouble, so they started looking for Liberals to taint. He figured, let's get them all at the same time to taint the entire institution."

Senator Marjory LeBreton was the Leader of the Government in the Senate at the time. She had risen from a clerical post in Conservative Party headquarters to become the Conservatives' leader in the Senate. She had dedicated almost her entire career with the party; she was staunchly loyal to it. For her, the party was everything; it was family.

Senator LeBreton's feelings were in step with those of fellow Conservative Stephen Harper, who became prime minister in 2006. Harper once told Marie he despised Liberals. It was an odd remark to make, or rather, it was an odd time to make this remark, as the two were representing Canada on an overseas trip as members of the small Canadian delegation attending Pope John Paul II's funeral in Rome in April of 2005. The tradition is that Canadian politicians on foreign soil maintain a unified stance and leave the partisan bickering at home.

"I don't know Harper very well at all, but for example, if you said anything about him in the press, you wouldn't be invited to any of his press conferences or other events. I don't know that he would have gone out of his way [to target Marie], but certainly, he wouldn't have discouraged Marjory from doing so."

And so it was that the political and legislative storm that was brewing was to unleash its fury.

# The Senate Expenses Scandal

IN JUNE 2013, Senate Government Leader Marjory LeBreton tabled a motion asking the Auditor General of Canada to review the expense accounts of all senators in light of the media uproar over alleged improper expenses claimed by Senators Duffy, Wallin, Brazeau, and Harb.

Their audits by Deloitte had been made public. Even though Deloitte stated that "the rules were unclear," all four Senators were perceived as "guilty" of administrative irregularities. Senator Harb resigned in the summer. Motions were tabled in the fall to "suspend without pay" Senators Duffy, Wallin, and Brazeau during an investigation. Marie rose to speak against those motions, placing another target on her back.

In the summer of 2015, Senator Charette-Poulin learned that as a result of this audit, her file was being referred to the RCMP. She was one of the lowest spenders in the Senate and had never claimed a housing allowance. She was ultimately exonerated two years later. But the investigation costed her dearly.

## The Bill to Reform the Senate

Accountability of public officials is essential. That goes without saying. And yet, the investigation by the Auditor General into the use of public funds by Senators was perhaps one of the harshest chapters in the history for the Canadian Senate. To Marie, it felt personal and tantamount to torture. Beyond the financial cost to her—including legal fees to the tune of $250,000—the ordeal highly impacted her mental health and her physical health.

One of the few senators who, from the outset, objected to the investigation was Anne Cools, an independent-minded woman with a deep regard for the Senate. For two days running in early June of 2013, Senator Cools challenged Senator LeBreton on the "Motion to Invite the Auditor General to Conduct Comprehensive Audit of Senate Expenses Including Senators' Expenses.[1]" Her interventions, which are recorded in *Hansard*, the official published report of Senate debates, are based on the definition of the Auditor General's role as outlined in the *Auditor General Act*.

---

1. This motion can be consulted online in the Debates of the Senate (Hansard), 1st Session, 41st Parliament, Volume 150, Issue 171: https://sencanada.ca/en/content/sen/chamber/411/debates/171db_2013-06-06-e

> "This motion is without precedent," states Senator Cools, adding, "there are no clauses whatsoever in the *Auditor General Act* that empower him to audit the Senate or the House of Commons. The House of Commons and the Senate are not departments of government, of the public administration; they are Houses of Parliament."

Without calling into question the notion of transparency and ethical responsibility of public officials, Cools questions the legitimacy of the audit and qualifies Senator LeBreton's motion as a political act with no legal basis. "This motion is without precedent," states Senator Cools, adding, "there are no clauses whatsoever in the *Auditor General Act* that empower him to audit the Senate or the House of Commons. The House of Commons and the Senate are not departments of government, of the public administration; they are Houses of Parliament." She reminds her colleagues that there is a distinction between Parliament (to whom the Auditor General reported as a Parliamentary Officer) and the public service (over whom the Auditor General had a responsibility).

In response to a question Senator Cools poses regarding constitutional law being used to justify the investigation, Senator LeBreton, Leader of the Government in the Senate, replies:

> Honourable senators, I indicated on Monday that I would move this motion. I put the motion before the Senate yesterday. I acted in my capacity as Leader of the Government in the Senate, but also as a member of the Senate and obviously as a person concerned with these issues in the last few months as all of us have been.
>
> I want to make it clear that I was motivated to do this—and I am sure any of us who are paying attention would know—for the sake of this institution, and the sake of the fine reputations of everyone in this institution who have been the subject of some considerable hostility by the Canadian electorate. This was in direct response to pleas from Canadians all over the country, tax-paying, hard-working Canadians, asking us to please take measures to make what we are doing here more transparent and accountable.

One would be hard-pressed to find fault with this display of respect for Canadian taxpayers or with the notion of transparency. However, it seemed to many that the audit was not simply an isolated measure designed to identify instances of the improper claiming of expenses by senators, but rather part of a broader effort by the Conservative government to undermine the Senate itself. Senator Cools noted: "Honourable senators, I rise to speak to Senator LeBreton's motion, which invites the Auditor General, Mr. Michael Ferguson, to audit the Senate and senators' expenses. It seems that this motion was suddenly conceived by the government leader and is being rushed through the Senate with improper haste[2]."

There is no record in Hansard of Senator LeBreton refuting Senator Cools' statements.

Senator Cools identifies major flaws in the mandate: "It is lacking as a term of reference for the Auditor General. It is very skimpy in detail. It also lacks definition, clarity and form." Later, she adds: "It does not even set a timeframe. It would appear that it is open-ended; it could go on for years and years. [...] I do not understand how such a motion can go forth with so little explanation and with so little substance and detail."

She concludes her statement of opposition to LeBreton's motion as follows:

> There is something very unusual and unprecedented about the fact that the Auditor General is being deployed not by the houses to audit the government and the administration [...] but by the government to audit a house of Parliament, the Senate. The system seems to have been turned on its head, and this bothers me. [...]
>
> [T]here is something very wrong, honourable senators, with all this. I do not believe for a moment that all this is caused because a few senators have perhaps—and we are not clear yet—done something wrong. People do wrong all the time, but, because of that, one does not have to willfully set out to weaken and discredit the institutions.
>
> [T]his situation is a very ugly one.

Senator Cools not only called into question the validity of the investigation but also points to political motivations.

"It does not even set a timeframe. It would appear that it is open-ended; it could go on for years and years. [...] I do not understand how such a motion can go forth with so little explanation and with so little substance and detail."

---

2. Elsewhere, we read that the Office of the Auditor General audited the House of Commons. The difference is that it audited the institution, but not members of Parliament.

> "I wish to confirm that the Royal Canadian Mounted Police has completed its review of the *Report of the Auditor General of Canada on Senators' Expenses* as it relates to you. They officially informed me that the matter is concluded with no further action being required."

She says publicly what others are thinking. Some even whispered that the motion brought forth by Senator LeBreton has been orchestrated by the Prime Minister's Office and meant to destroy the Senate. One senator, Céline Hervieux-Payette, even bravely stated in the Senate chamber that "the inquiry about our budget and things like that were [designed] to kill the institution and the people."

Most senators, however, were afraid to defend their colleagues; they feared they would be perceived as trying to cover up their own faults. Marie, despite being one of the lowest spenders in the Senate and despite never claiming the housing allowance, was told repeatedly by her liberal colleagues to not speak out as it would only bring her unwanted attention. Notwithstanding, in April 2014, Marie received several large binders from the Office of the Auditor General that included more than 800 questions she was required to answer. Then, in the summer of 2015, she learned that as a result of the audit, she was one of nine Senators referred to the RCMP.

On July 28, 2016, Marie received a letter from Michel Patrice, a senior Senate official. It read, in part: "I wish to confirm that the Royal Canadian Mounted Police has completed its review of the *Report of the Auditor General of Canada on Senators' Expenses* as it relates to you. They officially informed me that the matter is concluded with no further action being required."

Three years and millions of taxpayer dollars later, the Senate stood intact, though the reputation of individual senators and the Senate's standing with the public was left considerably damaged.

★ ★ ★

Since Confederation, there have been calls for Senate reform; countless newspaper articles and scholarly papers have been written on the subject.

The Senate expenses investigation are complex, but its genesis is tied to the foundation of the Reform Party in 1987 by Alberta political activist Preston Manning, son of Ernest Manning, who had been the Social Credit premier of Alberta for twenty-five years, from 1943 to 1968.

Grievances about the treatment of Western Canada by the federal government drove both father and son. The Reform Party's biggest slogan centred on a call for a "Triple-E" Senate—that is, a Senate that is equal, elected, and effective.

The party believed that the Senate was unbalanced and gave too much power to Canada's Atlantic provinces. For example, Prince Edward Island has four senators, while Alberta has six senators, as do Manitoba, Saskatchewan, and British Columbia. The population of each of the western provinces is higher than that of than the island province. Reforming the Senate so that each province had an equal number of senators (the same model is used in the U.S. Senate) would balance representation in the Senate.

Tom Flanagan, a political scientist, author, and at one point Stephen Harper's chief of staff, describes the Reform/Conservative case for an equal Senate in this way:

> The basic idea was that the West was outnumbered in terms of population. [...] Therefore, there needed to be some balancing institution to protect the Western provinces, and the Senate could have become that if each province had the same number of senators. [...] Then the Senate could have become a protector of regional interests. Without [equal representation], the regional interests of Western provinces like Alberta were likely to be overridden by the demands of larger voting majorities in Ontario and Quebec. [...] There were many other criticisms of the Senate—it was a patronage haven and senators were overpaid and abusing their expenses—but the primary reason [that there was a push for Senate reform] was the protection of regions against voting majorities concentrated in central Canada which would then dominate a parliamentary system.

The Reform Party believed that change was necessary if the Senate was to be made effective. They maintained that the Senate was, effectively, a useless parking ground for tired political hacks. This argument had great populist appeal,

> Harper wanted the Supreme Court of Canada to decide on three important changes: *Could Parliament change the rules setting term limits for senators? Could senators be elected rather than appointed?* And, in the extreme instance, *Could Parliament decide to abolish the Senate?*

and was fodder for the Reform Party's base in Alberta. The Party also wanted to have senators elected.

One of the party's young researchers and an acolyte of Preston Manning was Stephen Harper. Though he was brought up in the middle-class Toronto suburb of Leaside—he was at one point president of the Young Liberal Club at his high school—once he moved out West, Harper became a fervent Alberta nationalist. More Catholic than the Pope, as some would say. Harper's belief in Senate reform would make life a misery for the senators mentioned above.

It did not matter that the Reform Party wanted to reform the Senate; it did not matter that the people and media of Alberta were in favour of it. The *Calgary Herald* could run editorials until the oil runs dry, because reforming the Senate required—and still does—the approval of seven of the provinces representing 50 percent of the population. Recall Brian Mulroney's attempt to amend the Constitution, the Meech Lake Accord. Manitoba and Newfoundland scuppered that constitutional change. Senate reform would bring in bigger guns. No Quebec politician and no premier of Ontario would ever give up their Senate seats. Those provinces account for more than 50 percent of the population, and that is that.

The Reform Party, which had been re-branded as the Canadian Alliance, carried out a reverse takeover of the Progressive Conservative Party when the two merged in 2002. The new entity was called simply the Conservative Party of Canada. The term *Progressive* was clearly absent. When Stephen Harper and the Conservative Party won a minority in the 2006 federal election, he set out to reform the Senate, but failed to do so. After his 2011 election victory—this time a majority win—Harper sent his Senate reform proposals to the Supreme Court to rule on prior to any legislation being put to a vote. There appeared to be a precedent. All provincial legislatures had abolished appointed bodies that had acted as a Senate in provincial governments.

Harper wanted the Supreme Court of Canada to decide on three important changes: *Could Parliament change the rules setting term limits for senators? Could senators be elected rather than* appointed? And, in the extreme instance, Could Parliament decide to abolish the Senate?

The answer to these questions was a sound "No" from the Supreme Court of Canada on February 1, 2013.[3] The timing is interesting: it was four months later that the motion to bring in the Auditor General was tabled...

The *Globe and Mail* ran a headline that put the ruling into sixteen well-chosen words: "Unanimous provincial consent needed to abolish the Red Chamber; democratization would require at least seven yes votes."

The *Globe* reporters plucked the following excerpts from the decision the day after the ruling.

On the reason for the status quo: "The framers [of the Constitution] sought to endow the Senate with independence from the electoral process to which members of the House of Commons were subject, to remove senators from a partisan political arena that required unremitting consideration of short-term political objectives."

On non-binding elections: "The proposed consultative elections would [...] weaken the Senate's role of sober second thought and would give it the democratic legitimacy to systematically block the House of Commons, contrary to its constitutional design."

On Ottawa's argument: "[T]he purpose of the bills is clear: to bring about a Senate with a popular mandate. [...] Legal analysis of the constitutional nature and effects of proposed legislation cannot be premised on the assumption that the legislation will fail to bring about the changes it seeks to achieve."

On how to change the status quo: "[T]he provinces must have a say in constitutional changes that engage their interests. [...] The result is an amending formula designed [...] to protect Canada's constitutional status quo until such time as reforms are agreed upon."

On abolition: "Abolition of the Senate would [...] fundamentally alter our constitutional architecture—by removing the bicameral form of government that gives shape to the Constitution Act, 1867. [It] requires the unanimous

**The *Globe and Mail* ran a headline that put the ruling into sixteen well-chosen words: "Unanimous provincial consent needed to abolish the Red Chamber; democratization would require at least seven yes votes."**

---

3. Reference re Senate Reform, 2014 SCC 32: https://scc-csc.lexum.com/scc-csc/scc-csc/en/item/13614/index.do

consent of the Senate, the House of Commons, and the legislative assemblies of all Canadian provinces."

The Senate Reform Bill was dead before it went before the members of the House of Commons and the Senate. That left Prime Minister Harper frustrated. Reporter Tonda MacCharles outlined the situation in the *Toronto Star*:

> Prime Minister Stephen Harper shut the door Friday on a career pledge to reform the Senate after the Supreme Court of Canada ruled that there needs substantial provincial consent to introduce elections or term limits to the upper chamber and unanimous consent to do away with it altogether.
>
> In response, the government said it is dropping Senate reform and ruled out a referendum to build support to bring reluctant premiers onside as one of its own cabinet ministers, Maxime Bernier, and NDP Leader Tom Mulcair—who both advocate abolition—publicly urged Friday.
>
> The prime minister said he was "personally disappointed" in a ruling he says left the country "essentially stuck" with a scandal-plagued unelected Senate supported by "virtually no Canadian."
>
> The prime minister said no change will come to the 147-year-old Senate anytime soon because the court declared, according to Harper, "these are only decisions the provinces can take."
>
> "We know that there is no consensus among the provinces on reform, no consensus on abolition, and no desire of anyone to reopen the Constitution and have a bunch of constitutional negotiations," Harper said. He said the court had effectively determined "that significant reform and abolition are off the table."

This loss infuriated Harper, a man who had on many occasions made clear his contempt for the Upper Chamber. Senator Anne Cools, in remarks made in the Senate previously, reported how Prime Minister Harper's shockingly negative attitude toward the Senate was made plain to her:

> Honourable senators, I remember that a couple of years ago at a Christmas party I was absolutely flabbergasted when, outside, there was a press conference held by Mr. Harper and Senator LeBreton. In that press conference, on December 14, 2006, right outside the Senate door, David Akin from CTV made an inquiry to the Prime Minister, who responded, about the Senate: "I am always disappointed with that. You know, as a Western Canadian, I wake up every day and the Senate bothers me. I curse the Senate."

Clearly, a man with such deep convictions was not going to just let things go. He had lost that battle, but was not about to give up his war against the Senate.

Yet there was one minor victory for the Harper Conservatives. Parliament could change the property qualifications set out in the 1867 *British North America Act*, which states that the value of a senator's "Real and Personal Property shall be together worth Four thousand Dollars over and above his Debts and Liabilities," and that senators "shall be resident in the Province for which he is appointed."[4]

This is the 150-year-old legislative loophole that would be used to discredit senators.

In this, Harper found an unexpected ally. The NDP may have hated Harper, but they despised the institution of the Senate even more. They attacked several senators for absenteeism, though these insinuations were later disproven.

\* \* \*

Politics is a complex business.

"One of the political activities I was involved with during the years of the audit," remembers Marie, "was working closely with the NDP MP from Sudbury, Glenn Thibeault. I was trying to get him to cross the floor to the Liberals." In the end, while he did move to the Liberal Party, he joined the provincial Liberals in December 2014, where he became a cabinet minister, something he probably could never have achieved as an NDP member of either the federal or provincial legislatures. In retaliation, the NDP made remarks on its website about Senator Charette-Poulin, stating that she had the worst attendance record in the Senate and implying that her presence in the chamber cost more than it was worth.

The NDP was ultimately forced to issue a public apology to the Senator. "Liberal senator gets full apology from NDP for 'unfounded' attack—five months later," blared the headline in the *National Post*, hardly a Liberal Party house organ. It not only covered the apology but gave its interpretation for the reason for the attack: "In a January release, sent out as part of the NDP's ongoing efforts to

> In that press conference, on December 14, 2006, right outside the Senate door, David Akin from CTV made an inquiry to the Prime Minister, who responded, about the Senate: "I am always disappointed with that. You know, as a Western Canadian, I wake up every day and the Senate bothers me. I curse the Senate."

---

4. British North America Act, 1867 – Enactment no. 1: https://www.justice.gc.ca/eng/rp-pr/csj-sjc/constitution/lawreg-loireg/p1t11.html

> The NDP offers its sincere, complete and unconditional apologies to Senator Marie-P. Charette-Poulin for having spread unfounded information on the NDP website regarding her absenteeism and voting record.

discredit the Senate and push for its abolition, the party alleged Charette-Poulin had the worst attendance record of any senator since the 2011 election,"

The NDP apology to Senator Charette-Poulin, which is still available online[5], reads as follows:

May 15th, 2014
Honourable Senator Marie-P. Charette-Poulin

On January 21 and 23, 2014, several releases on the absenteeism of senators were posted on the NDP's website.

The NDP retracts all its remarks to the effect that Senator Marie-P. Charette-Poulin had the worst record of absenteeism in the 41st Parliament and about her lack of voting.

The NDP also retracts all its comments to the effect that each day that Senator Charette-Poulin spends at work costs the taxpayer $9,869.71.

Finally, the NDP retracts its comments to the effect that each vote by Senator Charette-Poulin cost taxpayers $35,556.16.

The statements made in the NDP's publications were false and unfounded.

The NDP offers its sincere, complete and unconditional apologies to Senator Marie-P. Charette-Poulin for having spread unfounded information on the NDP website regarding her absenteeism and voting record.

Sincerely,
Rebecca Blaikie
NDP of Canada President

Meanwhile, the Conservative government was becoming increasingly embarrassed by Duffy, Wallin, and Brazeau, and decided that these senators needed to be sacrificed in order to staunch the bleeding of the

---

5. https://www.ndp.ca/news/honorable-senator-marie-p-charette-poulin?_gl=1*1e3wmrg*_ga*MzA4NjEyNTIzLjE2OTA5MTAyNjc.*_ga_97QLYMLC56*MTY5MDkxMDI2Ny4xLjEuMTY5MDkxMDQyNi42MC4wLjA

Conservatives' reputation. The inclusion of Duffy in this group is interesting, explains the former Chief of staff to Stephen Harper, Tom Flanagan: "[Early in] his prime ministership he [Harper] pushed for Senate reform but was unable to get it. [So he started following] the traditional approach to appointments—treating them as patronage rewards.

"[Harper] needed an appointment from PEI, and Duffy was a prominent journalist who had become a sympathetic supporter of the Conservatives. [Y]ou could argue that Harper owed Duffy a favour because Duffy had torpedoed Stéphane Dion [the former Liberal leader]. But I think he became vindictive toward Duffy when he started causing so much trouble. Duffy ended up being put on trial and so on, and I think it was a payback for all the trouble that Duffy was causing."

Some have pointed to the fact that crusade against the trio was led by the government leader in the Senate, Senator Marjory LeBreton. In a *Maclean's* profile in 2013, Anne Kingston—like Wallin, a member of Toronto's media elite—described LeBreton's campaign against Mike Duffy and Wallin:

> On Wednesday, LeBreton stood in the Upper Chamber issuing a "False, false, false" rejoinder to Pamela Wallin's accusations, among them that she—along with Conservative senator Carolyn Stewart Olsen, Prime Minister Stephen Harper's former director of strategic communications—had waged a "personal vendetta" against her. The two were jealous of her success, Wallin claimed, and added that they "could not abide the fact that I was outspoken in caucus, or critical of their leadership—or that my level of activity brought me into the public eye and once garnered the praise of the prime minister. They resented that. They resented me being an activist senator."
>
> Wallin also accused LeBreton and Stewart Olsen of orchestrating "fourteen specific targeted leaks" to the media that left her reputation "in tatters." She called LeBreton a turncoat for reneging on a deal made during a May 17 "panicked phone call" to Wallin, along with Ray Novak, Harper's chief of staff. Both were speaking for Harper, who wanted her gone from the Conservative caucus, Wallin said. They agreed Wallin would say she was "recusing" herself and step down; ten minutes later LeBreton announced publicly Wallin had "resigned."
>
> LeBreton's rebuttal showed her to be a master of the faint-praise slam down. One example: "I hate to disappoint my colleagues, but I can't imagine Carolyn Stewart Olsen and I ever spent more than two minutes talking about Sen. Wallin," she said, a statement that suggests Wallin wasn't worth their time. LeBreton also raised the rampant rumours that Wallin had been angling for her job as government leader in the Senate while sloughing them off: "I was never threatened by Senator Wallin," she said.

> "I believe that every institution and organization needs to step back and review its governance on a regular basis. It can be every five years or seven years, but it must be done on a regular basis just to keep up with social, technical, and economic changes."

Her "rebuttal" to Duffy was more pointed, and more personal. [...] She even slammed his performance on *Mike Duffy Live*. [...] She said she was "bemused by his approach to politics, sometimes frustrated by his style of journalism—trading, as he did more often than not, on gossip and the latest hot rumour." She added, "Sometimes I was so disgusted that I felt like putting my foot through the TV set." She referred to the former journalist as a "great storyteller," code for "liar," as if she was accusing him of delivering "a whopper."

That article shows the kind of raw partisan feeling that could escalate into hatred of someone perceived as being on the other side.

★ ★ ★

Marie's views on Senate reform are fairly straightforward.

"I believe that every institution and organization needs to step back and review its governance on a regular basis. It can be every five years or seven years, but it must be done on a regular basis just to keep up with social, technical, and economic changes. That's number one, but number two is I really disagree with the way Harper went about Senate reform. When he wasn't able to do it his way my impression is that he decided to go after individual senators, including me, to try and ruin the institution by painting the Senate as systemically corrupt. Which it is not," says Marie.

Senator Charette-Poulin stood up in the Senate on Tuesday, November 4, 2013, and spoke out against the motion to suspend the three senators, without pay, for charges that had not been proven. It was a speech that angered the government side, in particular Senator LeBreton, the former Conservative leader in the Senate. And a stand that put yet another target on Senator Charette-Poulin's back. Slipping effortlessly from French to English, as one of the most fluently bilingual members of the Senate, she stated:

> Honourable colleagues, as we all know, for the past few weeks our parliamentary institution has been

dominating the headlines in print, electronic and social media. All of us have received many passionate messages from Canadians, not to mention the telephone calls to our offices and our homes, and the comments we hear every time we go out.

Like the rest of you, I would have preferred that we dominate the headlines for more constructive reasons than the current situation, but at least the controversy has given rise to an important debate in this chamber. Many senators have taken part in the debate on Senator Carignan's motions from the beginning. The three motions were followed by a government motion moved by the Deputy Leader of the Government in the Senate, Senator Martin.

Several interventions are based on the Act of Parliament, on the Constitution of Canada, on the *Canadian Charter of Rights and Freedoms* and on the Criminal Code. Others asked important questions about the risk that these motions could interfere or be perceived as interfering with the RCMP investigations that started in June 2013.

Therefore, I am just as uncomfortable with the government motion as with the three other ones. If these motions were adopted, the Senate could be accused of imposing severe punishment on three individuals while a process which is independent from the Senate, the RCMP investigation, was taking place, therefore interfering or obstructing justice.

The motions raise several questions, including these: are we not considered innocent until proven guilty in any administrative or judicial procedure? Could the motions have unforeseeable consequences? Will the motions to have our colleagues suspended without pay prevent them from having access to a legitimate defence, if need be? Is suspending a senator without pay against the present rules of the Senate? Are these motions contrary to the normal practices in Canadian public agencies and private businesses?[6]

> I am just as uncomfortable with the government motion as with the three other ones. If these motions were adopted, the Senate could be accused of imposing severe punishment on three individuals while a process which is independent from the Senate, the RCMP investigation, was taking place, therefore interfering or obstructing justice.

---

6. https://sencanada.ca/en/content/sen/chamber/412/debates/011db_2013-11-04-e

Senator Charette-Poulin continued:

> Honourable colleagues, as a member of the Ontario bar, I have taken an oath, and I take my oath very seriously. I would like to quote that oath, in part, to help you understand what governs my thinking with regards to this motion:
>
> I shall not pervert the law to favour or prejudice anyone, but in all things I shall conduct myself honestly and with integrity and civility. I shall seek to ensure access to justice and access to legal services. I shall seek to improve the administration of justice. I shall champion the rule of law and safeguard the rights and freedoms of all persons. I shall strictly observe and uphold the ethical standards that govern my profession. All this I do swear or affirm to observe and perform to the best of my knowledge and ability.

There followed an exchange with Conservative Senator Pierre Claude Nolin, who asked Senator Charette-Poulin if in her capacity as a human resources executive she ever had to suspend anyone.

> "I have a question for Senator Charette-Poulin. From what I understand—Senator Baker referred to this earlier today—you were once the human resources director for a large corporation. Is that true?"
> Senator Charette-Poulin: "You are correct. I was vice-president of human resources and industrial relations."
> Senator Nolin: "As part of your duties, did you ever have to take disciplinary action against employees who worked for you?"
> Senator Charette-Poulin: "I thank you for the question because I was hoping to be able to talk about that."
> Senator Nolin: "The answer is yes, then."
> Senator Charette-Poulin: "I would like to make a minor correction to your question. You asked whether I ever had to take disciplinary action. The answer is that there was a process. I experienced this very thing at a company where a number of employees were very public figures. From what I remember, the investigation process was quite extensive. During the investigation process, if the company determined that the case should be handed over to the RCMP—I personally handed cases over to the RCMP—the employee was suspended with pay."

The object of that exchange was to try and prove that suspending with pay was normal procedure in large corporations. But of course, the Senate is not a large corporation, and Marie did not believe the Senate had the right to suspend Duffy, Wallin, and Brazeau. She would be proven right, but it would take a tortuous route, a court decision, and the words of a former Supreme Court Justice to prove the Conservatives wrong. But at what a cost to reputations, health, and the respect of Canadians for Parliament itself.

Watching this from the sidelines was Sheila Copps. A veteran of six federal election campaigns, a cabinet minister, and a former deputy prime minister, she knows the world of Ottawa politics intimately. She certainly knows how tough that world can be. Copps was the victim of political skullduggery when she lost the Liberal nomination when her Hamilton, Ontario, riding was redrawn. Copps was also the victim of gross public sexual harassment on the floor of the House of Commons. John Crosbie had told Copps to "Just quiet down, baby," prompting her to reply, "I'm nobody's baby."

It is natural, then, that Copps would have a great deal of empathy for other parliamentarians facing unfair attack, including the senators caught up in the expenses scandal. "In retrospect, Duffy probably didn't realize how rough politics could turn out to be," she wrote in the Hill Times in February 2021. Copps said the treatment of Mike Duffy outraged her. She referred to Marjory LeBreton as Stephen Harper's "emissary in the Senate," and remarked that she was doing incalculable damage to reputations and lives.

"Lives were turned upside down because the prime minister [Harper] unsuccessfully decided that the best way to deal with the Senate was to make those senators completely rudderless and discredited and he got pretty close to doing that."

Copps described what happened to Senator Charette-Poulin as "brutal." She saw at the time that none of her Liberal colleagues in the Senate stepped up to defend her.

"At one point I said to Marie, 'Look, you can't sit there being battered in the media with nobody actually having a strategy. Why don't you have a fight-back strategy?'" says Copps. She puts the lack of support shown to Marie by her fellow Liberals in the Senate down to fear—that standing up on her behalf would only make things worse. "There was certainly an atmosphere of fear that if you stuck your head up to defend anybody, you'd be next. I think that's why her colleagues weren't as helpful as they could have been," says Copps.

> Marie did not believe the Senate had the right to suspend Duffy, Wallin, and Brazeau. She would be proven right, but it would take a tortuous route, a court decision, and the words of a former Supreme Court Justice.

> Watching this from the sidelines was Sheila Copps. A veteran of six federal election campaigns, a cabinet minister, and a former deputy prime minister, she knows the world of Ottawa politics intimately. She certainly knows how tough that world can be.

> "At one point I said to Marie, 'Look, you can't sit there being battered in the media with nobody actually having a strategy. Why don't you have a fight-back strategy?'" says Copps.

Senator Charette-Poulin recognizes that speaking against the motion to suspend some senators on the basis of allegations put a target on her back: "When I sat down after speaking against the motion, two conservative colleagues crossed the floor and said to me: 'You are going to pay for this.'"

She continues: "I recently remembered that those same colleagues had crossed the floor with the same threats in early 2010 when I paid tribute to Rémy Beauregard, CEO of Rights and Democracy, following his sudden death from a heart attack. The heart attack occurred following a lengthy board meeting where he was being accused of administrative irregularities by board members appointed by the Harper Government. I was invited to speak at his well-attended funeral at the Notre-Dame Basilica in Ottawa. I had worked closely with Rémy when he led the important Franco-Ontarian organization ACFO, and when he was a deputy minister in the Government of Ontario. Offering a tribute in the Senate was a must for me. But I paid a price."

# Enter the Auditor General

TO UNDERSTAND the investigation of senators' expenses, we must understand Michael Ferguson.

Michael Ferguson was the Auditor General (AG) of New Brunswick. During the provincial election of 2010, he criticized the Premier's policy on energy, liberal Shawn Graham. Ferguson was immediately removed as AG. The Conservatives won the election. Newly elected Premier David Alward immediately appointed Ferguson as Deputy Minister of Finance. A few months later, his name was put forward by a former university colleague working for a head-hunting firm in Ottawa, to succeed Sheila Fraser as Auditor General of Canada. His colleague knew that Ferguson and Harper shared a common hatred: liberals.

But Fraser was a tough act to follow. She was one of the most respected persons ever to hold the office and was listed as one of the five most trusted Canadians during her ten-year tenure. Also, Michael Ferguson did not speak French. This caused much consternation, particularly among Francophone parliamentarians. A requirement of the position was fluency in both official languages. Other Anglophone incumbents had been able to speak both English and French. For example, Sheila Fraser, despite her Scottish surname, grew up in rural Quebec, spoke French, and was married to a Francophone.

Michael Ferguson did not appreciate the grilling by parliamentarians when he appeared before the Senate, sitting in Committee of the Whole, for the approval of his appointment as an Officer of Parliament. "His anger was evident for all to see," recalls Marie.

## The RCMP

In the summer of 2015, the RCMP chose nine senators to investigate.

The audit—some would call it an attack—on these senators, and on the Senate as a whole, played to populist sentiment that the senators loll about in the parliamentary restaurant, getting rich at the expense of the taxpayer. The reality is that many senators, including Marie, take a pay cut and work longer hours as a senator.

It was a mystery to Marie as to why they chose her to be included among those nine. But not to her long-time executive assistant. "Natalie was the one who

> It was a mystery to Marie as to why they chose her to be included among those nine. But not to her long-time executive assistant. "Natalie was the one who made the analysis. Of the nine senators named, there was one senator per province, except for Alberta."

made the analysis. Of the nine senators named, there was one senator per province, except for Alberta," says Marie. These were Mike Duffy, (Prince Edward Island); Rose-Marie Losier-Cool (New Brunswick); Don Oliver (Nova Scotia); Bill Rompkey (Newfoundland); Patrick Brazeau (Quebec); Marie-P. Charette-Poulin (Ontario); Sharon Carstairs (Manitoba); Pamela Wallin (Saskatchewan); and Gerry St-Germain (British Columbia).

Alberta? No one.

★ ★ ★

Ray Bonin is quite blunt in his views on the Senate investigations: he believes that these senators were persecuted for political reasons. "In my fifteen years in Ottawa, I knew a lot of Progressive Conservatives. None of them would have done a dirty trick like that. I went to Ottawa at the same time as the Reform Party went there, and dirty tricks were a way of life for them. What I now see on CNN every day is akin to what I saw then from the Reform Party. Not quite as bad, but the need wasn't quite as dire," says Ray.

> "That was part of it. Like Trump, they would destroy a person like Marie Poulin's reputation to promote their cause of abolishing the Senate. Nothing would hold them back."

Years after the Senate investigation, he is still angry and does not contain his condemnation of the campaign to discredit the Senate and promote the Reform Party doctrine of an elected Senate. "That was part of it. Like Trump, they would destroy a person like Marie Poulin's reputation to promote their cause of abolishing the Senate. Nothing would hold them back.

"The first I heard of that was on the news. Friends of mine were starting to say, 'Oh gee, I didn't know she was like that.' I defended her from the beginning. I trusted her. I still trust her; having worked in caucus, I know that she didn't go along with little political games. With her, it all had to be up front and on the table. She was a fierce fighter, but everything was on the table. I would trust her with my life. I knew that there was no way there could have been a shadow of truth about what the Reform Party was claiming. It turned out that I was proven right."

★ ★ ★

Duncan Fulton ran Marie's bid for the presidency of the Liberal Party of Canada. As we know, defeating the party's chosen candidate, Tony Ianno, angered many Liberals, but Fulton says it also gave Marie Poulin a recognition factor she never had until 2006. "It probably elevated her status in the eyes of the Opposition research folks, who were Conservatives. Imagine you were in the Opposition research office and were drawing up the list of the top twenty Liberals. Previously, it would have been unlikely for Marie to have made the top twenty Liberals list. But becoming president of the party automatically put her on the list. In a way, it elevated her status within the party, but I couldn't say in the end if it contributed to the whole Senate hearing issue."

Erik Peters was Marie's colleague at the CBC when he was brought in by Pierre Juneau in the mid-1980s to clean up the financial situation that existed at the time. Peters once worked for the auditor general's office and went on to become the Auditor General of Ontario. His opinion of Marie echoes that of Fulton. "I was long gone when the audit of the senators occurred, but I was peripherally involved. When I was Deputy Auditor General of Canada, there were all sorts of things going on at the legislative level. We felt that the procedures for administering the financial affairs of the House and the Senate were very weak. However, it was also felt that we should not investigate because when you're an auditor, you shouldn't be investigating your employer," says Peters.

This was in the late 1970s. Back then, Peters says, there was not the political will to conduct an audit of senators. "I was surprised when they did engage the AG [to investigate the senators]. I was contacted by some of the senators who knew me from way back; they felt that the AG was leading a witch hunt. They asked me, 'Under what authority can they do that?' I said that once the Senate approved the audit then the AG had literally a free hand. Under the audit act, there was no right to withhold any information."

"Marie was very concerned. She had become a lawyer, and she was very taken by the concept of lawyer/client privilege. She felt somewhat put upon because she considered that the AG should not have access to what she considered

> "Previously, it would have been unlikely for Marie to have made the top twenty Liberals list. But becoming president of the party automatically put her on the list. In a way, it elevated her status within the party, but I couldn't say in the end if it contributed to the whole Senate hearing issue."

> "Marie was very concerned. She had become a lawyer, and she was very taken by the concept of lawyer/client privilege. She felt somewhat put upon because she considered that the AG should not have access to what she considered to be privileged information."

to be privileged information. I had to point out to all of them that, under the audit act, the auditor had the right to ask for information." says Peters.

What particularly alarmed the former member of the Auditor General's staff was the level of personal animosity shown by some members of the AG's staff, in particular the venom aimed at Marie. "After I left the office, there was a legislative change made by which the OAG was reporting quarterly and this created a whole shift in mentality and a lot of jockeying in the office to get their report to Parliament, so auditors became much more personally aggressive. I say that not just because of Marie's case but one of the roles I took on in retirement was that of Vice-Chair of the Audit and Evaluation Committee of Public Works. We had to deal with the OAG's people all the time and there were complaints coming up to us about the mentality there."

Erik Peters worked with Marie in a fiduciary capacity when they were both at CBC. He was shocked to discover the type of things she was charged with, charges that eventually disappeared.

> "There was a legislative change made by which the OAG was reporting quarterly and this created a whole shift in mentality and a lot of jockeying in the office to get their report to Parliament, so auditors became much more personally aggressive. I say that not just because of Marie's case."

"Marie was of high personal integrity while at the CBC, in my mind. She wasn't the kind of person who was going to cheat," says Peters. "Later on, she convinced me to join the Institute on Governance, which she was on. We worked very well together on that, and her integrity showed through even in that."

During this period one of Marie's friends, Don McCallum, said to her: "Marie, you're such an easy target. You're so open, and very visible and have always been active in the Senate. You spoke up about the motion against Duffy, Wallin, and Brazeau. You've got a target on your back, of course they are going to go after you."

Marie says she has always been a person who followed the rules. When she was in boarding school, her classmates used to chide her for sticking to the rules.

"The late cabinet minister Diane Marleau used to tease me," Marie remembers. When she would introduce me on the Hill, she would say, 'Marie and I went to boarding school together, and she was Miss Goody Two Shoes. She followed the rules, and I never followed the rules.'"

## Redemption

"The environment in the Senate became absolutely toxic in 2012, when the Conservatives went after Duffy, Wallin, Brazeau, and Mac Harb," Marie says, "They maliciously went after them. I still remember walking out of the Senate Chamber, making my way to my office, and bursting into tears, saying to Natalie, 'I feel as though I am witnessing a biblical stoning, but the stoning is being done with words. Colleagues of mine are making accusations and insinuations, and they are making them because the press gallery is full.'"

Senate stories seldom made the front page or the top of newscasts. Now they did.

"There's a press gallery in the Chamber of the Senate and most of the time there's nobody there, but when the story began leaking about Duffy, Wallin, Brazeau, and Harb, every day the press gallery was full," says Marie.

"Marie, you're such an easy target. You're so open, and very visible and have always been active in the Senate. You spoke up about the motion against Duffy, Wallin, and Brazeau. You've got a target on your back, of course they are going to go after you."

"'I feel as though I am witnessing a biblical stoning, but the stoning is being done with words. Colleagues of mine are making accusations and insinuations, and they are making them because the press gallery is full.'"

Family Christmas dinner at the Charette-Poulin home, 2012.
*Source*: Family Collection.

> "I remember saying to Marie that the stuff they did seemed inappropriate. She responded that while of course she could not condone wrongdoing, the issue was much broader and much more serious. It was about the process and the way the file was being handled which opened the door to potential and wide-ranging procedural abuses."

The attacks on the sitting senators, and their suspension from the Senate, outraged her. "During my absence, when I was recovering from my second stroke, a motion was tabled for the Office of the Auditor General (OAG) to audit the expenses of all senators. In the fall of 2013, the motion was tabled to have Duffy, Wallin, and Brazeau suspended without pay. I decided to speak up against this because I thought it was unjust and unfair. Nathalie was not comfortable with my speaking out because the Senate had become such a toxic environment, and she worried that people would try to retaliate. I told her I would not remain silent before this injustice and had to fight it."

Bob Underwood, who first worked with Marie at the Actra Fraternal Benefit Society (AFBS), which provides insurance services to actors and writers, commented on Marie's support for Duffy, Wallin, and Brazeau. "I remember saying to Marie that the stuff they did seemed inappropriate. She responded that while of course she could not condone wrongdoing, the issue was much broader and much more serious. It was about the process and the way the file was being handled which opened the door to potential and wide-ranging procedural abuses." Sheila Copps says that her comments made Senator Poulin a target as well as a victim.

Further, the former Deputy Prime Minister felt the obscure rules kept changing to trap senators. "At the time, the rules related to domicile [...] Then the Senate kept changing the goal posts [...] It went on and on." Take the charge that Mike Duffy was double-dipping, because as a senator from PEI he was charging for his living costs in Ottawa. "That was all planned by the government. At the time, the rules relating to domicile and ownership of land and all that dated back to the beginning of Canada; I think you had to own a property worth four thousand dollars or something. It was a joke," says Ms. Copps. "Then, what they kept doing in the Senate, was they kept changing the goal posts. When they found nothing in that external [Deloitte] audit, they came back and said they weren't going to accept that and were going to demand this money back from the Senators. It went on and on.

"At the time, Marie went to several senators and said, 'Look, why don't we try to counter this?' Nobody seemed willing to do this, so the ones who were indeed saying that stuck out. I went to the leader of the Senate and set up a special committee. He agreed but nothing came of it."

One senior senator said to her: "If I speak up about this it will look like I have something to hide."

★ ★ ★

Marie recalls: "At the end of March 2014, I received a number of huge, six-inch-thick binders, with eight hundred questions regarding every little expense I had claimed. We were told that we had to meet with the AG in two weeks.

"I was still working, and Nathalie was running the office full-time. I was attending Senate sittings, going to committee meetings, giving speeches, and meeting with lots of groups. We had planned a very intense May and June.

"Nevertheless, we worked 24/7 to respond to each query and then met with the OAG representative. It was a very difficult eight weeks. I continued to attend sessions in the Chamber and committee meetings, but my commitments outside of the Senate were all cancelled. Every meeting with the intimidating OAG agent was recorded. These meetings were intense: Nathalie felt we were treated like criminals. Based on the calls made to Nathalie and the disturbing behaviour of the OAG agent in my office, I now recognize that this was harassment.

"At the end of June 2014, following the eight weeks of meetings with a combative agent, the Principal Auditor General, Gordon Stock, running the audit, asked to meet with me. The agent was there, as was Nathalie. They asked for all my emails received and sent during the audit period. I answered that I would take the request under advisement and come back to them in a few days. I said that I would continue to cooperate with the OAG but that I needed to seek advice. The agent, who was sitting next to Gordon Stock, suddenly got up forcefully from her chair, and yelled at me: 'I'm going to get you no matter what you do' and walked out of the office. Gordon Stock got up, looking embarrassed, shook my hand and left. When I did seek advice from the executive of the Internal Affairs Committee, I was informed that no other Senator has been asked for copies of emails. The then Law Clerk of the Senate later added that Canadians should expect privacy when communicating with a parliamentarian. And that I should seek legal counsel."

Marie says she kept an electronic agenda, which other senators told her was a mistake. But they told her that more than a decade too late. "Some senators refused to use an electronic agenda because they knew that access could be organized, period. I found out about this practice only during the audit.

"It's a golden rule in politics: you don't share your agenda with anyone except with your executive assistant," says Marie. The reason was to separate Senate

> "I was trying to get him to cross the floor. I had quite a few meetings with him. There was no way I wanted the AG to know about those. That's why I paid about five thousand dollars back to the Senate when the audit started: I refused to divulge some of the names of the people I was meeting with."

business from party politics. A senator wears two hats: one a government legislator and the other a politician loyal to a party.

"One of the things I had been doing during the years of the audit was work closely with an NDP MP. I was trying to get him to cross the floor. I had quite a few meetings with him. There was no way I wanted the AG to know about those. That's why I paid about five thousand dollars back to the Senate when the audit started: I refused to divulge some of the names of the people I was meeting with. This amount included expenses for working meals, trips, and similar expenses. Nicole Proulx, then Director of Finance of the Senate, came to me during a committee meeting and asked me why I had repaid the money. She said to me, 'You are one of the strictest senators with all your expenses. You do not spend a lot, so why in the world would you want to repay some expenses?'

"I replied, 'Because I cannot divulge the names of the people I met with over lunch here and in Toronto.'

"I said to Nicole, 'When I arrived at the Senate, it was always the EA who filled out the administrative requirements, including requests for reimbursements. Natalie did all that work—like every other assistant did.' Natalie would be in contact with your staff and ask, 'Is this or that expense acceptable.'

"Nicole said, 'You are one of the few offices that when we give advice, you follow it… others would argue it.'

"She disagreed with me about paying back the expenses and wanted to give the cheques back to me. She had the cheques in hand. I said that a good friend, a professional auditor, had advised me to reimburse the expenses related to an activity, information about which I could not share.

She said I had received bad advice.

When Senator Céline Hervieux-Payette was in the same situation, she took a very different approach. "They came to me one day and asked with whom I had had lunch. I told them I'd never tell them. It was a private meeting with someone who wanted to deal with a senator. You can question whether I charged two or three hundred dollars for a meal, but you don't have to know who was there, and what were the circumstances. This is not your role.

You are doing the accounting. I met people and I have the budget for that, and I was respecting the limits of the budget so, that's all." She added: "My staff spent a lot of time on that, which disturbed the regular work in our office for the Senate. So, this was the most stupid thing and, as far as I am concerned, the external auditing should have been quite enough."

Michel Coulombe, who served on the board of the Regroupement des gens d'affaires de la Capitale nationale, a chamber of commerce, and who also served as Marie's accountant for decades, was shocked by the conduct of the Auditor General's young agent: "It's out of character for a professional accountant to behave like that, not to give the benefit of the doubt. I advised Marie to file a complaint to the Society of Chartered Accountants, but she didn't heed my advice. If I had had first-hand knowledge of that, my code of ethics would have obliged me to report it. I wouldn't have had a choice in the matter. If I didn't report an incident such as this one, I could have been charged myself. We have our own internal courts to deal with members. The benefit of filing a complaint is that they would have had to follow up with the agent, and a note would have been placed in her dossier."

Following her meeting with Stock and the OAG agent assigned to the file, Marie asked for advice from the Internal Economy Committee. She also sought outside legal advice. A wise decision, but one that would end up costing her and Bernard dearly, including their beloved house.

While the motivation of the Harper government and its Reform base to change or abolish the Senate was clear, what cannot be known is the reason for the evangelical-like zeal with which the Auditor General attacked the Senate.

★ ★ ★

When the story was related to Sheila Fraser, the former Auditor General, she was shocked at the reported behaviour. "It is totally inappropriate and there should be consequences. Even if you are dealing with the worst of the worst, you have to stay objective and unemotional in all

> "She disagreed with me about paying back the expenses and wanted to give the cheques back to me. She had the cheques in hand. I said that a good friend, a professional auditor had advised me to reimburse the expenses related to an activity about which I could not share the information. She said I had received bad advice."

> "It's out of character for a professional accountant to behave like that, not to give the benefit of the doubt. I advised Marie to file a complaint to the Society of Chartered Accountants, but she didn't heed my advice. If I had had first-hand knowledge of that, my code of ethics would have obliged me to report it."

of this. The whole thing became political just because of the people involved. That's why the Office of the Auditor General, when they take on these kinds of things, must be really sensitive to the potential outcomes of all of this stuff—to accuse somebody over postage stamps, really!" says Ms. Fraser. "I heard about that after the fact, but I wasn't involved in that audit or how it was scoped or anything. It just seemed ridiculous to me."

Ms. Fraser did an audit of the House of Commons, but she did it in a much different way. "Well, I got us into the House of Commons; they really didn't want the AG to do it. Around that time, in 2010 or something, all those issues were coming up in Great Britain about inappropriate expenses by the Lords and the members of Parliament—I recall the duck ponds and things like that.

"The Office had done an audit of the House of Commons in the early 1990s, so it was time that there be one. I thought it would be a good idea, and some of the members seemed to be in favour, but there was a lot of resistance. Finally, there was a newspaper article by Daniel Leblanc in the *Globe and Mail* about how Parliament was refusing us access. There was a huge public response to that, so they agreed for the office to come in and do an audit.

"We did an audit of systems and practices: Did they have good financial controls in place? What were the hiring practices? And all the usual stuff. There were a few issues there but nothing scandalous at all. So, then we thought, *maybe the Senate*, but by then I was out of office. It took so long that I was out of office before the report was even tabled," says Ms. Fraser. She says she would have done the Senate audit using the same method used to look at the House of Commons.

★ ★ ★

In the middle of this crisis, another occurred. A truly terrifying one. A potentially life-threatening one.

A few minutes before ten on the morning of October 22, 2014, Nathan Cirillo, a young reservist of the Argyll and Sutherland Highlanders of Canada, was guarding the

Canadian National War Memorial with two other young soldiers. It was a ceremonial guard duty, and the rifles they carried were unloaded.

One shot in the back. Corporal Cirillo staggered. Two shots, both from a 30-30 Winchester 34 lever-action hunting rifle. That rifle can kill a deer at two hundred metres, a bear at thirty metres. Nathan Cirillo was shot point-blank. He fell to the ground and would soon be dead, not knowing why he had been shot or by whom.

The two other soldiers, who were for all intents and purposes unarmed, could not help their murdered colleague.

The murderer, Michael Zehaf-Bibeau, rushed across the street to Parliament Hill entering the Centre Block unchallenged. He pushed his way past an unarmed security guard and began roaming the Halls of Parliament. Within minutes, the House of Commons and the Senate were in lockdown.

Soon, all downtown Ottawa was shut tight.

Under the Peace Tower: panic stations. No one knew if the gunman was alone or part of a mass assault.

Marie was meant to be in her Senate office at 10 a.m., but had been delayed in a meeting at Gowlings.

Her Senate office was located behind the Senate Chamber in the Centre Block, about twenty metres from where the armed intruder was shot by Kevin Vickers, the Sergeant at Arms of the House of Commons. Marie's long-time executive assistant, Natalie Grimard, was terrified, as was just about everyone in the building. Prime Minister Stephen Harper was said to be hiding in a cupboard in the caucus meeting room.

At Gowlings's offices, a few blocks away, no one knew of the crisis yet.

"Senator Charette-Poulin, Natalie is on the phone. She is very upset; she said she has to talk to you. It's an emergency. She said, 'Don't leave Gowlings office,'" said Marie's legal assistant.

"I took the call. Natalie was yelling, crying, saying, 'Don't move, don't come. There's a killer in the building. We don't know how many they are. They are just outside my door, Senator. I have locked the door, and I am under the desk. Don't leave Gowlings!'"

> "I took the call. Nathalie was yelling, crying, saying, 'Don't move, don't come. There's a killer in the building. We don't know how many they are. They are just outside my door, Senator. I have locked the door, and I am under the desk. Don't leave Gowlings!'"

Natalie went on. "I was so worried; I thought you had been killed because you were supposed to have been on your way at the same time as this attack on Parliament Hill."

Marie recalls what happened next.

"We didn't know anything yet. I went back to the meeting and told everyone what Nathalie had told me. All the lawyers went to the window. We saw a huge commotion at the Cenotaph, but we didn't know what was going on. I said that they didn't know if there was more than one gunman. People were asked not to leave the meeting rooms where they were."

Meanwhile, in Centre Block, the halls were filled with gunfire. Kevin Vickers took the pistol from his drawer and he, along with RCMP Constable Curtis Barrett, challenged the gunman. At the end of the confrontation, Zehaf-Bibeau lay dead.

An atmosphere of deadly crisis still infected both Houses of Parliament, though. Immediately after word got out about the attack, heavily armed tactical teams were sent to help defend Parliament Hill. An RCMP SWAT team, dressed in military camouflage, carrying submachine guns, entered Marie's office. They told Natalie to grab her purse and leave. They escorted her out the back door; from there, though, she was on her own.

Natalie was not allowed to take her car. She ran in her high heels to the Château Laurier. The doors were locked, and she was not allowed in. She ran down Rideau Street, but not a shop, restaurant, or coffee shop would give her shelter. No one knew what was happening. She would have been better off back at Centre Block.

She ran the length of Rideau Street, more than five kilometres, to her mother's apartment in Vanier, where she finally took refuge.

This dramatic incident had a long-term effect. The trauma of that day's events, combined with the tension Marie and her staff were already experiencing as a result of the intense pressure being applied by the OAG, created massive amounts of stress. It seemed that things could not get any worse.

And then they did.

A few weeks later, Natalie's husband was diagnosed with Amyotrophic lateral sclerosis (ALS). Less than three months later, Natalie went on sick leave. It was the stress of the investigation, the constant demands for records, and the justification for things as small as stamps.

"We were in the middle of the Auditor General's scouring our records. There was all that stress, but there was more than that," Marie remembers. She was worried about Natalie and her health, both physical and mental. Natalie, like Marie, had suffered a great deal of stress.

The attack on Parliament Hill added tension to a traumatic situation. "At the time, I never thought about the fact that the attack on Parliament Hill, which happened in October 2014, took place at the height of the audit. After that horrible experience, Natalie went on sick leave. The pressure was intense. That's when my family doctor said to me, 'If you don't leave the Senate now, I'm going to be taking you out feet first.' I was already seeing a psychologist at the time. I think I had the symptoms of a battered woman."

## Lies Live Forever on the Internet

> The evil that men do lives after them;
> The good is oft interred with their bones.
> —Marc Antony's funeral oration from *Julius Caesar* by William Shakespeare

Shakespeare died over four hundred years ago, and he could never have conceived of the harm that search engines, could do, though he got it right in the famous lines above.

Despite being cleared of any wrongdoing, Senator Charette-Poulin is still represented online as dishonest, where past accusations made against her still live and old articles have never been erased or corrected.

With the aid of powerful online search engines, users can source articles that might otherwise have been long forgotten. Abandoned web pages can be discovered too. Whether or not the information preserved on those web pages and in those articles is true, whether the misinformation, the libel, has since been recanted, is irrelevant. What "lives after" is the "evil."

> "At the time, I never thought about the fact that the attack on Parliament Hill, which happened in October 2014, took place at the height of the audit. After that horrible experience, Natalie went on sick leave. The pressure was intense. That's when my family doctor said to me, 'If you don't leave the Senate now, I'm going to be taking you out feet first.'"

> "Many newspaper articles cast doubt about my integrity. It was like a seed that was sown by the Conservatives. And today, years later, the articles are still there, even though I have been entirely exonerated. And don't forget that I have never been called by a journalist for a comment since, even though I was hounded by reporters throughout the investigation."

"Many newspaper articles cast doubt about my integrity. It was like a seed that was sown by the Conservatives. And today, years later, the articles are still there, even though I have been entirely exonerated. And don't forget that I have never been called by a journalist for a comment since, even though I was hounded by reporters throughout the investigation," says Marie.

One of the most hurtful rumours that appeared in the media involved allegations that Marie had used the resources of her office to benefit her husband's career as an artist. Ten years before Marie was even named a senator, Bernard was receiving commissions such as painting the portrait of Governor General Jules Léger and his brother Cardinal Paul-Émile Léger. He has also painted Prince William, Duke of Cambridge, heir to the British throne. He is not a man who needs help, and Marie never gave him any, apart from, in his words, "constant love and encouragement."

Marie feels that papers in Sudbury, Toronto, Ottawa, and across the country carried news stories that were planted by her enemies, or people who wanted to soil her reputation and downgrade the authority of the Senate in general.

A particularly egregious example is on the CBC's website, of all places, presenting the file in the opening paragraph as fact, without verifying whether the information was true:

> In a report released today, it was shown that former Sudbury Senator Marie-Paule Charette-Poulin was one of the three cases with the highest sum of questionable claims, which were among the nine referred to the RCMP. The audit found that Charette-Poulin had "conflicting or insufficient information" for more than $130,000 in claims, questioning whether some of her travel expenses were for her work as counsel for a law firm, to visit family members or to support her husband's business activities. The audit details that she has repaid $5,606 of those questionable expenses.[1]

---

1. https://www.cbc.ca/news/canada/sudbury/former-sudbury-senator-charette-poulin-has-more-than-130k-in-questionable-expense-claims-1.3106472

Marie speaking at the Queen's Jubilee Dinner in Sudbury, 2012. *Source*: Family Collection.

Marie received no phone call asking for comment. Despite the Auditor General subsequently exonerating her, there was no retraction, correction, or removal.

*  *  *

Jean Leroux was a freelance researcher who wrote speeches for Marie and helped her identify Franco-Ontarians who might be put forward for the Queen Elizabeth II Diamond Jubilee medals. Marie wanted to ensure the thirty candidates were worthy recipients and not merely friends getting handouts.

Leroux managed the entire Diamond Jubilee medal project. As part of his assignment, he had to make sure that the pool of thirty candidates included men and women equally, and that candidates came from a wide group of occupations and backgrounds. Jean was ideally suited for the freelance job, as he was the owner of a small headhunting firm that specialized in Franco-Ontarians. He had the connections.

> Leroux was far from the only one to feel that the Auditor General's display of excessive minutia was scandalously tantamount to government boondoggle and machinations.

Leroux did more than just the Jubilee Medals contract for the senator. Over a two-year period, he did a great deal of other work, including speech writing and research. Of the $130,000 of expenses incurred by Senator Charette-Poulin that were questioned in the report, most were for the work done by Jean Leroux. While the Auditor General's report did not name Jean Leroux, it queried every one of his invoices, doggedly disregarding the way all senators operate. All senators hire freelancers to do the kind of work Jean Leroux did for the senator.

"I couldn't believe how the Auditor General attacked Jean Leroux in their report on me. Those expenses were over a two-year period" says Marie. "Jean Leroux refused to meet with the Auditor General's staff because he said the investigation was a partisan attack on me and didn't want to be party to it. He told me: 'This is totally political, Marie, and no matter what I say they are not going to believe me.'"

This was far from being the scandal it was made out to be. But more importantly, Leroux was far from the only one to feel that the Auditor General's display of excessive minutia was scandalously tantamount to government boondoggle and machinations.

★ ★ ★

Mitch Spiegel, one of Marie's lifelong friends, is a hard-nosed businessman whom one would expect to come down hard on any perception of government waste.

"Eight years ago almost to the day, we ran a World Rowing Tour here in Sudbury. We had people from sixty countries doing long-distance rowing and they were here for a week. I tried to get our local municipal leaders to come and address the people, but I couldn't get any. So, I called our senator, Marie, to come and join us at the final dinner and bring greetings from the federal government. Well, it was one of the things that the stupid auditor general picked up on. It's like being audited by the CRA. Who is innocent?" says Mitch. "It was a witch hunt and that's all it was. I think some of them deserved what they got, but I think Marie got a bum rap."

Marie's friend Shirley Westeinde also believed Marie was unfairly treated and is still shocked by the dirty politics and how these affected her friend.

"It was horrible; I encouraged her to resign because she was having health issues and I could tell it was just draining her. [...] I still can't believe this could happen. [...] It seemed to be a hate thing that went on," says Shirley. "They were digging into every expense of every senator and publicizing it in the paper. And it wasn't just Liberals, it was Conservatives too that the OAG was going after. How Stephen Harper could have gained anything by that, I don't know. Whether we'll ever find out who was really the one who got it started and why they did it, I have no concept."

The official accusations were not the only problem.

There was also the hearsay—and of course, hearsay originates somewhere, though it's sometimes difficult to determine the source of the political skulduggery. But leaking "information" to curry favour with journalists in the "you owe me one" world of dirty dealing does happen in the political realm.

One evening, Marie was having coffee with Claude Carignan, who had taken over from LeBreton as leader of the Conservatives in the Senate. Marie was explaining to Senator Carignan how the Office of the Auditor General had called Heenan Blaikie, where Marie had worked, and requested copies of all her expense claims, to check these against her Senate expense claims.

"The OAG observed that there was not a single case of overlap or a single instance of double-dipping. But the fact that the OAG had obtained that info from my former firm troubled me, especially since the person they questioned felt intimidated by the style of the request and the attitude of the OAG representative," says Marie. "I told Senator Carignan that I felt the Auditor General was insinuating that I was double-dipping with the firm."

As she told this story to Senator Carignan, someone appeared in the doorway. He was a young political aide attached to his office. Was he the source of the leak that ensued? Who knows? But certainly, the story was shared with a newspaper, and this coverage was picked up by wire services. It made its way to the regional papers of Northern

> "Eight years ago almost to the day, we ran a World Rowing Tour here in Sudbury. We had people from sixty countries doing long-distance rowing and they were here for a week. I tried to get our local municipal leaders to come and address the people, but I couldn't get any. So, I called our senator, Marie, to come and join us at the final dinner and bring greetings from the federal government. Well, it was one of the things that the stupid auditor general picked up on."

> "They were digging into every expense of every senator and publicizing it in the paper. And it wasn't just Liberals, it was Conservatives too that the OAG was going after. How Stephen Harper could have gained anything by that, I don't know."

Ontario. The story was a lie, twisted and untrue, but it made great copy.

Marie found out about the article when an embarrassed Senator Carignan appeared at the door of her Senate office on the day of publication. "Marie, I did not leak our conversation, I promise you," Marie recalls him saying, adding, "He was very emotional."

Could Marie have found a way to remove or redress this print and online misinformation, lest these articles haunt her forever? One would hope so, but in Canada, that is not as easy as it sounds.

In Europe, there is a Right to Be Forgotten law. Reputation.ca carries this description of the law: "The right to be forgotten is the right to have private information about a person removed from internet searches and other online directories under some circumstances. In 2014, the European Union (EU) enacted 'the right to be forgotten' privacy law, which allowed people living in the EU to request removal of Google search results that were deemed no longer relevant or inadequate," says Jamie Watt, of Navigator Limited, who works on restoring the reputation of his clients.

> "Google has received millions of de-indexing requests, but reports conclude that fewer than 45 percent of those requests have actually been resolved. Although the law requires Google to remove links from its search results in Europe, this has not translated to other countries, including Canada."

"Since the ruling took effect, Google has received millions of de-indexing requests, but reports conclude that fewer than 45 percent of those requests have actually been resolved. Although the law requires Google to remove links from its search results in Europe, this has not translated to other countries, including Canada."

The Canadian federal government has promised similar legislation, but so far, nothing has been proposed. Canadians can go to court and file a libel action, but that option is expensive and a roll of the dice. Google has fought back. The EU's top court ruled in 2019 that Google did not have to delist entries worldwide that it has struck from its European website.

"Currently, there is no obligation under EU law for a search engine operator who grants a request for dereferencing made by a data subject [...] to carry out such a de-referencing on all the versions of its search engine," said the European Court of Justice ruling. And the tech giants have no intention of changing unless governments force them to.

\*\*\*

There are good things about Marie online, of course. Given her accomplishments and all the work she has done for so many, how could there not be?

One can learn, for instance, of her accomplishments at Radio-Canada/CBC and at the Senate, as well as how she has served the community and in turn been recognized for her service over the years.

She received many awards, including the Marcel Blouin award for best radio morning program in Radio-Canada (1983), the Médaille du Conseil de la vie française (1988), the Ordre de la Pléaide distinction (1995), an honorary Doctor of Law degree from Laurentian University (1995), the insignia of the Officier de l'Ordre national de la Légion d'Honneur de la France (2003), the insignia of the Order of St. John (2004), the Trille de Platine award (2008), and the Personnalité Richelieu International (2008). She served on a variety of boards of directors, including Bell Globemedia, hospital boards, university and college boards, chambers of commerce, arts and culture boards, and the United Way. She was a member of the Implementation Committee for Bill 8 in Ontario, and a founding director of La Cité collégiale and of the Regroupement des gens d'affaires (RGA). She was the first woman to chair the RGA.

Marie welcomes the President of the United States of America, Barack Obama, to the Senate, 2009.
Source: Government of Canada Archives.

We also discover that she is a member of the board of governors of the ACTRA Fraternal Benefit Society, and of the advisory board of Canada's CEO of the Year Award. She was the Canadian president of the Fédération Canada-France, and as Vice-Chair of the Canada-Japan Inter-Parliamentary Group, she was a member of the Asia-Pacific Parliamentary Forum.

As a senator, she was a member of the Senate committee on Internal Economy, Budgets and Administration, and the Senate committee on National Security and Defense. As well, she was a past member of the committee on Banking, Trade and Commerce. She chaired the Senate committee on Transport and Communications and the subcommittee on Communications; leading the review of Canada's national and international position in communications and telecommunications. She was the first Francophone woman to chair the Senate Liberal caucus, and the first senator to chair the Northern Ontario Liberal caucus.

# The Aftermath of the Inquiry

THE NEGATIVE EFFECTS of the Auditor General audit on Senate expenses on Marie were enormous.

"The auditor general's investigation lasted over three years—and it was unrelenting. It occupied all of my days, seven days a week. It took a huge toll on my health. My family doctor—Dr. Lyne Pitre, an unbelievable professional—began seeing me early on every two weeks because she could see the impact the situation was having on me. I had already had two previous strokes. She was the one who told me I had to go see a specialist, a psychologist, to be given tools on how to deal with this stress," says Marie.

"This situation took a toll not only on me, but also on Bernard and our daughters and their families. It was a very intense time."

Bernard comments: "We came together as a couple—we have always been extremely close and loving, despite ups and downs throughout the years, but this one was *the* down. It was unexpected, undeserved, and I had to calm down a lot and just make sure that Marie was doing okay during all the shit because she had to live through it every day.

"It wasn't so much tension as it was pain, and I had to quell my anger because I am a lot more brash and irrational in my feelings. My response was, 'Don't fucking touch my wife and kids.' I cannot forget, nor could I forgive, but Marie can and always does. She could still talk to people who were tearing her apart like wild animals. She takes it and smiles and treats them as human beings, which is totally impossible for me to do. I will not shake these people's hands; I will not look them in the eye; I do

> "She takes it and smiles and treats them as human beings, which is totally impossible for me to do. I will not shake these people's hands; I will not look them in the eye; I do not want to see their faces; and I don't want to deal with them. I know what they did to my wife, and I know what it did to our kids."

> "What was really interesting to me too was that the Liberals also seemed to shun the Senate in that period; they sort of turned their back on the Senate. It was almost like the Senate was going through a very bad period in terms of its reputation and I'm not sure if that was deserved."

not want to see their faces; and I don't want to deal with them. I know what they did to my wife, and I know what it did to our kids."

Elaine and Valérie, of course, suffered a great deal during the period when Marie was under attack. Bernard continues: "The kids know who their mother is, and what was being done to her in the press was probably as bad if not worse than what was being done to her in Parliament. It affected them because it was public, and it was everywhere. But there was never any doubt for them about who their mother was and what she did or did not do. They saw the total unfairness of it all, and something we had taught our kids never to do was to be unfair to anyone else."

Marie adds, "They were very relieved when I decided to take early retirement. I think it was a huge relief for everybody, being out of the spotlight. It was all consuming."

★ ★ ★

Her colleagues at Gowlings could see the toll it was taking on her health.

"The Senate inquiry was going on and it really did affect her, I could see it in her face," says Wayne Warren, managing partner at the law firm. "Marie was extremely professional about all of it, she was always concerned about any impact on the reputation of the firm more than even her own reputation. She had legal counsel, and she was pushing back on what was going on in the Senate, but over time you could see the impact on her, the stress."

Though Marie kept her problems at the Senate separate from her work at Gowlings, her colleagues could not help hearing about the Upper Chamber investigation—it was, after all, making the headlines at the time.

"As a member of the public, it seemed pretty unfair to me," remembers Warren. "It seemed to be highly politically motivated, sort of a finger-pointing exercise of the Conservative Party to distract the public from some of the issues that they had at the time. What was really interesting to me too was that the Liberals also seemed to shun the Senate in that period; they sort of turned their back on the Senate. It was almost like the Senate was going through a very bad period in terms of its reputation and I'm not sure if that was deserved."

Marie did not know that one of the outside lawyers she was working with her on her Senate file was a long-time Conservative, but in the end it did not matter. He was working for his client, not any political party. He was, however, invited to Conservative functions, and at one of them he heard slanderous remarks about his client, Marie.

"I came into his office with Bernard on one occasion," Marie recalls, "and he said that something had happened last night that he had to tell me about.

"'I was invited to have a drink with some of the staff in Stephen Harper's office,' he told me. 'As you know, I'm a Conservative.'

"I said, 'I've never asked myself that question.'

"He said he came from a long line of conservatives and it is part of his family. Then he said, 'Today, I am ashamed of the Conservative Party.'

"'What are you talking about?' asked Marie.

"Marie, I saw these young people toast your demise. They named you. They didn't know I represent you. I wouldn't have believed it if I hadn't heard it and seen it with my own eyes. Marie, I'm not that type of Conservative, you have to know that," he said.

Shaken, he promised to work even harder on my case now to be sure that justice be done, adding, "This is totally political."

"Dealing with all that was so hard," says Marie, "and that's where the help from the psychologist was important; she gave me tools on how not to be consumed with a problem.

"I'll give you one example: she would say, 'When you're walking outside, feel your feet when you are walking, listen to what you are hearing around you, be more sensual when you are walking, so your mind rests a bit because your mind is totally consumed with what you are living.'

"But can you imagine what Duffy went through? My situation is mild compared to what Mike went through. It does become all-consuming, it eats your heart and your mind, and you become nearly dysfunctional because there's always something happening every minute of every day and your schedule is blown up.

> "Marie, I saw these young people toast your demise. They named you. They didn't know I represent you. I wouldn't have believed it if I hadn't heard it and seen it with my own eyes. Marie, I'm not that type of Conservative, you have to know that."

> "But can you imagine what Duffy went through? My situation is mild compared to what Mike went through. It does become all-consuming, it eats your heart and your mind, and you become nearly dysfunctional because there's always something happening every minute of every day and your schedule is blown up."

"I realized how easy it is to mount a well-organized and well-planned campaign to harass a person and to intimidate a person and to bully a person. I think it was Judge Vaillancourt who said, 'I think this is the best military exercise I have ever seen; it's so well-orchestrated.'

"On the personal side, I was afraid to go out. That's the thing that really struck me. The objective was to shame me. One of the things I discovered was that when you are being shamed publicly you are sitting alone. You begin to believe that you have done something wrong even though you haven't.

"One time, we went to dinner at the home of friends. I was sitting alone with the hostess. She turned to me and said, 'What you are going through is simply hell and I'm so sorry to hear it.'

"They had lost a daughter a number of years previously, and I was thinking of that when I said, 'My hell is not like your hell; your hell is much worse.'

"I nearly fell off my chair when she answered, 'Oh no, your hell is much worse; it's your reputation.'

"I still see her telling me that today. It shocked me. My plan was to fight to regain my reputation with family, friends, and colleagues.

"There were so many leaks to the press, lies being given to the press, and ultimately they weren't able to prove anything or that I had taken even a penny, yet they were printed.

"My other lawyer said to me, 'Because of the press, Marie, you're going to have to accept the fact that you will be getting hate mail. It happens to all my clients, and I just wanted to give you a heads up. It's really rough when you start getting hate mail.'

"About a month later, and this was during the worst part of all this, I brought a file to him containing seventy-two emails and hand-written notes that I had received in the past month.

"'Hate mail?' he asked.

"'No, it's love mail. From people who said they didn't believe what they read in the press because they had known me for many years.'

"He took the file and looked at it, saying, 'Marie, I have never seen this in all my professional life. You have a really strong supportive network. I don't think one can become a crook overnight,' he joked."

*　*　*

There were many people who were supportive. Marie offered her resignation to Gowlings, the law firm where she was a partner, but they refused to accept it. Marie insisted, saying she did not want the firm's name sullied by the investigation.

She also offered to resign as a governor of the Actra Fraternal Benefit Society (AFBS), the pension and insurance arm of writers and performers. Its CEO Robert Underwood refused her resignation. "David Ferry [chair], David Atkins [another governor], and I talked her out of it because I think we collectively agreed it was good for us to keep her on board and it was good for her head to maintain a positive relationship with one of her boards where she was respected and supported," says Underwood. "And of course, any accusations of inappropriate expenses were entirely dismissed."

It was the same at the Advisory Board of the CEO of the Year Award, which is operated by Caldwell Partners. "She had asked [me if I thought that she should] step down while she was going through the audit, and I said, 'Look, Marie, that's your decision, but I want to make perfectly clear that you have the full support of Caldwell and my support while you are going through this,'" says John Wallace, CEO of Caldwell Partners. "I have a position that, when I'm a colleague and a friend of somebody I stick by them. I knew she was going through a very stressful period and I wanted her to know that she would remain on the CEO Advisory Board."

John Wallace was shocked that after Marie was exonerated, the Senate refused to reimburse her for substantial legal costs. "As a Canadian citizen, I say the government has a right to investigate things. But if they find that somebody is exonerated, I would expect that someone would bear the cost of the defence," says Wallace.

The Senate investigation not only compromised Marie's personal life but also her family's financial well-being. She

> "She turned to me and said, 'What you are going through is simply hell and I'm so sorry to hear it.'
> "They had lost a daughter a number of years previously, and I was thinking of that when I said, 'My hell is not like your hell; your hell is much worse.'
> "I nearly fell off my chair when she answered, 'Oh no, your hell is much worse; it's your reputation.'"

> "I have to tell you that I wanted to spend that money because I knew it was well invested. Bernard convinced me that my reputation was worth protecting, and that I had worked too hard to let it be tattered."

spent a lot of money on her two lawyers. It was necessary as matters had been referred to the RCMP, and no one knew where this was going. A criminal offence is a terrifying thing, both for a politician and, especially, for a lawyer. Marie was both.

"One of my lawyers had to do a lot of research, making calls and asking questions of many contacts. I think he found this case very difficult because it was so political. The final tally of all the legal fees, if memory serves correctly, was a quarter of a million dollars, and even by that time we didn't know if we would be continuing or not. I have to tell you that I wanted to spend that money because I knew it was well invested. Bernard convinced me that my reputation was worth protecting, and that I had worked too hard to let it be tattered," says Marie. "We didn't know where this was going with the RCMP in the fall of 2015."

It was only in July 2016 that Marie received a letter stating that the RCMP had completed its review and that no further action was required.

"We decided to sell our house and move to a less expensive one. I wanted to be sure we still had enough money to keep paying the lawyers. To this day, Bernard and I still think it was very well-invested money," says Marie.

At that point, Marie raised the question of being reimbursed for staggering legal fees when in the end no charges had been laid and there was no finding of any improper conduct.

"Senator Carstairs and I began talking. She was the former leader of the government in the Senate, and our issue was the reimbursement of our legal fees. Hers were about eighty thousand dollars, and she was being asked to reimburse about twelve thousand, but she decided that as a matter of principle there was no way she was going to pay that. She knew darn well that those were legitimate expenses.

"There is a policy in the Senate on how your legal expenses are reimbursed. But because it wasn't linked to 'legislation,' she was told that she could not get them reimbursed. She appealed the decision. What she said publicly about her case applies exactly to my own case because we were both in the same situation. She was refused, but what's interesting is that although the committee recognized that there had been serious injustices perpetrated upon the senators in question, they weren't going to reimburse them."

### Jocelyne Bourgon: "It inflicted huge pain on her"

Jocelyne Bourgon was the first woman Clerk of the Privy Council from 1994 to 1999. She did not know Marie from that period, but the two women are friends today, and they discussed the file.

Ms. Bourgon is circumspect in her analysis of political events—a carry-over from her non-partisan post as Clerk of the PCO—but she knows the toll the investigation took. "It's a complicated story; I think she was in terrible pain but I also think a private conversation is private so I would not go too far there. It inflicted huge pain on her. It was a very stressful and painful chapter of her life."

### Sandra Pupatello: "Business and politics are different"

An Ontario MPP who held many Cabinet posts in the Ontario Liberal government, Sandra Pupatello now works in the upper reaches of Canadian business. She feels business and politics are different. "Well, one is covert, and one is overt. Politics is covert, which makes it tougher, and everyone pretends to be one thing. But in business, it is what it is: 'Of course I want to take all your money,' and it's very upfront and open, and that's really the difference. There's a lot less bullshit in business, if I may. Everybody knows what the game is and what the end game is," says Pupatello.

She says that in politics, people pretend to be nice.

"You don't want to be upfront or open about what your real agenda is. I was told early on when I got involved in politics that I was too honest to be in politics. But I discovered sixteen years later that if more people were [honest], we [politicians] wouldn't have the terrible reputation that we do."

Sandra Pupatello thinks Marie is one of those people who were perhaps too open and too trusting in aspects of her political career. Certainly, the investigation came as a shock.

> "I think she is one of the most versatile, competent, diligent, creative, and bright people in public policy that I [have come] across. She had a tremendous capacity to advocate without pushing in a counter-productive way."

## Hugh Segal: "What am I doing here?"

Hugh Segal was a Conservative senator. He was a longtime Progressive Conservative, with the emphasis on the *progressive*. He was an aide to former Tory leader Robert Stanfield in the early 1970s and chief of staff to Prime Minister Brian Mulroney in 1992 and 1993. But it was a Liberal prime minister, Paul Martin, who named him to the Senate in August of 2005, a measure of how respected he is across party lines.

When the Auditor General started his investigation into Senate expenses, Hugh Segal spoke up in the Red Chamber. It took a lot of guts, and he became persona non grata with the PMO. He had a lot of time for Marie, going back to his time with Prime Minister Mulroney.

"When I was chief of staff to Mr. Mulroney, and we were doing the negotiations for the Charlottetown Accord after the failure of Meech Lake, she was in the Cabinet office, where she had replaced Dan Gagné, the associate secretary of Cabinet for communications, because of her broad background with Radio-Canada and her fluent bilingualism," says Segal. "Before the negotiation cycle was finished, Marie became the main player and contact in the Privy Council Office. As chief of staff working the political side of the negotiations around Charlottetown, I was in regular contact with Marie. We met two or three times a week and would have attended some of the same planning meetings up in PCO."

In the Senate, Hugh Segal represented Kingston and Eastern Ontario, a part of the country with a sizeable Franco-Ontarian population. He consulted Marie on issues involving Franco-Ontarians, and they worked together on committees. There was no partisan animosity between Senator Charette-Poulin and Senator Segal.

"I have known her for a very long time, going back to her days at the Radio-Canada/CBC: I think she is one of the most versatile, competent, diligent, creative, and bright people in public policy that I [have come] across. She had a tremendous capacity to advocate without pushing in a counter-productive way. She made steady progress on the files about which she was concerned: the appointment of senior female leaders to more important posts in the public service; ensuring that in public policy there was always an important caveat about the effect of any particular policy on the North or Francophone minorities; or legitimate opportunity for women. I just thought she was superb, always did and still do."

This is a man who did not think Marie Poulin was guilty of the offences the Auditor General was asking about, day after gruelling day.

"The auditors applied a level of forensic auditing that is tied to the presumption of guilt. That's where they started. Sometimes you get a mood in the country where a group of people are deemed bad actors without substantive evidence. Based on the work done by Deloitte and the RCMP, whose incompetence is legion in my view, the alleged worst actor was Duffy, with thirty-one criminal charges. And yet, he was acquitted—of *all* charges—on April 21, 2016. This discrepancy between allegations and outcomes eloquently demonstrates just how badly Deloitte and the RCMP did their job. Clearly, they didn't give a damn what they did to people's reputations."

The three-hundred-page or so ruling by Ontario Court Justice Charles Vaillancourt is definitely worth the read.

"I have said this in the Senate: 'In a Banana Republic, the prime minister of the day calls the police and tells them to investigate the following people. In a democracy, with the non-partisan administration of justice, you may get a request from a politician, which in and of itself is inappropriate. Still, the commissioner of the RCMP has a duty to determine whether there is probable cause. If there isn't probable cause, then they have a duty to say to the prime minister or chief of staff, 'There is no basis for a criminal investigation in this circumstance.' Period, full stop. And that is not what the commissioner at the time did.

"One of the reasons I stepped out of the Senate was because, having voted against what I thought was the violation of basic principles, and realizing that I was the only Conservative to do so, I said to myself, 'If there's anything we Tories believe in, it's these principles of peace, order, and good government: presumption of innocence, the rule of law, due process, and independent police. If I'm the only Conservative who feels strongly enough to

> "Based on the work done by Deloitte and the RCMP, whose incompetence is legion in my view, the alleged worst actor was Duffy, with thirty-one criminal charges. And yet, he was acquitted—of *all* charges—on April 21, 2016. This discrepancy between allegations and outcomes eloquently demonstrates just how badly Deloitte and the RCMP did their job. Clearly, they didn't give a damn what they did to people's reputations."

> "In a Banana Republic, the prime minister of the day calls the police and tells them to investigate the following people. In a democracy, with the non-partisan administration of justice, you may get a request from a politician, which in and of itself is inappropriate. Still, the commissioner of the RCMP has a duty to determine whether there is probable cause. If there isn't probable cause, then they have a duty to say to the prime minister or chief of staff, There is no basis for a criminal investigation in this circumstance.' Period, full stop."

vote against this motion brought in by the Conservatives, then what am I doing here? Why would I be spending my life with this crowd when I could be of service doing other things in other ways?'"

"One of the factors that contributed to me leaving the Senate was how Marie was treated. I said to myself that if that is what this institution is all about and that's how prime ministers want to act and if that's where we are on the presumption of innocence and if even the members of the Senate cannot be presumed to be innocent, why would I hang around?"

Hugh Segal resigned from the Senate on June 15, 2015, days after the Auditor General report, dated June 4, 2015, was submitted. He passed away on August 9, 2023. Marie took the train to Kingston to attend visitation at the funeral home."

### Senator Linda Frum: "They needed to find a villain"

One day, Fiorella from Rinaldo's Salon was cutting Marie's hair. In fact, there were two women senators at Rinaldo's: Liberal Marie Poulin and Conservative Linda Frum.

Senator Frum approached Marie and, without being prompted, apologized to Marie for the way she was being treated in the Senate. It was a very human moment. And emotional. So emotional that Marie remembers the date it happened.

"It was June 21, 2017. She apologized for what had been done to me and said that she was sorry she hadn't stood up for me. I said to her only one thing: 'Apology accepted, Linda.'"

Pressure must have been quite high for Senator Frum not to defend Marie, given how she speaks of her. "One thing about Marie that really made me love her occurred when we were on a trip to Bahrain and Saudi Arabia. I was a brand-new senator. There were six senators on that trip. At the first one of our meetings, where we were meeting the counterparts in the Sharia Council in Saudi Arabia, I started walking into the room. She took my hand and said, 'No, dear, we do this in the order of seniority, and you're last.' She was number five, and I was number six.

Marie with Senator Linda Frum in Saudi Arabia (on their Blackberrys) while their camel ride awaits, 2011.
*Source:* The Senate of Canada Archives.

"The way that she did it, this piece of etiquette and decorum and protocol, was so gracious and warm and thoughtful. She didn't make me feel bad by saying, 'You're doing it wrong.' She did it with grace, and it was obvious after she said it that there was a protocol, and I wasn't following it. No one else would have said anything to me. They would have let me look like an idiot, but she said, no, no, no, here's how it's done."

Senator Frum's travels with Marie left her with little doubt that she was a woman of integrity.

What I know about Marie is that she is a very ethical person. One of the things I find so endearing about her is that she was among the most non-partisan people, and I know I am talking about an arch-Liberal when I say that. On a human level, she has a goodness of spirit about her, and to see her raked over the coals like that was hard to watch. My impression was that she was one of

> "My impression was that she was one of their early audits when they were in their hyper-vigilant mode at the beginning, and they needed to find a villain. Her dossier came up early, and I think that by the time they got to people at the end, they began to realize that 'Okay, it's not just a den of thieves.' But she was an early victim."

their early audits when they were in their hyper-vigilant mode at the beginning, and they needed to find a villain. Her dossier came up early, and I think that by the time they got to people at the end, they began to realize that "Okay, it's not just a den of thieves." But she was an early victim. But even if people had done things wrong, and I don't want to minimize the importance of fiscal responsibility, the whole tone of the investigation was out of whack. The punishment did not fit the crime, and the public outrage was way overboard and overwrought. People's lives and reputations were destroyed and, in many cases, extremely unfairly.

Frum is very careful about her own expenditures. As an author and the daughter of a famous Canadian, the CBC's Barbara Frum, she says she knows if she were caught doing anything wrong, there would be a strong feeling of *schadenfreude*—pleasure derived by someone from another person's misfortune—in the press gallery. She recalls being queried in an audit about seventy-five dollars in postage expenses. It felt, she says, "a witch hunt."

### Justice Robert Del Frate: "That was totally uncalled for"

Justice Robert Del Frate was plain Bob when he and Marie first met at Laurentian University. They were part of a group of close friends that hung out together. They share the type of friendship that lasts for life. Old friends just know the character of the people they are close to.

Bob Del Frate said he was surprised when Marie became a senator because he always thought the outgoing Marie-Paule Charette might run for Parliament. "I knew she was very involved with the Liberals. She did a heck of a job; she raised a lot of money, and she organized the Liberal Party when they were having real financial problems. One year after she took over, they raised something like ten million dollars.

> "She did a heck of a job; she raised a lot of money, and she organized the Liberal Party when they were having real financial problems. One year after she took over, they raised something like ten million dollars."

"Marie-Paule is such a charming person; if she wants you to do something, she has such an ability to make you want to volunteer. How she does it, I don't know; it's just her personality. She is very soft and very convincing.

At Laurentian University, she would call me up at times because I was Chair of the Laurentian University Board, [and Marie was on Laurentian's Board of Governors], and she would ask me what I thought of this or that. I gave her my opinion, and we were always very frank with each other. She would say, 'What if we considered this?' and most times, if not all times, her point of view prevailed because it was so sensible and so reasonable."

It shocked him when Marie was put under the Auditor General's spotlight, and stories about her began appearing in the press. "That was totally uncalled for. I have known her for a long time; she is probably one of the most honest people around and a hard worker. It was a real shock because I couldn't see her doing anything untoward. Marie-Paule's reputation was and still is beyond reproach in my view," says Justice Del Frate.

## Monsignor Jean-Paul Jolicoeur: "In the wrong place at the wrong time"

Another long-time Sudbury resident, who has known Marie since childhood, is Monsignor Jean-Paul Jolicœur. He was shocked when he read newspaper accounts of what she was alleged to have done, which is cheating.

"First of all, it was heartbreaking because I knew Marie. It hit me in a very special way because I could feel her suffering—it didn't affect just her but her family, and people here in Sudbury, people who had known her, worked with her, and grown up with her. She didn't deserve that, but the thing is, she was in the public eye, and there was all this turmoil going on in the Senate and Parliament Hill. You had senators Wallin, Duffy, and Brazeau mixed up in that thing too. Everyone was shooting arrows at whoever they could find," says Monsignor Jolicœur.

As a priest, he is a man used to listening to people's problems. He knows attacks such as this can have a devastating effect on mental health. Marie survived, and he thinks he knows what helped her.

"You have to have people around you that you can trust, people you listen to, and people who will listen to you. I don't think you can survive that alone. Number one was the support of her family, and secondly, I think her faith, because her faith is strong. That's not something you would publicly say of a politician or someone in the public eye, but I'm sure that her family, faith, and values helped her. Her parents were strong characters, used to having to fight for survival. And she is strong. Maybe this was not the first crisis in her life, but it was a public crisis. She had to fight, and she had to believe in what she was, and she had to believe in herself. Others believed in her also."

Father Jolicœur said she had that strength throughout her life.

"Just look at her life path, from childhood to the Senate: the obstacles and challenges that she overcame even before she was a senator; and before the audit, she managed to further her education while being a senator. She had a strong will and determination and the knowledge that she was not guilty. With that you can get through almost anything. People were backing her in the local community. I never heard anyone here in Sudbury saying, 'Oh, that's just Marie.' I think they separated the politician from the person, and the person was good, and she did not deserve that. She was just in the wrong place at the wrong time."

### Milton Shaffer: "She should be proud"

On a similar matter, Bernard shared the perception of his discerning ninety-eight-year-old mentor Milton Shaffer who loved news and discussing history. Aware that Marie was undergoing a targeted and what he deemed an illegitimate audit as an election tactic, based on a prior determination of guilt, he stated: "If the likes of them are attacking the likes of her, she should not be afraid. Rather, she should be proud."

### Senator Vivienne Poy: "Hyphenated Canadians"

Vivienne Poy was named to the Senate by Jean Chrétien in 1998, three years after Marie took her seat. Poy was a fashion designer for many years. Eventually, she sold the company and went back to school, earned a master's degree and was in the middle of her PhD in history, which she eventually completed at the University of Toronto, when Jean Chrétien called her to the Senate.

She and Marie were Senate seatmates for several years. The two of them hit it off. "Marie is a very friendly and straightforward person, the kind of person who I always like because I'm very straightforward too. I tend to get along with people who say what they mean, and they don't have to agree with me."

Poy represented Toronto and Asians across Canada, in much the same way as Marie represented Northern Ontario but also Franco-Ontarians as a whole. They did not have that much in common on the surface, but that is not the way Vivienne Poy saw it. "I was the first Asian to be named to the Senate, and that bothered a lot of people. That was especially true because I was a woman from a minority as well as an Asian. But there were also a few senators who were very accepting of me, and Marie was one of them. I

> "Her parents were strong characters, used to having to fight for survival. And she is strong. Maybe this was not the first crisis in her life, but it was a public crisis. She had to fight, and she had to believe in what she was, and she had to believe in herself. Others believed in her also."

> "If the likes of them are attacking the likes of her, she should not be afraid. Rather, she should be proud."

remember one time she saw a very nice article about me in one of the national newspapers. She phoned me. She has a very generous heart," says Poy.

Poy always objected to people calling immigrants "hyphenated Canadians." "I remember one time I asked, as a French Canadian, had she ever been called a hyphenated Canadian, and she said no. She was completely surprised. I'm a Canadian; I'm not a hyphenated Canadian," says Poy.

She recalls Marie asking her to take her place on a visit to Indonesia. "I appreciated that because while we were in the Senate, on the Foreign Affairs Committee, the guys, mainly the guys, would not let me go on the trips, even if it was in parts of the world that I knew quite well. It was because they wanted opportunities to travel. Marie didn't worry about that, being a very confident woman, and if you are confident, you don't have to worry. I appreciated that because it was a great opportunity for me. I was representing Canada as one of the few members of the Senate who went, and I was asked to speak." says Poy.

All that to say that when it came to the Senate expenses scandal, Vivienne Poy felt she knew Marie-Paule Charette-Poulin well enough to be convinced she had done nothing wrong.

"I knew why the Conservatives did it. It was because Harper hated the Senate, and he wanted to target a few, including some of their own, and wanted to tarnish the reputation of senators." When asked if she was surprised, coming from business, just how dirty politics could be, she replied, "Oh, totally. Did I learn? I was never involved with politics before, but I'm a fast learner. When I got to the Senate, I knew who would be supportive of me and who to stay away from. Absolutely. It is totally horrible."

## Senator Braley: "We are all being tarred and feathered"

Another senator who was disillusioned by the state of the system was David Braley. A long-time Conservative supporter and generous donor to the party, Braley was named to the Senate in 2010 by Prime Minister Stephen Harper.

Braley was a businessman who owned several sports teams, including the Hamilton Tiger-Cats, the BC Lions, and the Toronto Argonauts. He was the only person ever to own two CFL franchises at the same time. One of the bills that came to the Senate when he was there was Bill C-290, a private member's bill to allow "single sports betting." People would be allowed to bet on a single game. Senator Braley supported the bill but, a man of principle, he recused himself from the vote. In the end, it never passed.

The Senate scandal disgusted David Braley. When he discovered the evil that was being done, he could not abide being associated with it. He resigned from the Senate on November 30, 2013. He told a newspaper that the investigation into the Senate was hurting the reputation of the Red Chamber. "We are all being tarred and feathered as a result."

Marie heard a more detailed story straight from Senator Braley. "I remember meeting him in the corridor one evening. I asked him how he was doing, and he said he wasn't doing so well. I asked why, and he said, 'I think this place is sick. I'm a businessman, and I'm losing precious time here.' I asked what he meant, and he said, 'This place is toxic.' This was when things were starting with Duffy, Wallin, and Brazeau. He added, 'Marie, this is awful. People are going after people for innuendos; I can't believe it.' He retired officially a few days later. It's too bad because as a businessperson, he could contribute a lot, but he was just so discouraged," says Marie. "He didn't care about the politics; for him, it was a matter of integrity, humanity, goodness."

### Jim Gordon: "Politics can be very dirty"

Though newspaper headlines in the *Sudbury Star* and other papers painted a terrible picture of the goings-on in the Senate, including the unsubstantiated claims against Marie, many people in Sudbury did not believe them.

One of her supporters was Jim Gordon. "I know politics can be very dirty," says the former mayor. "It was a shame for Senator Charette-Poulin because she was a very hard-working person and not the type that would try to take advantage of her position. She just wasn't that kind of person. I always saw her as a woman of high ideals and passion for what she was doing. She was passionate about life. Whenever you talked to her, you could see that she was rooted in her values. At the time, the Senate was being run administratively in a very loosey-goosey way."

### Honourable Pierre Pettigrew: "Life under a glass"

Pierre Pettigrew held six Cabinet portfolios under two prime ministers, Jean Chrétien and Paul Martin, from Foreign Affairs to International Trade. In the year 2000, he headed up a trade mission to Algeria, Morocco, Spain, and Portugal.

Senator Charette-Poulin was part of the official Canadian delegation. When Pettigrew was called back to Ottawa, Marie took over the leadership of the mission.

The former Liberal Cabinet minister has worked at high-level posts in government and politics. "In politics, you live life under a glass. When you've had a bad week in business, on Saturday night when you have dinner with your friends, they don't know, and you don't have to talk about it. But when you've had a bad week in politics, it's front page in the media and it is top news, and all your friends know it," he says. "The meanness in politics sometimes comes from your own colleagues because of the rivalries around the Cabinet table, but in business, people who are normally your allies will fight with you and it will be your competition who will be meaner sometimes. They are two different universes altogether."

By the time of the Senate investigation, Pierre Pettigrew was out of politics and busy with a successful business career. Of course, once a political animal,

As a member of a Senate delegation to Morocco, Marie paid a courtesy call on the Crown Prince of Morocco who, a few weeks later, acceded to the throne as King Mohammed VI, 1999.
*Source*: The Government of Canada Archives.

always a political animal. And he watched the machinations over the Senate from the sidelines.

"Being a Liberal, I disagreed with Mr. Harper on many fronts. I was not a supporter of Senate reform the way he was proposing it," says Pettigrew. "I was extremely saddened by the whole affair. Those claims of administrative irregularities seemed to be based on rules that were not very clear."

## "I impute no bad motives to any of the senators."

On May 14, 2015, the Standing Committee on Internal Economy, Budgets, and Administration, named Former Supreme Court Justice Ian Binnie Special Arbitrator to "consider the justification for expense claims made on behalf of a number of senators put in question by the report of the Auditor General dated June 4, 2015." The mandate of the special arbitrator was to "determine whether

Marie with former President (2007–2014) and Prime Minister (1984–1986 / 1995–1996) of Israel, Shimon Peres, 1999.
*Source*: CIJA Collection.

the Senator in fact received an overpayment or made an improper use of the Senate resources" focussing on the period of April 1, 2011, to March 2013.

Less than a year later, on March 21, 2016, Former Supreme Court Justice Ian Binnie released his findings in a 221-page report, which can be found online.[1]

Binnie outlines the administrative apparatus under which the Senate of Canada operates, along with its *Senate Administrative Rules*, *Senators' Travel Policy 2012*, and *Special Arbitration Rules*, and others. He states that senators occupy a position of public trust and are expected to conduct themselves accordingly— with integrity, accountability, honesty, and transparency. Senators are presumed to have acted honourably in carrying out their administrative functions. The use of public funds by senators must only support Parliamentary functions, including public and official business and partisan matters, but excluding the election of a member of the House of Commons during an election, or private business interests of a senator or a member of their household. The definition of these functions must be broad and not inhibit senatorial work on issues considered to be important to the country, as "many Senators fight a lonely battle on an issue

---

1. https://sencanada.ca/media/93482/arbitrationreportsenatorsexpenses-e.pdf

which is regarded by the public to be of little significance until it explores into public prominence." Expenses must be reasonable, and weigh cost against need and public benefit. A level of discretion, judgment, common sense is required.

While Former Justice Binnie disagreed with some of the judgement calls senators made in their interpretation of policies and procedures in the use of public funds, he clearly stated that "I impute no bad motives to any of the senators." This quote became the title of the press release announcing the release of the report and made national headlines.

This was cold comfort for the Senators whose personal and family lives had been turned upside down, whose reputations lay in tatters, whose careers were compromised, whose important and useful public service work had been interrupted, and whose personal finances were, in many cases, severely compromised because of the inordinate amounts in legal fees required to defend themselves.

One could argue that it was also a terrible loss for the Senate of Canada: beyond the attack on its reputation and its usefulness, it had lost the keen minds of some of the brightest leaders in the country.

How does one account for all of this? We'll perhaps never know.

What we do know, however, is that this investigation cost Canadian taxpayers an unthinkable amount. In the wake of the Auditor General report, voices of condemnation rose from throughout the country. *The Huffington Post* published, on June 16, 2015, an op-ed piece by University of Calgary Professor Lee Tunstall:

> The auditor general spent around $23 million on this investigation and found less than $1 million in questionable expenses—out of $180 million worth of expenses investigated. So, we, the ever-patient, ever-indulgent taxpayers, spent $23 million to find out that 0.5 percent of Senate expenses were questionable. Should we be outraged? Yes, by the dollar cost of the investigation, and by the cost to the reputation of Canada's upper house.

"The auditor general spent around $23 million on this investigation and found less than $1 million in questionable expenses—out of $180 million worth of expenses investigated. So, we, the ever-patient, ever-indulgent taxpayers, spent $23 million to find out that 0.5 percent of Senate expenses were questionable. Should we be outraged? Yes, by the dollar cost of the investigation, and by the cost to the reputation of Canada's upper house."

In iPolitics.ca, Ian MacDonald published a piece titled "The AG and the Senate: $23 million to catch $1 million? Are we kidding?":

> It isn't just senators' reputations that are on the line—it's Ferguson's as well. Leave aside for a moment the nine senators referred to the RCMP; should Binnie dismiss his conclusions about many or most of the Senate 21, Ferguson's reputation for competence—not to mention that of his consultants—would be in trouble. He'd need to consider his own future at that point, if only for the integrity and standing of the AG's office.

Senator Cools, in relation to a distinct matter, would later characterize the Senate expenses investigation as follows: "Honourable senators, this indulgent and extravagant use of public funds on this Senate audit was wholly unjustified and wholly unnecessary."

For her part, Marie had this to say: "One of the things Former Supreme Court Justice Ian Binnie said was that the Auditor General never took into consideration the fact that the Senate and the House of Commons are not only institutions for legislation, but they are also political institutions. Expenses related to political activities are acceptable. I used to belong to a party, and we were allowed to expense meetings like a caucus meeting in BC or Halifax—these are all acceptable expenses. For many of the meetings senators have, you don't want to say who you meet with because it's political. But the AG did not realize that or simply didn't want to recognize it."

It is perhaps ironic that the investigation by the Auditor General into the inappropriate use of public funds by the Canadian Upper House ultimately led a much larger waste of public funds, by the very institution that was supposed to protect public monies.

The silver lining, if any is to be found in this dark chapter in Canadian history, was perhaps the fact that the Senate made several significant administrative and other changes in the wake of the Auditor General and special arbitrator reports designed to modernizing procedures, oversight, openness and accountability in the use of public funds, including "tightening expense provisions for travel, hospitality and procurement; requiring proof of residency; implementing a new Ethics and Conflict of Interest Code that ranks among the toughest in the Commonwealth; and the establishment of an independent Office of the Senate Ethics Officer. The Senate is also committed to introducing changes such as a more detailed model of proactive disclosure and more independent oversight measures."[2]

---

2. https://sencanada.ca/en/content/sen/chamber/421/debates/221db_2018-06-14-e

\*\*\*

In 2018, the Senate of Canada was called upon to debate the right of the Auditor General to gain access to the financial records of Petro-Canada, then a Crown corporation.

Senator Cools recalled the overreach of the Office of the Auditor General in its investigation of the Senate, the political motivations, the exorbitant cost, and the terrible damage it wrought:

> The audit of the Senate and senators was [...] bad politics [...] very bad politics. [This] unique political and constitutional embarrassment [...] humiliated and diminished the Senate and senators, whom this June 2015 audit report maligned. In particular, I speak of the thirty senators, each of whom was willfully and personally identified, individually by name, in this audit report. I repeat: Each of these senators was named and blamed. Until then, I had never encountered any such actions in any auditor general's report—and believe you me, I have read many of them.[3]

Speaking of the Auditor General's decision to refer the investigation of nine senators to the RCMP, Senator Cools commented:

> [T]he Auditor General's 2015 audit report provided no explanation whatsoever as to just why concerns about expense claims respecting primary residence warranted referral to the RCMP for criminal investigation, whereas those related to other claims did not. Similarly, there is no indication as to why the Auditor General's prevention from reaching an audit opinion was an indicator that there were issues deserving the heavy hand of criminal investigation that is necessary to lay criminal charges that engage criminal prosecution in all of its full force and gravity.[4]

> "[T]he Auditor General's 2015 audit report provided no explanation whatsoever as to just why concerns about expense claims respecting primary residence warranted referral to the RCMP for criminal investigation."

---

3. https://sencanada.ca/en/content/sen/chamber/421/debates/221db_2018-06-14-e
4. https://sencanada.ca/en/content/sen/chamber/421/debates/221db_2018-06-14-e

> "I don't know why he [Harper] did it, but his meddling into the affairs of the Senate was a big mistake for him. It's not the job of the prime minister to get involved in the agenda of the senators. They form a house of reflection, and they have their own rules and their budget."

As an aside: Marie never claimed the housing allowance during her twenty years as a member of the Upper Chamber.

Senator Cools concluded her remarks by noting that it was the very painful personal cost felt by the senators named that was the most concerning result of the audits:

> I shall use my last minute. We can never know the pain and the anguish and the agony that those senators went through when they were informed that their files were being handed over to the police. I knew all of those senators, and I would say I was very close to some of them. And, I tell you, I stood by them, and I made sure I supported them through that miserable agony and ordeal that they were put through for absolutely no reason.[5]

★ ★ ★

Looking back, the Reform Party's old idea of changing the Senate was a failure. It had been one of the ambitions of the likes of Preston Manning and his acolyte Stephen Harper, when they carried out a reverse takeover of the old Progressive Conservative Party, following the debacle in the 1993 election when Jean Chrétien's victory reduced the once-proud Tory party to two seats.

Speaking on the subject in 2020, Mr. Chrétien says it was a fool's errand from the start. "I don't know why he [Harper] did it, but his meddling into the affairs of the Senate was a big mistake for him. It's not the job of the prime minister to get involved in the agenda of the senators. They form a house of reflection, and they have their own rules and their budget."

He adds it is easy to criticize the Senate, but it remains a permanent feature of Canadian political life. "You can be for it or against it, but there is nothing you can do about it. To abolish the Senate, you need the consent of all the provinces. The small provinces think that if there were to be a major crisis, having more senators than their population

---

5. https://sencanada.ca/en/content/sen/chamber/421/debates/221db_2018-06-14-e

[qualifies them for] could be of help to them. So, even if you wanted to abolish it, it would be very difficult. You could debate it ad nauseam, but any change would have to have the consent of the ten provinces. And to have the ten provinces to agree on something, it would take a lot of work, my friend."

# Elaine and Valérie

ELAINE AND VALÉRIE grew up with a working mother and a father who could work as a successful portrait artist staying at home. There were no nannies for Valérie and Elaine. Today, Valérie lives in Toronto, while Elaine lives a quiet life in the country.

Valérie, who was eight years younger than Elaine, admits to teasing her big sister when they were younger. When Elaine brought a boyfriend home, Valérie could be a bit obnoxious.

Elaine is very different from her sister Valérie. "Being younger, my sister grew up in that political world a little bit more than me. When I think of my sister I think of a mini-mom; I picture both her and my mom together on their Blackberrys. We used to get together for dinners, and they would get going on politics. I'd feel like going next door or going for a coffee somewhere because I'd be so bored." There is little doubt that political talk at dinner irritated Elaine, but Valérie and Marie could not help themselves.

Valerie remembers: "When I first started in politics, I was probably the closest to my mother. To a certain extent, politics brought us closer together. It ticked off my sister that all we did was gossip about politics—who we knew and what we had heard and all those kinds of things—it drove my sister nuts," says Valérie. "Elaine is the opposite. She has no patience for it, and she used to say, 'No political talk at the dinner table.' I guess it was pretty annoying for others who weren't a part of it, but people in politics tend to do that when they are in the middle of it all."

## Elaine

Elaine and her husband live in a small town in Quebec, about a forty-minute drive from Ottawa, just outside of Gatineau between Ottawa and the Laurentians. Their idyllic country house is on a small river. Elaine works from home three days a week and one day a week she travels to a nearby town where she is a coordinator for a centre that trains and helps caregivers.

She connects the work she does and her attitude to life to her mother, even though in many ways they are different people.

"I have pondered this question of shared similarities, of the scope of her influence, and the inspiration she has given me. My mother is a pioneer woman. She

Marie's favourite place is in or on the water, despite occasional bouts of sea sickness, 1997. *Source*: Family Collection.

has started professional projects such as CBON with sheer creativity, determination, and enthusiasm. She has shown me that anything is possible if you really want it. That has been a tremendous gift. It influenced the start-up of my business in 1998 and now a community social program for caregivers," says Elaine.

"Also, one of my mother's qualities is that she finds ways to bring people together, to connect them to one another. This is now an essential part of my work, creating communities of support. Her influence is far greater than one can see."

Elaine realized early on that her mother was a hard-working, hyper-achieving person. At some stages in her life, especially when she was a teenager, it was difficult. "When you're young, you only think of your own needs. Sometimes, when my mother wasn't home because she was at work and at engagements, I would give her the cold shoulder when she came home. I suppose I felt, 'You weren't there when I was ready.' I'm sure it wasn't easy for

> "One of my mother's qualities is that she finds ways to bring people together, to connect them to one another. This is now an essential part of my work, creating communities of support. Her influence is far greater than one can see."

her, but when I became an adult, I realized that she had actually made a lot of sacrifices. She was the breadwinner. She had to travel when she was directing all the radio stations in the regions. In those years as I was a teenager, she was gone half the time so that was [difficult]. However, my father was a great presence. He's amazing. I was very lucky."

Still, says Elaine, "one of my mother's dearest qualities is her generosity. She would give the shirt off her back to someone in need! And she has always treated people around her with special attention and respect. I remember her talking about offering meat pies to the security guards on Parliament Hill at Christmas time. They loved her! And now she makes food for people in their building who are living alone during the pandemic. Both my parents have taught my sister and I the importance of giving the gifts you have been given to others. That has made a lasting impression."

Valérie and Elaine are different from one another, but they share not only unconditional love for Marie, but for Bernard.

"My dad has the resilience and patience of Job. He has been my mother's number one cheerleader since the day they met. I essentially spent my youth looking for a husband like my dad. My husband is very similar to my dad. My dad has a reserved streak, and he leaves the limelight to my mom. He's the backroom cheerleader. She never would have survived any of the crap she has been through without him. I think their love story is beautiful," says Valérie.

"They fall in love all over again every day; it's really cute. He totally accepts her for who she is. He has his moments of being frustrated with her, of course, because she's impatient and stubborn and she cooks up these plans. But he's there to support her through them. I spent every single day after school in his studio, so he and I are super close, more on the emotional level. She and I are close on the professional stuff. I have a very similar makeup [in my marriage] to what my parents had: all the things that drive me bonkers about my mom, I have as traits."

"I think it is part of her work ethic, she has really high standards. She doesn't believe in retirement. She doesn't

> "One of my mother's dearest qualities is her generosity. She would give the shirt off her back to someone in need! And she has always treated people around her with special attention and respect. I remember her talking about offering meat pies to the security guards on Parliament Hill at Christmas time. They loved her! And now she makes food for people in their building who are living alone."

Marie is introduced to the Prime Minister of the United Kingdom, Tony Blair, by Prime Minister Jean Chrétien. Also in attendance are Minister Denis Coderre and Senator Frank Mahovlich, 2001.
*Source*: Photograph by Jean-Marc Carisse.

have many hobbies: she reads, she swims, she walks, but I think my mother is a bit of a workaholic. It's where she gets her values, her sense of worth. I think her identity is based on work and if you took that away there would be a big void for her."

Even when her mother was named a senator, she was uneasy. "I remember when my mother was appointed to the Senate. She took me out to lunch to celebrate. I reacted very badly, though—I wasn't discouraging or anything, but I've always disliked politics and so I wasn't enthusiastic at all," says Elaine.

"Still, and I think that everything that is put on our plate is put there for a reason, to give us the opportunity to grow. That's my perspective on life."

Elaine has her own thoughts about the attacks her mother suffered during the audit. Unlike her mother and her sister, Elaine is not political at all. And what happened to her mother at the end of her tenure in the Senate confirmed her dislike of politics. In her words: "It's a dirty business. It's just really unfortunate that her career in the Senate ended the way it did because she worked so hard. I think that maybe she had to work even harder because she was a woman in a man's world a lot of the time. You know, things like that rob you of your sense of self. It's hard to have to reconstruct that at an age where you should be ending your [work life] and being comfortable. The repercussions are immense. They are financial and your sense of self and your reputation, it's big."

As a woman who wrote a book on the ravages of PTSD, Elaine thinks her mother may have suffered symptoms akin to traumatic stress at the peak of the Senate investigation. "I saw her. She wasn't well. It was very challenging to see her like that. She has always been the strong, resilient person. I was really concerned about her when she was going through the audit. But then she got help and it seems that she's managed to overcome things. But I really don't know where she is at in her healing process. It's clear, however, that it all had an impact," says Elaine.

> "It's just really unfortunate that her career in the Senate ended the way it did because she worked so hard. I think that maybe she had to work even harder because she was a woman in a man's world a lot of the time."

## Valérie

Valérie's first job was with the Office of the Superintendent of Bankruptcy, part of Innovation, Science and Economic Development Canada. It was not a good fit. Valérie saw that working with people who were in a desperate stage of their lives—going bankrupt—took a toll on the office culture. "These poor women who worked there were essentially counting down the days of the week, and I kept thinking to myself, 'There's no way I can do this for the rest of my life' so, I ended up in a minister's office as a receptionist and worked my way up from there," says Valérie.

Valérie landed the job without her mother's help. Poulin is a common enough name that it would have been unlikely that the Minister's staff would have made the connection. Valérie did go to her mother's Senate office to tell her about the opening, asking her mother not intervene on her behalf, even though Marie had no intention of doing so. But Marie encouraged her to accept the job if offered, even though Valérie's friends were telling her that a receptionist's job was a comedown for a university graduate.

"It's just the opposite," Marie told her daughter. "Receptionists are key people in every organization." Marie then gave her three rules to follow:

"Rule number one: learn how to make good coffee and—please, it's so important—welcome people. You have the opportunity of offering people a good cup of coffee and they will so appreciate it."

"Rule number two: buy yourself some wrapped candies and put them in a beautiful bowl on your desk. You will be a source of dialogue because people come in, they take a candy, and then, to remain polite, they will chat with you. And you will receive information like you wouldn't believe, and in politics, information is power."

"Rule number three: never repeat confidential information to anyone. Stay away from gossip. But when you receive something that you think would be useful to your minister, you only go to one person with it."

"Valérie said, 'To your minister?'"

Marie replied, "No, you go to the chief of staff, and you never divulge your source. You simply say that you have information that might be useful to the minister. Give him the information and then leave and that's it."

Valérie started working for Don Boudria, a Franco-Ontarian like her parents. She was not a receptionist for long. Valérie is outgoing, friendly, clever, and was a natural for the political world. She volunteered for work when political staffers would go on holidays, and soon she was a legislative assistant, speech writer, and press secretary. She worked her way up to director of communications for one minister. In Ottawa, she worked for Don Boudria, Andy Mitchell, Sue Whelan, and Joe McGuire. But political work has no job security.

"We all got fired when Stephen Harper was elected," says Valérie. "I made my way to Toronto with a bunch of people from Ottawa, and I started working at Queen's Park. McGuinty benefitted from a bunch of Liberal staffers showing up in Toronto at the time."

"I joined Sandra Pupatello's office as her director of communications, and then after that, I moved with her when she was at Education. I followed her when she became the minister of Economic Development. At that time, I was asked to be her chief of staff. So, under thirty, I became chief of staff to Sandra Pupatello in Ontario," says Valérie.

"I spent about a year with Sandra, then I was asked to be Madeleine Meilleur's chief of staff at Community and Social Services, as well as Community Safety and Correctional Services. Those were the two ministries we did together. Madeleine and I are still very close today. My mom has described her as being my second mother. We became so close that when we did business together people thought we were a mother/daughter duo travelling together. I was her chief of staff for about six years."

Madeleine Meilleur agrees that she and Valérie got along very well. "She has that contagious laugh. She's very social and very loyal. And she's a hard worker. She is like my daughter. And you know, as chief of staff there can be no secrets. And, of course, like her mother, she is beautiful," says Madeleine.

She recalled the Senate expenses audit and the RCMP investigation. "By that time, Valérie was not my chief of staff anymore. I knew Marie, yes, but I had to

Marie and Bernard alongside the Speaker of the Senate Noël Kinsella, and his wife Ann at the Negev Dinner in Ottawa, at which Barbara Walters was the keynote speaker, 2011. *Source*: Negev Dinner Archives.

stay away from her because, as the Attorney General of Ontario, I was involved. I made sure that I didn't speak with her. I read the papers like anybody else. I also told my deputy minister that Valérie was my chief of staff at one point. I felt sorry for what had happened to her and how it impacted her and her family. When these things happen to a politician, it's not only the politician that suffers; their friends, their family, and their spouse suffer too. I felt sorry for Marie; it tarnished her reputation."

Her mother's troubles in the Senate worried Valérie. "I informed my boss of what was going on with my mother because I didn't know if she was going to end up on the front page of the paper—the bank was always worried about their reputation. My boss had a political background, so he understood. Yet I was worried about the politics at the bank. And above all, I was worried about my mother. The audit was horrific. My mother is a personality that you don't meet very often: she oozes niceness and positivity and having worked in a lot of these political environments with women, I know that some of them can be awful and brutal and mean."

Valérie retired from the political world before her mother did. "After I came back from maternity leave with my daughter Claire in 2011, I knew that I had

Valérie and animals are always one.
*Source*: Family collection.

plateaued in the political sense, having done every job in a minister's office. I became concerned about work/life balance when one of my daughter's first words was Blackberry. I knew something had to shift."

Valérie switched to the Toronto Dominion Bank. She enjoyed life in the corporate world for the six years she was there. She was in the Community Relations Department. "That's essentially the philanthropy wing of the bank. I had the privilege of helping to donate the bank's money, which was a pretty amazing job. I had no idea that even existed," says Valérie.

Valérie then moved to RBI as an executive, then to St. Joseph's Hospital Foundation as VP. She now works as an executive at the energy company Greenfield Global.

# A Busy Post-Senate Life

SENATOR MARIE-PAULE CHARETTE-POULIN resigned from the Senate in 2015. Doctor's orders. At the same time, she left her law practice at Gowlings. "I had gone through a tough period in the Senate, and my health was deteriorating so, following doctor's orders, I took a step back from both professional commitments."

She had already had a minor stroke, yet she found making the decision difficult. Duncan Fulton remembers discussing it with her and telling her: "Marie, you can stay and fight for two years and probably be exonerated, but it's going to cost you a substantial amount of your savings to do that. You have to ask yourself how you want to spend the next twenty years of your life. Do you want to spend the next two or three years in a daily bitter grind in the trenches, being attacked and defending yourself and incurring huge expenses? Or retire from the Senate five years early, take most of your pension with you, and have a really great quality of life?"

"In the end I think she made the right decision to move on."

This was not a woman who was going to sit back, read, and spend winters in Florida, however. After all, she was only seventy years old.

"I decided to get another job."

Doing so, however, took some doing.

"I was totally absolved and exonerated; the nightmare was finished and behind me. I started meeting different people while I was looking for work. I had helped a lot of people during my years, and so I tried calling in a few favours. I was disappointed, though, by those for whom I had done huge favours," says Marie.

"One of the people I consulted was Mr. Chrétien, and that's the point he raised with me. He said, 'Marie, you're

> "You have to ask yourself how you want to spend the next twenty years of your life. Do you want to spend the next two or three years in a daily bitter grind in the trenches, being attacked and defending yourself and incurring huge expenses? Or retire from the Senate five years early, take most of your pension with you, and have a really great quality of life?"

Marie with her coffee and newspapers and Laurier, with his milk bowl, begin their day, 2013.
*Source*: Family Collection.

over forty-five, and in Ottawa these days, if you're over forty-five, you're not good anymore.'

"I said, 'Mr. Chrétien, you're over forty-five, and you're working full time at Denton's.' I said that what really doesn't help is the fact that I'm a woman. He agreed.

"So, it wasn't easy, but I finally found a friend who helped me. The Institute on Governance (IOG) retained my services."

Marie found a full-time position with the IOG; the not-for-profit had a contract with the federal government to help renew governance in Iraq. Marie had landed a job that was incredibly interesting and took full advantage of her unique experience.

"The president of the Institute at the time, Marie-Antoinette Flumian, was a former deputy minister and just a brilliant woman. She knew the project in Iraq so well, and she had surrounded herself with excellent people. The new constitution of Iraq gave the government the option to establish an upper house, and she hired me because of my experience in the Senate," says Marie.

The IOG has three mandates: training for public governance and leadership; research; and advisory responsibility. It was that third area that Marie and her team were involved with.

"We were advising and working with the leaders in Iraq on the implementation of their new constitution. It was such a unique opportunity for me," says Marie.

Harmony Sluiman, who worked with Marie at the IOG, speaks highly of Marie's role in organizing the visits of the delegations of Iraqi women leaders who came to Ottawa to learn about the Canadian governmental model. Madeleine Meilleur, who held several Cabinet positions in Dalton McGuinty's Liberal government in Ontario, worked with Marie at the IOG. She, too, speaks highly of Marie's ability to connect the Iraqi delegations with government officials and politicians in Ottawa. "When we had these delegations coming from Iraq to Ottawa, she was the one organizing all the events on the Hill, meeting with ministers and senators, and attending question period. The delegation from Iraq had a private meeting with Jean Chrétien which was supposed to be for half an hour and we had an hour and a half with him. The delegation was very impressed to have had this time with him."

Speaking of Marie as a person, Sluiman says, "She took me under her wing. She was warm and friendly, and she listened. One moment that really stood out to me: she and I were touring around Parliament Hill. It seemed she knew everyone in every hallway. It didn't matter if they

Marie and Valérie, 1979.
*Source*: Family collection.

were administrative staff or senior officials or security personnel; she knew them and she knew their names and they remembered hers. I thought that was just such a special quality. I remember thinking, That's the person that I want to be. I thought that was so powerful."

Marie receiving an honorary business degree from Collège Boréal President Denis Hubert-Dutrisac, 2013.
*Source*: Collège Boréal Archives.

Meilleur echoes Sluiman's opinion, describing Marie as "a mentor to the young employees at the IOG. She was a natural big sister to them, and they would ask her for advice."

The job also involved travelling to the war-torn country on a regular basis. "I went several times, confirmed Marie. At the time, the level of security was reasonable. We always stayed in an area in Iraq known as the Green Zone, which is where you find the government offices and the embassies of all the countries. It was an opportunity to experience a fantastic culture. I fell in love with the people, the country, and its food. We had to learn the whole history of what happened to the country. We worked closely with very senior officials in Iraq," says Marie.

"This was a country that had finished one war and yet was still fighting against ISIS. The infrastructure of the country had been very badly damaged, and the people had suffered—and continued to suffer—a great deal. I had never been in a post-war country in my life, and the destruction of formerly beautiful areas, beautiful houses, broke my heart. Violence and war don't benefit anyone."

Trained in social work, Marie was particularly sensitive to what she saw of the misery that war had wrought. "I could see that there was so much work to be

> "I could see that there was so much work to be done, not only in Baghdad but in other areas that I had the opportunity to visit. There are profound internal divisions like you find in any other country. There are generational gaps; there are those who knew the Hussein regime and those who didn't. It's a work in progress. Security remains a big issue, and that's one of the reasons why the IOG had to stop going."

done, not only in Baghdad but in other areas that I had the opportunity to visit. There are profound internal divisions like you find in any other country. There are generational gaps; there are those who experienced the Hussein regime and those who didn't. It's a work in progress. Security remains a big issue, and that's one of the reasons why the IOG had to stop going while I was still working for it—security became an issue once again," says Marie.

Given that the trips to Iraq are no longer possible, Marie becomes editor of the IOG newsletter for the last three months before her departure from IOG. "I loved it because I came back to my roots—broadcasting and communication. Every month, the newsletter would publish an interview with a well-known person in Ottawa. I interviewed former Governor General David Johnson, Marie-Claude Bibeau, Minister of International Development, and Greg Peters, Black Rod of the Senate. I just loved doing those interviews," says Marie.

Nevertheless, there was a dark side to Marie's experience at the IOG. Looking back, she has come to believe the IOG was one of the most negative places she ever worked. There was one senior person who mocked her constantly. She did the same to others members of the small staff. You know the type: they camouflage ridicule as humour. It is an insidious form of bullying. There was a formal inquiry into the culture of harassment and bullying, but there is little reason to name names here.

### Canadian Senior Artists Resource Network

"I was invited to lead the Canadian Senior Artists Resource Network (CSARN) in 2019. It's a young not-for-profit dedicated to the cultural industry. It supports experienced professional artists of all disciplines, including musicians, painters, actors, singers, composers, writers, and more. It works to ensure that these elder professional artists remain relevant, connected, and informed. I am especially proud of our mentoring program, our Salons, conferences, and webcasts. Interestingly, the pandemic has put the wind in our sails. Via Zoom we now reach artists across the country, no transportation involved," says Marie.

Marie was connected to CSARN by one of her wide range of contacts: Bob Underwood, the recently retired CEO of AFBS, the Actra Fraternal Benefit Society, the pension and group insurance arm of Actra and the Writer's Guild. The chair at CSARN was retiring, and they needed a replacement right away.

"We needed somebody with profile, somebody with Ottawa exposure who could pick up the phone and call the Department of Heritage and actually get someone to listen to her," Bob explained. "Marie was familiar with CSARN because of her husband Bernard, who is an internationally renowned painter. And Marie, God bless her, puts everything into anything that she does. I talked to her about it, and once she understood what was involved, she said she'd be happy to do it. So that's how we got Marie."

Marie explains: "Because it was such a small and young organization, it required someone who was very hands-on. Bob asked me if I would be interested in coming to CSARN. I trust Bob so much that I said yes right away. He said, 'Okay, come in next week.'

"I just got hooked because it is a not-for-profit with a mandate for senior artists and for younger artists too. It is very important to me that older people do not lose their relevance," says Marie. "I am also convinced of the truth of the French adage, 'La culture c'est ce qui reste quand on a tout oublié.'" [Culture is what remains when everything else is forgotten.]

Marie also believes that Bernard profoundly shaped her appreciation of the arts: "Bernard has had a huge influence on me because I have discovered and been able to appreciate the hard work, the learning, and the discipline it takes for a professional. He has opened my eyes to the importance of creativity not only in the arts, but in any field of work."

Bernard, however, believes that Marie always possessed an appreciation for and respect of artists and all those working in the cultural industries. "Marie was already involved in radio when I became an employee of Radio-Canada. She treated the [radio program] engineers as artists as much as she treated her on-air people and her researchers as artists. That's why they always strived to do their best. Everyone

> "She treated the [radio program] engineers as artists as much as she treated her on-air people and her researchers as artists. That's why they always strived to do their best. Everyone was treated with enormous amounts of respect. Everybody loved working for her. Her radio shows were the best on air, and they won awards. She encouraged every person who was a creative to be as creative as they could be."

> "CSARN has an additional responsibility, to advocate for elder professional artists in an environment where ageism is rampant. It is simply at the right place at the right time. It gives us the opportunity to set up systems where the experienced professional artists can remain relevant today by the fact that they are still producing, number one; and number two, helping ensure their talent is recognized; and three, they have an opportunity to pass on that knowledge as mentors."

was treated with enormous amounts of respect. Everybody loved working for her. Her radio shows were the best on air, and they won awards. She encouraged every person who was a creative to be as creative as they could be. They came out even better than even they expected and even mentioned it when we celebrated the fortieth anniversary of CBON on Parliament Hill. She has the capacity to organize and structure an environment in such a way that creative people can be the best that they can be. That certainly didn't come from me. I was an unknown in her world until I entered Radio-Canada."

"Eventually we met, married, and had kids," continues Bernard. "That's when we discovered each other as creative people. But Marie has respect for people from the bottom all the way up to the top. She was perfectly endowed with all the talents and skills that were required to do the tribunal for self-employed artists, plus whatever other jobs she has done in her life."

Marie acknowledges that her experience, skills, and connections allow her to make a contribution to the work CSARN does. "CSARN has an additional responsibility, to advocate for elder professional artists in an environment where ageism is rampant. It is simply at the right place at the right time. It gives us the opportunity to set up systems where the experienced professional artists can remain relevant today by the fact that they are still producing, number one; and number two, helping ensure their talent is recognized; and three, they have an opportunity to pass on that knowledge as mentors. Through mentorship, they contribute to the upcoming excellence of younger professionals. That's why CSARN has so much meaning for me."

Marie stepped down as the lead of CSARN at the end of 2022. She had reached her core objectives: the development of a strategic plan, a reform of the governance structure, the inclusion of team members from across the country, additional funding from private corporations, and a new brand, moving from the "Canadian Senior Artists Resource Network" to the "Canadian Artists Network" (CAN). "We CAN," says Marie to underscore the efficiency of the new branding, "because creativity lives forever."

Senator Charette-Poulin has also been on the Advisory Board of the Canada's Outstanding CEO of the Year Award for more than twenty years. It is a program run by Caldwell Partners, the executive search firm. "Senator Poulin was asked to join because she is one of those rare people who has a very broad perspective and understanding of leadership," says John Wallace, the CEO of Caldwell Partners. "She brought a research-based perspective on leadership, and she has demonstrated that every year in our selection process. She has been a vigorous participant in all our decision-making."

During the summer of 2023, Senator Charette-Poulin received two new invitations, which she has accepted. She has joined the Sandstone Group, based in Ottawa, as Senior Associate. The Group is co-chaired by Kevin Bosch and Nareesh Raghubeer. It specializes in matters of public affairs, government relations, crisis communications and issues management, procurement, public policy and in legislation before Parliament.

She has also joined the senior team at Saint Paul University, in Ottawa, as a "Parliamentarian in Residence" working with the President, the deans, the professors to ensure better information and connections for students with Parliament, the public service, the diplomatic community, professional firms, NFPs, social services and businesses.

In all Marie's professional roles, clear communication has been critically important. As has been said many times by people who have worked with her, Marie has an astonishing ability to connect with people, to talk to them. Fundamental to that ability is the degree of respect that she consistently displays toward those she has dealings with. Her way of interacting with others is, of course, rooted in who Marie is as a person, but her training and experience as a social worker have also played an important role in Marie's professional success.

Reflecting on the role social work played in her life, Marie observes: "I think that social work provides a lot of training for interviews and research, and in broadcasting you need both. So, there was a lot of the training I received in social work that I was able to use at CBC, that's number one. Number two, I would say that social work also makes you understand the importance of empathy. In broadcasting, if you are going to work with and develop a good team, if you are going to bring out the best in each team member, you need to have real empathy for them. The other thing that social work does is it gives you the ability to analyze situations from various angles—socially and economically. In broadcasting you always have to remember your production, be it radio, television, or social media, is not in the middle of nowhere. It's in the middle of a context and so, as a social worker, you automatically analyze and if you can't analyze, you go get the data. Nothing exists in a vacuum."

Of course, social work is something that proved to be of great importance in Marie's personal life. Marie notes, "The thing that linked us so closely was

> "The thing that linked us so closely was that Bernard had worked in social work. He worked with children with emotional disturbances for years. Each of us knew the social work environment in the Ottawa area and we knew people that we didn't know each other knew. So, we had that additional link, which was very strong."

★ ★ ★

Marie Poulin's life has been one of service and achievement. While never boasting about it, Marie has achieved a number of major firsts: among them, the first founding station manager at Radio-Canada; the first female Francophone senator from Ontario; the first woman Francophone president of the Liberal Party of Canada.

She never set out to do those things; she just worked hard and got there.

Even as a child in Sudbury, Marie-Paule Charette set herself goals. When she attended Laurentian University, a Jesuit philosophy professor told her not to work so hard, since she was only at Laurentian University to "find a husband." That made her work even harder, and she graduated magna cum laude. Marie-Paule loved Sudbury and her roots there, but she longed to see the wider world. That took her to the Université de Montréal, where she got a degree in social work, and Berkeley in California.

It was in California that she discovered the meaning of betrayal, something she would encounter again in life. She dropped daily use of her second name, returning to Canada an impoverished single mother. But she was educated and refused to settle for the life fate had handed her.

In Ottawa, Marie found a job as a social worker, but soon decided social work was not for her, as she became too emotionally involved with the people she worked with. She moved on and joined Radio-Canada/CBC, where she had a brilliant career as a producer in Ottawa. Marie was then asked to build and run a new French-language radio station in Sudbury. That was such a success that she was promoted to be a senior executive in Ottawa, managing the CBC's regional broadcasting across the country. Following that, Marie became Vice-President of Human

Marie with former Governor General David Johnston, sharing Northern Ontario memories, 2018.
*Source*: Marie Charette-Poulin / Newsletter of the Institute on Governance.

Resources and Industrial Relations, where she brought together thirty-three different unions and avoided a major strike.

After her success at the CBC, Marie moved to a senior communications post at the Privy Council Office, where she learned how the country was governed. From there she was asked to become the first CEO for the quasi-judicial tribunal for self-employed artists, the Canadian Artists and Producers Professional Relations Tribunal.

Following that, Marie began a career in the Senate. She never lobbied to become a senator and was surprised when Prime Minister Jean Chrétien made the offer. She loved working in Parliament. The process of making laws so fascinated Senator Charette-Poulin that she returned to law school so she could better understand the law itself. Not content with all that, Marie also seized the opportunity to become president of the Liberal Party of Canada when that position became available. As president, she reformed the way the party raised

The Poulin family, 1996.
*Source*: Family Collection.

money, encouraging small donations—as little as five dollars—from ordinary people.

There is a saying that all political careers end in tragedy. That was true for many senators of her era. Marie and several other senators became targets, part of a politically motivated attack on the institution of the Senate itself, an attack disguised as an audit of the senators' expenses.

Even a former Auditor General was critical of the way the audit of the Senate was handled. Two judges, including a former Supreme Court justice, came down hard on the methods used and motivations for the audit of senators' expenses; particular criticism was aimed at the way in which nine senators from nine provinces were treated in the audit. Senator Charette-Poulin and her colleagues were absolved of any wrongdoing—but it left lives and careers in tatters, and the Canadian taxpayer with a 23-million-dollar bill.

Again, as she had while studying at Laurentian University, Marie refused to play the victim.

She is a survivor and has a busy post-Senate life. She worked with the Institute on Governance, the not-for-profit awarded a contract by the federal government to help organize the new government in Iraq, which meant trips to war-torn Iraq and work with legislators there.

Today, Marie's major commitments are to Saint-Paul University as Parliamentarian in Residence and to the Sandstone Group as Senior Associate, while remaining involved as a member of five boards and advisory councils, including the Actra Fraternal Benefit Society.

Marie-Paule Charette-Poulin is a woman of great achievement. She has served as a social worker, a pioneering radio programmer, a media executive, the

Bernard and Elaine, 1976.
*Source*: Family collection.

**Marie-Paule Charette-Poulin is a woman of great achievement. She has served as a social worker, a pioneering radio programmer, a media executive, the president of the Liberal Party of Canada, a lawyer, and a parliamentarian in the Senate of Canada. She has sat on the boards of a number of corporations, organizations, and not-for-profits. In all these roles, she has accomplished something truly extraordinary: great personal achievement *through* public service.**

president of the Liberal Party of Canada, a lawyer, and a parliamentarian in the Senate of Canada. She has sat on the boards of a number of corporations, organizations, and not-for-profits. In all these roles, she has accomplished something truly extraordinary: great personal achievement through public service.

It is a life of service and achievement for a woman who has never slowed down.

The Poulin family, 2019.
*Source*: Family Collection.

# List of Interviewees

| # | Names | Positions |
|---|---|---|
| 1 | Mohammed Abdulkareem | Head of the Institute on Governance (IOG) office in Baghdad, now working in the Ottawa office |
| 2 | Al Albania | Founding CEO and owner of ACART Communications |
| 3 | Serge Arsenault | Journalist, Radio-Canada, radio and television, sportscaster, CEO of the Montréal Marathon, owner of Serdy Video and Canal Évasion, Canadian race organizer for North American cycling, awarded a WorldTour licence for the Grand Prix Cycliste de Québec et de Montréal |
| 4 | Michael Atkins | Businessman and journalist, founding CEO of Laurentian Media Group |
| 5 | Norman Bacal | Lawyer, author, speaker, Co-managing Partner at Heenan Blaikie LLP |
| 6 | Raymond Bonin | Member of Parliament (Liberal) from Greater Sudbury (ret.) |
| 7 | Honourable Jocelyne Bourgon | Canadian public servant, Deputy Minister of several departments, Clerk of the Privy Council; first woman to hold this office, and CEO of Public Governance International |
| 8 | Honourable Sharon Carstairs | Senator (Liberal), Leader of the Government in the Senate, President of the Liberal Party in Alberta, Leader of the Opposition in Manitoba (first woman to hold such a position in any Canadian legislature) |
| 9 | Ronald Caza | Lawyer, Founding Partner at Caza Saikaly, preeminent litigator in Ontario, recipient of Best Lawyers in Canada Award |
| 10 | Pierre Champagne | Partner at Gowling WLG, Ottawa |

| #  | Names | Positions |
|----|-------|-----------|
| 11 | Gilles Charette, PhD | CEO of Québec Iron and Titanium (retired) – brother |
| 12 | Sheila Copps | Member of Parliament (Liberal), Deputy Prime Minister and Minister of several portfolios, columnist |
| 13 | Michel Coulombe | Chartered Accountant, Partner at Marcil Lavallée |
| 14 | Right Honourable Jean Chrétien | Prime Minister of Canada (1993–2003) (Liberal) |
| 15 | Peter Crisson | Businessman, Bermuda |
| 16 | Peter Daniel | CBC journalist, Communications Advisor to the Department of Finance, OECD, NATO |
| 17 | Honourable Justice Robert Del Frate | Superior Court of Justice of Ontario (ret.), lawyer |
| 18 | Perry Dellelce | Lawyer, Founder, and Managing Partner of Wildeboer Dellelce LLP, Chairman of the Canadian Olympic Foundation |
| 19 | Honourable Justice Robert Desmarais | Superior Court of Justice of Ontario (retired), lawyer |
| 20 | Lorena Dudley | Hotelier (Parker House Suites, Sudbury), municipal employee for the City of Greater Sudbury – niece |
| 21 | John Duffy | CEO of Neate Roller Ltd. (retired), former CFO at the Liberal Party of Canada |
| 22 | Honourable Mike Duffy | Senator (Conservative then Independent), journalist, author |
| 23 | Tom Flanagan | Author, Conservative political activist and professor, advisor to Prime Minister Harper |
| 24 | Shimon Fogel | CEO of the Centre for Israel and Jewish Affairs (CIJA) |
| 25 | Matthew Fraser | University professor in Paris, Editor-in-Chief of the *National Post* |
| 26 | Honourable Sheila Fraser | Auditor General of Canada (2001–2011); first woman to hold this office |

| # | Names | Positions |
|---|---|---|
| 27 | Honourable Linda Frum | Senator (Conservative), author, and journalist |
| 28 | Duncan Fulton | CCO of Restaurant Brands International, former president of Canadian Tire's sports division, Senior vice-president of Corporate Affairs, advisor to Premier McKenna of New Brunswick and Prime Minister Chrétien, campaign manager in Senator Poulin's bid for the presidency of the Liberal Party of Canada. |
| 29 | Jim Gordon | Member of Provincial Parliament (Conservative) and Minister of Government Services in Ontario, Mayor of Sudbury (1976–1981 and 1991–2003) |
| 30 | Natalie Grimard | Executive Assistant to Marie Poulin (1992–2015) |
| 31 | Honourable Céline Hervieux-Payette | Senator (Liberal), Leader of the Opposition in the Senate, lawyer, businesswoman |
| 32 | Tom Jackson | Entertainer, actor, singer, Member of the Canadian Senior Artists Resource Network (CSARN) Board |
| 33 | Bruce Johnson | Lawyer in Doha, Qatar |
| 34 | Monsignor Jean-Paul Jolicœur | Diocese of Sault Ste. Marie |
| 35 | Guy Laflamme | Executive in Residence and Professor, Telfer School of Management and Toulouse Business School, Executive Director and Producer of "Ottawa 2017" |
| 36 | Steve Loubier | Constable, Senate of Canada Security |
| 37 | Honourable John Manley | Parliamentarian (Liberal), Deputy Prime Minister, Minister of several portfolios, lawyer, CEO of the Business Council of Canada (2009–2018), Senior Business Advisor at Bennett Jones |
| 38 | Janice Marshall | Executive Assistant to Senator William Rompkey and Researcher to Senator Poulin |
| 39 | Daniel Mathieu | Radio host at Radio-Canada, first morning man at Sudbury's CBON station when it opened in 1978 |

| #  | Names | Positions |
|----|-------|-----------|
| 40 | Don McCallum | Businessman, former owner of Bravo Dental Products, real estate investor |
| 41 | Madeleine Meilleur | Member of Provincial Parliament (Liberal), Minister of several portfolios as well as Attorney General of Ontario, Senior Advisor at the Institute on Governance (IOG), lawyer, nurse |
| 42 | Don Mitchell | Lawyer and corporate executive, Corporate Secretary and Communication Director at Boise Cascade, Chair and President of Samsung Canada |
| 43 | Michel Morin | Radio host at CBON in Sudbury, executive at Radio-Canada, Director of the Fédération des communautés francophones et acadienne du Canada (FCFA) |
| 44 | Right Honourable Brian Mulroney | Prime Minister of Canada (1984–1993) (Progressive Conservative) |
| 45 | Donald Obonsawin | Deputy Minister of several portfolios in Ontario |
| 46 | Eric Peters | Internal Auditor at CBC/Radio-Canada, Auditor General of Ontario, Senior Advisor at the Institute on Governance |
| 47 | Honourable Pierre Pettigrew | Parliamentarian (Liberal), Minister of several portfolios, Managing Partner of Deloitte Canada, and Executive Advisor for International Activities |
| 48 | Valérie Picher | Vice-President Community at St. Joseph's Health Centre Foundation, Head of Government Relations in Canada for Restaurant Brands International, Associate VP Community Relations TD Bank, Chief of Staff to four ministers (Government of Ontario), Director of Communications/Press Secretary for several ministries (Government of Canada) and the Canada Foundation for Innovation |
| 49 | Bernard Poulin | Visual artist, author, teacher, composer, sculptor, mentor – Marie's husband and best friend |

| #  | Names | Positions |
|----|-------|-----------|
| 50 | Elaine Poulin | Award-winning entrepreneur, author of *North of Darkness*, a book on PTSD, pianist, composer, coordinator/trainer, support and training at a centre for caregivers |
| 51 | Honourable Vivienne Poy | Senator (Liberal), businesswoman, author, and philanthropist |
| 52 | Sandra Pupatello | Member of Provincial Parliament (Liberal), Minister of several portfolios, Director of Business and Global Markets, Price Waterhouse Coopers |
| 53 | Pierre Racicot | Senior executive at CBC/Radio-Canada, Member of the Board of Actra Fraternal Benefit Society |
| 54 | Honourable Hugh Segal | Senator (Progressive Conservative), Chief of Staff to Premier Davis then to Prime Minister Mulroney, Master at Massey College of the University of Toronto, journalist, and author |
| 55 | Harmony Sluiman | Outreach and Communications Coordinator at the City of Ottawa, Senior Researcher at the Institute on Governance |
| 56 | Donna Speigel | Psychologist, teacher, rower (Sudbury) |
| 57 | Mitch Speigel | Businessman, contractor (Sudbury) |
| 58 | Gregory Tardi | Parliamentary Counsel, House of Commons, law professor (Osgoode Hall, Queen's University) |
| 59 | Laurent Thibault | President/CEO Canadian Manufacturers Association (retired) |
| 60 | Bob Underwood | CEO of the Actra Fraternal Benefit Society (retired); member of the Canadian Senior Artists Resource Network Board |
| 61 | John Wallace | CEO, Caldwell Partners, Member of the CEO of the Year Advisory Board |
| 62 | Doug Ward | Vice-President of CBC Regional Services (retired) |
| 63 | Wayne Warren | Managing Partner, Gowling WLG |
| 64 | Reverend Sister Rachelle Watier | Superior General, Grey Nuns of the Cross (Sisters of Charity), Principal of Collège Notre-Dame in Sudbury |

| #  | Names             | Positions                                                                                              |
|----|-------------------|--------------------------------------------------------------------------------------------------------|
| 65 | Jaime Watt        | Executive Chairman of Navigator Ltd., political strategist (Conservative), columnist                   |
| 66 | Shirley Westeinde | Co-owner of Westeinde Construction, first woman president of the Canadian Construction Association     |

# Biography and Memoirs

The focus of this series is to feature the life and work of prominent Canadians whose distinctive contributions have marked our society and history. This series tells their life stories, life's work and recounts the times in which they were active. Combining scholarship with an accessible voice, the Biography and Memoirs collection is contributing to building an archive of Canadian achievements in culture, science and beyond.

**Recent Titles in the Biography and Memoirs Collection:**

Michel Bastarache and Antoine Trépanier, What I Wish I Had Told My Children, translated from the French by Julie da Silva, 2023.

Stéphane Desjardins, La famille Fermanian : l'histoire du cinéma Pine de Sainte-Adèle, 2022.

Constance Backhouse, Deux grandes dames : Bertha Wilson et Claire L'Heureux-Dubé à la Cour suprême du Canada, 2021.

Monique (Aubry) Frize, A Woman in Engineering: Memoirs of a Trailblazer, 2019.

Michel Bastarache and Antoine Trépanier, Ce que je voudrais dire à mes enfants, 2019.

David M. Culver and Alan Freeman, Saisir sa chance : mémoires de David M. Culver, 2018.

Ruey J. Yu, Journey of a Thousand Miles: An Extraordinary Life, 2017.

Michel Bock, A Nation Beyond Borders: Lionel Groulx on French-Canadian Minorities, 2014.

Jacqueline Cardinal and Laurent Lapierre, Taking Aviation to New Heights: A Biography of Pierre Jeanniot, 2013.

For a complete list of our titles, please visit:
**www.press.uOttawa.ca**